A Traveler in Indian Territory
The Journal of
Ethan Allen Hitchcock

The American Exploration and Travel Series

MAJOR GENERAL ETHAN ALLEN HITCHCOCK
From a photograph.

A Traveler in Indian Territory

The Journal of Ethan Allen Hitchcock, late Major-General in the United States Army

Edited and Annotated
by
GRANT FOREMAN

Foreword By MICHAEL D. GREEN

UNIVERSITY OF OKLAHOMA PRESS
NORMAN AND LONDON

Library of Congress Cataloging-in-Publication Data

Hitchcock, Ethan Allen, 1798–1870.
    A traveler in Indian territory : the journal of Ethan Allen
Hitchcock, late major-general in the United States Army / edited
and annotated by Grant Foreman ; foreword by Michael D.
Green.
        p.   cm.—(The American exploration and travel series : v.
75)
    Originally published: Cedar Rapids : Torch Press, 1930.
    Includes index.
    ISBN 0-8061-2840-2 (alk. paper)
    1. Indians of North America—Indian Territory.   2. Indians of
North America—Relocation—Indian Territory.   3. Indians of
North America—Government relations.   4. Indian Territory—
Description and travel.   I. Foreman, Grant, 1869–1953.
II. Title.   III. Series.
E78.I5H57   1996
323.1'197073'09034—dc20   95-46136
                                                                          CIP

A Traveler in Indian Territory: The Journal of Ethan Allen Hitchcock is
Volume 75 in The American Exploration and Travel Series.

The paper in this book meets the guidelines for permanence and durability
of the Committee on Production Guidelines for Book Longevity of the
Council on Library Resources, Inc.ⓐ

1 2 3 4 5 6 7 8 9 10

To
BESSIE B. CROFFUT

Contents

CHAPTER I

Major Hitchcock Arrives at Fort Smith — Description of the Post — A Steamboat Warming — An Indian School — On the Military Road — A Wilderness Home — Refuge from a Storm — Arrival at Fort Gibson — Rumors — Indian Traders — Union of a Cherokee and a Quakeress — Indian Government — Buffalo — Horse Racing at Fort Gibson — Wild Cat . . . .

CHAPTER II

Cherokee Customs — A Journey to the Capital — An Indian Home — Cherokee Piety — An Indian Council — John Ross, the Executive — Legislative Committees — The Indian's Religion — The Home of an Indian Merchant — Sequoyah — Park Hill — An Incident of the Seminole War — Civilization of the Cherokee — Killing of Boudinot . .

CHAPTER III

Cherokee Evening Service — Judge Bushyhead — Cherokee Customs — Joseph Vann — Change in Cherokee Conditions — War on Whiskey — Osage Visitors Astonish the Cherokee — Iniquity of Osage Treaty — Preëminence of Osage Horse Thieves — Cherokee Statistics — Legislative Discussions — Cherokee Decorum — Punishment — Return to Fort Smith — By Steamboat to Webber's Falls . . . .

CHAPTER IV

Mackey's Salt Works — Lynching a Soldier — Return to Tahlequah — Sequoyah or George Guess — In-

CHAPTER XIII

Illustrations

MAP OF INDIAN TERRITORY

∼1842∼

Compiled by Grant Foreman
Traced by Will Blake

CIMMARON

C

NORTH

CANADIAN RIVER

CEDAR OR LITTLE E

WALNUT CREEK

WASHITA RIVER

FORT HOLMES

CHOUTEAU'S
TRADING HOUSE

RUSH CREEK

C H I C K A S A W

WILDHORSE CREEK

TRAIL

FROM TH

WASHITA

BEAVER CREEK

MUD

SHAWNEE, DELAWARE AND KICKAPOO

WALNUT

RED RIVER

CREEK

CREEK

WARREN'S
TRADING POST

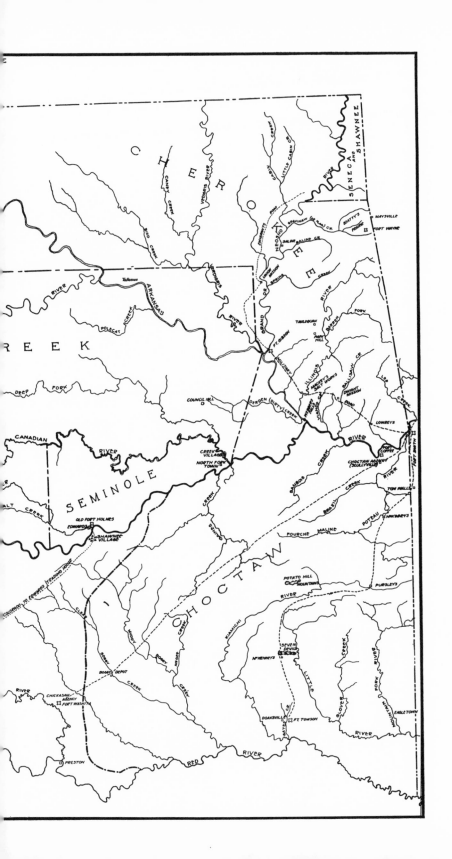

Foreword

Grant Foreman, an attorney by training, became Oklahoma's most prolific historian. Born in Illinois and educated in Michigan, in 1899 Foreman moved to Muskogee, Indian Territory, to accept a staff position with the Commission to the Five Civilized Tribes. Better known as the Dawes Commission, it had been created by Congress in 1893 to negotiate allotment agreements with the governments of each of the Five Tribes. In 1903, after four years of appraising and classifying land and arbitrating conflicting claims, Foreman left the commission to enter the law office of Judge John R. Thomas. Foreman married Thomas's daughter, Carolyn, and inherited Thomas's law practice. He became wealthy through wise investing and, in the early 1920s, retired from the law to devote all his energies to historical research and writing.

Foreman wrote or edited nineteen books and more than eighty articles, but the four books that constitute his history of Indian Territory are certainly his most important. Published between 1930 and 1934, they represent a phenomenal research challenge. In an age before the National Archives, photocopying machines, and microfilm on interlibrary loan, Foreman and his wife traveled to government offices, dug old records out of dusty boxes, hired typists to transcribe letters and documents, and purchased enough materials to assemble an enormous private library. Somewhere along the way they encountered W. A. Croffut's *Fifty Years in Camp and Field: Diary of Major-General Ethan Allen Hitchcock, U.S.A.* (New York, 1909) and Bessie B. Croffut, owner of the voluminous Hitchcock collection from which her husband had culled snippets for his book. Recognizing the value of Hitchcock's observations—his diaries are among the first to document conditions in Indian Territory after the removal of the five Southern tribes—Foreman cited them in one of his books, *The Five Civilized Tribes* (Norman, 1934). With a light editorial touch, he then prepared the Indian Territory section of the Hitchcock diaries for the publication of the first printing of the present volume.

Published in 1930 as *A Traveler in Indian Territory*, this journal covers the period between November 1841 and March 1842, when Hitchcock was investigating charges of massive fraud in the supply of provisions to Indians—particularly Cherokees and Chickasaws—after removal. The government decision to inquire into these charges, and the selection of Hitchcock to conduct the investigation, is a matter of some interest. Hitchcock's reputation in the War Department was that of a scholar, a careful investigator, a perfectionist, and an honest man. He was also something of a moralist. After his 1836 tour of duty in Florida against the Seminoles, for example, Hitchcock came to believe that the treaties that stipulated their removal to Indian Territory had been fraudulently achieved, that the army's mission to defeat and expel them was wrong. This experience, along with others in the frontier army, also convinced him that in general the Indians were more sinned against than sinners. Never backward about expressing his views, Hitchcock reported his opinions to the War Department at length and in detail.

Hitchcock, a Whig, believed he had suffered for his political loyalties at the hands of the Democratic administrations of Andrew Jackson and Martin Van Buren. The election of William Henry Harrison in 1840 was most welcome, however, because the president appointed Hitchcock's brother-in-law, John Bell, as Secretary of War. Bell resigned with the rest of the cabinet in the fall of 1841, but his replacement, John Spencer, also appreciated Hitchcock's advice. For months after his return from Indian Territory, Hitchcock served Spencer as a special advisor on Indian affairs.

The Whigs generally had opposed Indian Removal when Congress debated it in 1829–30. Henry Clay had tried to make Jackson's Indian policy a campaign issue in his unsuccessful race for the presidency in 1832, and the succeeding years demonstrated that removal had been achieved only at an astronomical cost in human lives, suffering, and money. No historian has ever attempted to compute the cost in money, but it was clear at the time that huge overruns occurred through fraud. The removal treaties obligated the government to compensate the Indians for the possessions they left behind, pay the costs of transport and subsistence en route to Indian Territory, and provide provisions and other help for the first year after removal. To fulfill these obligations, the government used private contractors, and the opportunities for illegal profiteering were manifold. Responding to specific allegations, Secretary Bell instructed Hitchcock to investigate what had happened and then document his findings in a full report.

Foreman notes in his "Introduction" that Hitchcock's report was so explosive, so incriminating of friends of the administration, and so sensitive, that the government suppressed and ultimately destroyed it. Foreman was half right. On April 28, 1842, Hitchcock submitted his report, with one hundred documents attached, to Secretary Spencer. Spencer was overwhelmed and worried about two things: first, Hitchcock's investigation might be perceived as unfair because he never interviewed any of the contractors charged with fraud, and second, information contained in his report could compromise negotiations about to begin with the Cherokees on a related problem. Therefore, on Spencer's advice, President John Tyler refused to submit the report to the House Committee on Indian Affairs. This ignited an argument between the president and the committee over their respective powers and pre-rogatives, the nature of executive privilege, and the right of the peoples' representatives to know. But a year later, after concluding the negotiations with the Cherokees, the president submitted the report to the committee, which published Hitchcock's report together with the acrimonious exchange of charges and countercharges twice. (The report and accompanying documents may be found in the U.S. Congress Serial Set, House Document 219, 23rd Congress, 3rd Session, Serial 416; and House Report 271, 23rd Congress, 3rd Session, Serial 425.)

Hitchcock's report is a detailed exposé of repeated fraud and corruption and contains much information of historical interest, but the real gem is his journal, reproduced here under the able editorship of Grant Foreman. Hitchcock was in Indian Territory for only a few months, but while there he spent many hours talking with Indian people of every description about their lives and experiences. He attended council meetings, slept in peoples' homes, and shared their food, and in his journal he describes all these experiences, supplementing the entries with information on how they looked and what they wore. Hitchcock was particularly fascinated by politics and the institutions of government, and students of American Indian history place great value on his descriptions of Creek and Cherokee political organization.

A Traveler in Indian Territory has been out of print for decades. This new printing is long overdue and most welcome.

MICHAEL D. GREEN

LEXINGTON, KENTUCKY

Foreword to the First Edition

Of the many tawdry chapters covering the relations between our government and the Indians perhaps the sorriest was the removal of the eastern tribes to the territory now embraced in Oklahoma. By nearly all who had anything to do with it this undertaking seems to have been used as a means of the most cold-blooded, systematic looting of public and tribal moneys and was accompanied by a cynical disregard for human suffering and the destruction of human life which were its immediate, and remote, consequences. Maj. Caleb Swan says of the majority of the whites living in the Indian country in Alabama in 1790 that they "are the most abandoned wretches that can be found, perhaps, on this side of Botany Bay; there is scarcely a crime but some of them has been guilty of." In the removal we seem to have an exhibition of the actions of just such an element when placed in a position of power and given access to the property of ignorant and dependent peoples.

Since, as the event showed, the national administration was willing to look the other way while this criminal operation was in progress, it made a curious blunder in permitting the injection into such a situation of an investigator as little disposed to whitewash iniquity as was Ethan Allen Hitchcock, the writer of the present diary. A man of refinement, of literary and philosophic instincts, of unimpeachable honor, of broad humanitarian sympathies, and of unflinching courage, one who could not be seduced by effervescent hospitality and the treacherous temptings of "good fellowship" or browbeaten by the braggadocio of frontier ruffianism, he pursued his investigation with military promptness and precision and with more than military intelligence. Granted a man of this type, and there could be but one result had the administration been honest in its pretensions, the immediate dismissal of a large part of the personnel remaining in the service who had been entrusted with the expenditure of the removal funds and extensive prosecution of contractors who had benefitted by them. The fact that it did not allow the report to be made public and its mysterious disappearance from all official files proves at one and the same time the honesty of the report and the dishonesty of the national administration of the period. The present diary gives some idea of the scandalous condition of affairs in the Indian country, and is a testimony to the candor and penetration of its writer, but, aside from the insalubrious event with which he was so largely concerned, it furnishes historians one of those close insights into the *mores* of an age which turn up only too seldom.

General Hitchcock's interest in everything about him is especially illustrated in those sections of the diary dealing with Indians and their customs, and in a separate paper devoted to the Creeks which is incorporated into the present volume as Chapter VIII. So far as the latter tribe is concerned, the Hitchcock documents must henceforth be placed side of those of Bartram, Swan, and Hawkins among the original sources essential to an intelligent understanding of primitive tribal conditions. They yield to other authorities only in the one point of age. Mr. Foreman has therefore performed a service to ethnologists as well as to historians in giving this diary a publicity richly deserved and all too long delayed.

JOHN R. SWANTON.

WASHINGTON, D.C.

Introduction

Ethan Allen Hitchcock, an eminent American soldier, was born at Vergennes, Vermont, May 18, 1798. His mother was a daughter of the famous Ethan Allen. A graduate of West Point in 1817, Hitchcock was first an instructor there and afterwards commandant of the Corps of Cadets in that school. He was engaged in the Florida wars where, by his tact, diplomacy, and fair dealing he gained the confidence of the Indians and was credited with ending in 1842 the bloody campaign that decimated both red and white contestants. In the Mexican War he served first with General Taylor in the North, and later with General Scott; he engaged in a number of actions and on August 20, 1847, received the brevet of colonel for gallant and meritorious conduct in the battle of Molino Del Ray. As inspector-general of General Scott's army, he mustered out the volunteers at Independence, Missouri. He was made colonel of the Second Infantry, April 15, 1851, and commanded the Pacific Division from that date until 1854. He resigned from the army October 18, 1855, and located in Saint Louis, Missouri, where he was engaged chiefly in literary pursuits during the remainder of his life, interrupted only by the Civil War, when he was commissioned major-general of volunteers. After nearly fifty years of service in the army, he died at Saint Louis, Missouri, August 5, 1870.

Prior to 1839, Major Hitchcock was stationed for a

time in Saint Louis, where he acted as disbursing officer of the funds expended in the Indian service; at this post he was instrumental in discovering and arresting frauds by Indian agents at stations on the upper Mississippi. In 1838, legislation by Congress required his post to be filled by a civilian and as Major Hitchcock naturally declined to resign his station in the army, he terminated his service in Saint Louis, to the great regret of his superiors. In the spring of 1841, Major Hitchcock declined the appointment of commissioner of Indian Affairs, and a few months later he was assigned to the important duties that took him among the Indians in the West.

General Hitchcock was a man of literary taste and scholarly accomplishments, and kept a journal during his entire life which forms a voluminous chronicle of passing events.

He made extensive contributions to military history, and wrote often and vigorously for publication on passing events and matters of professional importance. He was a profound student and writer on recondite philosophy, and in the intervals of an active career gave to the world eight volumes on abstruse and esoteric subjects. Because of his acquaintance with the Indians and their history, and his judicial contemplation of events, he was assigned by the War Department, September 29, 1841, to a most important duty in Indian Territory.

Following the passage in 1830 of President Andrew Jackson's measure known as the Indian Removal Act, the Government launched the huge undertaking of removing the Indians from the East to the country west of the Mississippi River. So-called treaties were negotiated with influential, often venal, and sometimes

representative members of the tribes. Choctaw removal
was first got under way and a large part of the nation
was moved during the years 1831, 1832, and 1833. The
Creek Treaty of 1832 inaugurated the migration of
part of that tribe soon after, but the majority held back
and were finally removed by force in 1836. The Chickasaw were emigrated during 1837. The removal of the
great majority of the Cherokee Nation by virtue of the
fraudulent treaty of 1835 was accomplished by force as
a military measure during 1838 and 1839. A few hundred members of the Seminole Tribe were removed,
most of them as prisoners; so that by 1840 more than
sixty thousand, a large majority of the membership of
these tribes, were located in Indian Territory.

Large bodies of these Indians were sent west under
contractors who obligated themselves to feed the emigrants on the road. Others were removed by the Government, but all were rationed by contract with white
men who were required to maintain stores along the
way, and provision was made to subsist nearly all of
them for a year after removal, while they were adjusting themselves to their new environment and growing crops for their sustenance.

Some of these contracts were honestly performed so
that the Indians traveled in a measure of comfort; but
out of this great undertaking there came accounts of
profiteering and fraud committed on these helpless Indians. These charges created such a scandal that the
Government was driven to make an investigation, and
in the effort to find a suitable person to perform that
duty in the field, selected Maj. Ethan Allen Hitchcock.
When he came to Indian Territory he was not only
attentive to the subject under investigation, but he was
interested in all he saw about him; and following his

custom when circumstances permitted, he made notes
of all he saw and heard, and of the impressions he
received. During his stay in Indian Territory he filled a
series of nine note books that he carried in his pocket.

It is obvious from the reading of these notes that they
were not intended for publication, but nevertheless
Major Hitchcock performed a distinct service to the
student of history by the interest and industry which
induced him to set down his impressions.

These diaries made in Indian Territory form only a
small part of the manuscripts written by the General,
which came into the possession of Mrs. W. A. Croffut,
of Washington, D.C., the niece of General Hitchcock's
widow, and to whom the editor of these notes is indebted for the privilege of publishing them. They are
now part of the archives of the Manuscript Division of
the Library of Congress; and acknowledgment is made
to the officials and attendants there for facilities
afforded.

Bribery, perjury and forgery were the chief
instruments employed in the infamous transactions
investigated by Hitchcock. Due bills were issued by
contractors to the Indians, and then bought back at a
fraction of their value. Short weights, issues of spoiled
meat and grain, every conceivable subterfuge was employed by designing white men on ignorant Indians.
After the investigation was made, Colonel Hitchcock
prepared a report with one hundred exhibits attached,
which he filed with the Secretary of War; committees
of Congress tried vainly to have it submitted to them, so
that appropriate action could be taken; but it was
stated that too many friends of the administration were
involved to permit the report to become public. It disappeared from the files and no trace of it is to be found

in the voluminous correspondence on this subject now in the files of the Office of Indian Affairs.[1]

Major Hitchcock received his commission on September 28, 1841, and the next day departed from Washington by stage; on October ninth, by steamboat, he reached Lexington, Kentucky, where he attended a dinner given in honor of Henry Clay. Nearly five weeks later, on November 12, his boat arrived at Little Rock, Arkansas, where there was much curiosity about his business, news of his coming having preceded him. Some of the beneficiaries of the frauds he was to investigate were living in Little Rock. "One Indian agent," he wrote, "came here so poor that a man with a $400 claim against him was glad to settle for $100. Now he owns a considerable number of negroes and has offered $17,500 for a plantation." Major Hitchcock ascended Arkansas River, and after a three days' boat trip, for which he paid thirteen dollars, he reached Fort Smith,[2] November 21, 1841.

[1] Chairman Cooper of the House Committee on Indian Affairs called on the Secretary of War for the report; when the refusal of the Secretary was received, a violent debate took place in the House on June 4, 1842 (Congressional Globe, vol. xi, 579, ff.; Croffut, W. A. *Fifty Years in Camp and Field* [New York, 1919], 156, ff.). In Croffut's excellent life of Hitchcock, *ibid.*, he quotes from entries made by the Colonel in his diary while waiting in Washington to render such further service as should be required of him, in connection with his report; instead of being called on he was shunned by officers connected with the Indian service; and Secretary of War Spencer told him the "House should not have the report without his heart's blood."

[2] Fort Smith was begun in 1817, by the location there of a detachment of riflemen under command of Maj. William Bradford, who, in connection with Maj. Stephen H. Long, selected a site for the post at the mouth of the Poteau River, where the Osage boundary line from the north intersects the Arkansas River. These troops had been ordered to this point in an effort to abate hostilities between the Osage on the one hand and the whites and Cherokee on the other. It was named for Gen. Thomas A. Smith. It was the farthest west outpost for several years, and long remained a celebrated military establishment on the western frontier. Fort Smith was abandoned in

1824 when the troops were sent up the Arkansas River to begin the establishment of Fort Gibson. In 1840 a new fort was begun near the site of the original Fort Smith and construction was continued for a number of years (Army and Navy Chronicle, April 23, 1840). Hitchcock observed the new Fort Smith near the site of the original post, under construction "of masonry in the form of a pentagon, its sides bisected and the point advanced a short distance. Bastions at the angles, 20 paces face and 12 flank, 100 semi-curtain. The walls are about 7 feet high and 4 feet thick. It is some 200 or 300 yards from the river, not on the highest ground, which is some 150 yards east and overlooks the wall; the work as it now stands is not defiled from this commanding point. The wall is to be 14 feet high." Here Major Hitchcock notes the meeting with Col. John Drennen who was afterward appointed Superintendent of the Southern Indian Superintendency, with his headquarters at Fort Smith. "Col. Drennen urges the continuation of troops at Fort Wayne; he says if they are removed he shall be disposed to move with his family from Van Buren, his present residence. Colonel Drennen was the proprietor of Van Buren which is 5 miles by land and 10 by water from the Arkansas line West." For extended accounts of Fort Smith and Fort Gibson see Grant Foreman, *Pioneer Days in the Early Southwest*, (Cleveland, 1926); *Indians and Pioneers* (New Haven, 1930).

GRANT FOREMAN

MUSKOGEE, OKLAHOMA

INTERNATIONAL INDIAN COUNCIL AT TAHLEQUAH, CHEROKEE NATION, CONVENED BY JOHN ROSS IN JUNE, 1843. Painted by John Mix Stanley. Courtesy of Smithsonian Institution, Bureau of American Ethnology.

MARY JANE ROSS

From a portrait. Courtesy of her son Hubbard Ross.

JOHN ROSS

From a photograph taken late in life. Courtesy of Smithsonian Institution,
Bureau of American Ethnology.

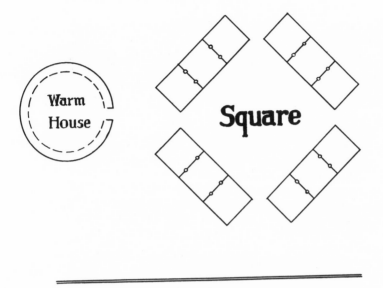

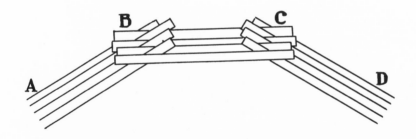

BUILDINGS AT CREEK BUSK GROUND
From sketches made by General Hitchcock.

A Traveler in Indian Territory
The Journal of
Ethan Allen Hitchcock

Chapter I

Major Hitchcock Arrives at Fort Smith – Description
of the Post – A Steamboat Warming – An Indian
School – On the Military Road – A Wilderness Home –
Refuge from a Storm – Arrival at Fort Gibson –
Rumors – Indian Traders – Buffalo – Horse Racing at
Fort Gibson – Wild Cat.

Fort Smith, 22nd Nov. — Reflecting upon the conduct of Col. Wharton Rector,[3] Paymaster, yesterday, I
am inclined to suspect him, tho' I had not thought of
him before he exhibited a fear of my mission in this
country. He pretended to be offended with my not
drinking with him, which I had twice declined doing
and he asked if I never drank. I told him I preferred
not drinking and did not drink when I could avoid it,
that I only drank a glass of wine at dinner table. He
said I had a right to do as I pleased, but he thought at
first I had refused to drink with *him*, and then he went
on in a very miscellaneous manner, being under the
influence of liquor at the time. This passed at the steam-

---

[3] Wharton Rector Jr., frequently called Colonel Rector, was appointed
paymaster in the army in 1836 with rank of major and died February 8,
1842, in his forty-second year, mourned by a large circle of friends; he was
buried at Van Buren, Arkansas, with military honors, the funeral services
being conducted by Maj. William W. Lear of the garrison at Fort Smith.
Major Rector was one of a very numerous and distinguished family of
Arkansas. Of German origin, the Rector family first migrated to Virginia,
and early in the nineteenth century part of the descendants joined in the
movement to the West; some of them reached Arkansas by way of Illinois
and St. Louis; Major Rector was a son of Wharton Rector, and a brother of
William V. and Elias, and more remotely related to many other Rectors in
Arkansas.

boat yesterday morning on her return from Fort Coffee.[4] The fact is, that the day before yesterday there was a horse race at Van Buren and the captain of the boat, *Arkansas*, invited the ladies and gentlemen on board at a sort of steamboat warming. The ladies went on board early in the afternoon, but the gentlemen attended the horse race and came to the boat, many of them highly "excited"; in truth some were very drunk including Col. Drennan and Thos. G. Wilson and Colonel Rector was also excited. He was evidently prepared to be suspicious of me, for he knows I broke up some speculators on the upper Mississippi and he fears I am here on a mission to rake up misdemeanors in this country. He was suspected of selling U. S. money in 1838 & had great difficulty in explaining the transaction on a call from Col. Benton[5] in the Senate – so I heard. Now, I think he wishes to brow-beat me and drive me off the track, as their own slang has it. We met again yesterday at Major Lear's quarters and he renewed his remarks, Lear being on a sick bed in one room and his wife sick in an adjacent room. He was more drunk on this occasion and I became grave and silent, when his brother, seeing his folly, called him away and after a few moments he went away; Lear apologised for him that he had never seen him in that situation before. That I don't like him is true, a renegade as he is from St. Louis and desperate in his feelings as he certainly is. He suspects he is not respected because he ·feels that he has

---

[4] Fort Coffee was established in 1834 on the south bank of the Arkansas River, at Swallow Rock about fourteen miles above Fort Smith. It was five miles from the Choctaw Agency, and was planned as the point of debarkation for Choctaw and Chickasaw emigrants coming up the Arkansas River by boat.

[5] Thomas H. Benton, United States Senator from Missouri from 1821 to 1851.

forfeited respect and he has found himself so successful in bravado heretofore that he has purposely sought
a quarrel with me. I hope not to see him again.

P. M. Col. Rector called this morning and apol-
ogized for his conduct yesterday, expressing the deepest
mortification. I at once told him that it was of no
importance and desired him to think no more of it.
He expressed the deepest regrets also to Lt. West.

Dwight Mission,[6] at Jacob Hitchcock's [7] (my cousin
from Brimfield, Mass.), Nov. 23, 1841. Left Fort
Smith this morning and entered the Cherokee nation
on horseback. Dined 17 miles at a Mr. Lowry's [8] a
Cherokee High Sheriff. Lowry not at home — his wife
gave me venison, bacon, eggs, fresh butter and good
corn bread on a table covered with a perfectly clean
cotton cloth, in crockery ware (coffee, sugar and milk
must be included), and she charged but two bits –
fifty cents for two, for I had a guide with me. Lowry
lives in a good log house floored and well secured
against weather. His wife, about 30, large but good
looking woman neatly dressed in a check frock. Her
little girl about 10, also neatly dressed in check. There
was nothing to distinguish appearances from those of
many of our border people except the complexion
(Cherokee) and superior neatness. Saw a spinning
wheel and some hanks of spun cotton hanging in the

---

[6] Dwight Mission was established within what is now Pope County,
Arkansas, among the Cherokee Indians, in 1820. Upon the removal of the
Cherokee in 1828 and 1829, from the present Arkansas, Dwight Mission also
was removed and school was reopened on the first of May, 1830. It was
located within two or three miles southwest of the present Marble City,
Oklahoma, near the military road constructed from Fort Gibson to Fort
Smith.

[7] Jacob Hitchcock was one of the missionaries at Dwight Mission, who
came west in 1820.

[8] George Lowrey lived on the military road where it crossed Skin Bayou.

passage between the two log houses under one roof.

Country today, wooded, mostly oak, not very dense except in the bottom along the river. Upland soil, medium, country rolling near the mission, almost hilly and rocky. Passed several log houses, with enclosures of several acres — upwards of 100 in one instance — trees merely girdled and left to decay. Saw corn and pumpkins, hogs, fowls and cattle, two waggons and some oxen and horses; a fine looking negro at Lowry's was "snaking" in trees with two yoke of oxen. The trees entire and nearly as large as my body.

24th, visited the school; Miss Hannah Moore from Connecticut, is a teacher; about 25 years of age not overly handsome, has about 36 scholars, all girls except one, ages from about 6 to 16, quite fair, some with light hair and eyes, recited in arithmetic, plain addition and multiplication examples. Saw some writing, pretty fair and heard some respectable reading – I mean for any school. Girls behaved well, were under good discipline, well but plainly dressed. The whole expense of this establishment is paid by the Board of Foreign Missions at Boston. Teachers have no salary but are provided with everything. Stores sent from Boston on estimates yearly from this place. Actual expense here for farming, etc., paid by drafts on Boston. I do not think I saw any but mixed blood in school.

Scott's 5 miles from Fort Gibson,[9] 2 P.M. I came

---

[9] In the spring of 1824, depredations by the Osage upon the whites, and disorders between them and the Cherokee had increased to such an extent that General Winfield Scott on March 8, ordered Colonel Arbuckle to remove his troops from Fort Smith to the mouth of the Verdigris. The removal was accomplished during the month of April and the troops were located at the best boat landing place in the vicinity, which was on the left bank of the Grand River. The troops were quartered in tents until log houses could be erected in which they were comfortably established by the succeeding year, and the post was first called Cantonment Gibson. It was located below the

from the mission yesterday 14 miles [10] to Mackay's [11] on the Illinois where I remained last night. Mackay, a white man, was sick and I did not see him or his family (half breeds) except a little girl. Thompson, a fine looking half-breed and a very active man speaking good English, received and entertained me. There were 3 Arkansaw horse drovers at the house. They were returning from the Creek Nation, where they had been with horses, but had sold but a few and were going back by the way of Tallequa,[12] the Cherokee capital, where there is to be a national council next Monday ('tis Thursday now). Mackay is building an addition to his house and will soon have a very comfortable house two stories high of squared logs with regular windows and doors, the former fitted with sashes and glass. The second story is low but affords good sleeping rooms. There were 5 double beds in one of them — feather beds resting on cords binding a proper bedstead, one sheet to each bed, with pillows in cases, a mackinaw blanket and coverlet to each. It rained vi-

hill upon which the modern Fort Gibson was constructed during the Civil War.

[10] Major Hitchcock is traveling over the first road constructed within the present State of Oklahoma. This military road was authorized by Congress in March 1825, and the survey was completed by the Seventh of November of that year. The road was authorized from Fort Gibson to Little Rock but only that part from Fort Gibson to Fort Smith was completed by autumn of 1827. This road to some extent followed an old Osage trail and crossed Illinois River near the old salt works about seven miles north of the present town of Gore. From Fort Gibson to Fort Smith the road measured 58 miles.

[11] Samuel Mackey made salt at a spring on the Illinois River, a few miles above the modern Gore, Oklahoma.

[12] Tahlequah, the capital of the Cherokee Nation was established at the springs near where the Cherokee tribe first met to counsel after the removal of the large body of the eastern faction of the tribe in 1839. Tahlequah was incorporated as a town in 1843 by the Cherokee government and is the oldest incorporated town in the State of Oklahoma.

olently, accompanied with lightning and thunder soon after I reached Mackay's and the first room we were put in was soon wet and we were directed to the upper room of the next half of the house, the roof of which was complete. Negro girls set a table for supper and breakfast, pork steak, bacon, corn bread, coffee, sugar, milk, crockery ware, charge one dollar, myself and horse. Rode this morning 13 miles to this place in a cold wet wind occasionally sleet and snow, stopped in a snow storm almost frozen and it has continued to storm more than an hour. A more disagreeable ride I do not remember to have had.

Scott was absent when I arrived at his house but came in after an hour or two with another man and immediately after dinner they, both white men, began playing "all fours" over a chair bottom, the back broke off. Scott had a lame hand but played with one hand and cursed and swore almost every other word. I had determined, on account of the bad weather to pass the night there, but was so much disgusted that I ordered my horse, saddled him myself, paid half a dollar and set off with snow and sleet in my face and came to Fort Gibson; where I now am for the first time. It is on the left bank of Grand River some two miles from its entrance into the Arkansas. I approached it over a prairie of some 2 miles or more with a strong cold wet wind blowing right in my face.

I hear, vaguely, that the union of the two parties of Cherokees, Ridge and Ross parties is of doubtful continuance that Ridge's friends are inveterate against Ross whose life is not safe. Ross' enemies charge him with selfishness and with squandering the public money, favoring his brother Lewis and other relations.

Fort Gibson 26 Nov. 1/4 after 8 A.M. and at length

I hear the first bell for breakfast at McDermot's hotel, a little better than at Capt. Roger's at Fort Smith, where we breakfasted at 9. Saw Col. Mason last evening and Dr. Maxwell, received well; spent the evening with Mason, who was formerly a Captain in the old 8th Infantry with me in 1820-21 at Bay of St. Louis. He thinks Ross a rascal, i.e., an artful, cunning, shrewd, managing, ambitious man. Tells me that some Cherokees had privately leagued and determined to put to death three of Ross' principal supporters, Taylor, McCoy and Lynch living near Beatty's prairie. On comparing notes and facts we concluded that Ross and his friends must have deceived the Council into the order they gave for the payment to Vann, some 500,000$ by representing that the money would be paid from the Treasury of the U. S. whereas it was paid from the Cherokee fund. The arrival of Ross [13] recently in the nation suspended the purpose of putting his friends to death until they can hear what is to be communicated by Ross. I am inclined to think that Ross is merely ambitious of elevating his nation into perfect independence. It is known that he wishes all the U. S. troops withdrawn. Mason thinks that Fort Wayne (Beatty's Prairie) should be continued if it be designed to establish the cordon of posts projected along the frontier.

Later-Shewed Col. Mason [14] my letters of instruction

[13] Ross had been in Washington looking after the adjustment of the affairs of the Cherokee growing out of the treaty of 1835 and their enforced removal.

[14] Richard Barnes Mason was born in Virginia; commissioned major of the Dragoon Regiment March 4, 1833, lieutenant-colonel, July 4, 1836, and colonel, June 30, 1846. With the Dragoon regiment he saw considerable service at Fort Gibson and was in command there at the time of Colonel Hitchcock's visit. In 1848, Colonel Mason was in command of the Tenth Military Department with headquarters at Monterey, California. He died July 25, 1850.

today and explained some facts tending to the proof of great frauds having been committed in this country in feeding Indians. He was very much astonished.

Some Cherokees and Creeks trade with Comanches – pack out one or two hundred dollars worth of goods and buy horses, etc. Comanches steal negroes sometimes from Texas and sell them to Cherokees and Creeks. The latter have been known to pay $400 and $500 for a negro.

P.M. introduced myself to Mr. Field a Cherokee half-breed, a merchant who has just returned from the north with a wife, a quakeress of Philadelphia and with *two* Cherokee half-breed daughters (16 and 17) or (15 and 17) who have been educated in New England.[15] Mr. Field invited me into his apartment and introduced me to his family. He is about 40 years of age and his wife may be 22 or 3, an intelligent fair looking woman. He looks like a white man and his two daughters are very fair and one very pretty. His language is as good as that of any country merchant I ever saw. I had not been told he was a half-breed and supposed he was a white man and hearing his daughters speak of having been at Keene, New Hampshire, I asked Mr. Field if he was from that State. His daughters smiled and he answered at once that he was an Indian born and bred in Alabama. I could then see a tincture of the Indian complexion but his whole de-

---

[15] One of these daughters was Amanda Fields who married Delos B. Sackett, afterward inspector-general of the United States army. The other was Elizabeth who married William Shorey Coody a distinguished member of the Cherokee tribe; of this union besides others is the daughter Ella, now Mrs. Ella F. Robinson of Muskogee. Richard Fields' daughters were educated at Keene, New Hampshire, where they lived several years in the home of Mr. Parker one of the teachers in the school attended by them. Young Mrs. Fields, formerly Henrietta Ridgeway of Philadelphia, was Fields' second wife.

meanor and language bespeak a gentleman and a man of independence and character. I begin to see how it is that the Cherokees are noted for their progress in civilization; it is the effect of the Crawford plan.

Mr. F. says the people elect the members of the Committee and Council for two years; they elect the sheriffs also, two committees and council and one sheriff for each of the 8 districts. The people elect the principal chief and assistant principal chief; and the committee and council act upon the nomination of the judges by the principal chief. They have a Supreme Court and Circuit Courts and other inferior Courts. The present committee and council is the first under the new constitution.[16] In cases of appeal from the Circuit Court, the papers are sealed and passed by the Sheriff to the upper court. All proceedings are recorded.

My object in speaking to Mr. Field was to inquire the object of the expected meeting of the Council. He could not tell me but says that the people have expected a considerable per capita sum (under the New Echota treaty)[17] and that if it be not received there must be difficulty and that Mr. John Ross will be held to a strict account. He does not intimate that the Cherokees will make any difficulty with the U. S. about it. He asked me if I knew what the amount was for distribution. I told him I did not know, but that I had heard it esti-

---

[16] After the removal of the Cherokee from the East a new constitution was drawn up at Tahlequah September 6, 1839, and adopted by the tribe.

[17] This treaty was executed at New Echota, Georgia, December 29, 1835, with supplementary articles concluded March 1, 1836. The treaty' was negotiated mainly by John F. Schermerhorn with a minority of the Cherokee tribe under circumstances repugnant to the wishes and sentiments of the great majority of the tribe. The principal feature of the treaty was that providing for the removal of the tribe which was opposed by the great body of the Indians and required a large force of the military to execute it.

mated at less than half a million. He said that he wished there was nothing remaining for the payment of money to the *"common people"* only made them dissipated and yet, said he, its a hard case to say a man shan't have what is due him because he'll make a bad use of it.

Lt. Carleton says there are a number of Indians in the Creek country about a hundred miles west of this who were driven out of Texas and took refuge in the Choctaw country from which they were driven by Gen. Arbuckle and that the Creeks received them, but that they are in a deplorable condition without powder and without corn. They are wanderers from several tribes.[18]

Lt. Carleton says there is no buffalo east of the Cross timber which is a range of timber varying from 1 to 10 or 15 miles in width, stretching from Texas north a great distance more than 100 miles west of this point, Fort Gibson.

Fort Gibson 27th Nov. A.M. Snowing and the ground white. Yesterday it was very cold and windy. The wind has declined and the sun will disperse the snow. . . .

12 M. Have seen Capt. Burgwin [19] of the 1st Regt. of Dragoons. He is just from Fort Wayne and confirms the report of a league against Lynch and others who have voted against the wishes of the Ross party. Lynch secludes himself, but it is understood that he will appear at the approaching council supported by fol-

---

[18] These were remnants of the Cherokee, Shawnee, Delaware, Kickapoo, Quapaw, and Piankashaw tribes.

[19] John H. K. Burgwin was graduated from the United States Military Academy, July 1, 1830; he became second lieutenant of the First Dragoons March 4, 1833, and afterwards saw much service at Fort Gibson; he was made captain of the First Dragoons July 31, 1837, and on February 4, 1847, during the Mexican War in the assault of Pueblo-de-Taos, was mortally wounded while gallantly leading, and skilfully directing the attack. He died on February 7, 1847, at the age of 36.

lowers. Ross, I think will see his policy in restraining his friends from acts of violence.

Col. Mason says the equipments for his command are the worst possible. His carbines blew off the stock and will not stand 20 fires. His saddles are made of *pine* and break with the ordinary weight of a man and let the whole weight upon the horse's backbone. He can twist and break his bridle bits with his own hands with the greatest ease and the leather of his bridle reins is of a loose spongy texture ruined on being wet, etc. Complains of it constantly without effect.

Mr. Field says great numbers of Cherokees have never been paid or indemnified for losses on their removal. He told me of a tradition among the Cherokees that about a hundred years ago the Chickasaws moved from the coast of Carolinas and settled by permission of the Cherokees on the upper Tennessee River under a promise to aid the Cherokees in defense against the northern Indians, Shawnees and others. After a time it was discovered that the Chickasaws pretended to go on war parties against the northern Indians but made great circuits and struck the Cherokees and robbed them. The Cherokees gave a great green corn dance and invited the Chickasaws arranging a Chickasaw next to a Cherokee all around a circle and at a signal the Chickasaws were nearly all murdered.

One-half past 8 P.M. Mr. Arnold Harris (Sutler) invited me to dinner today at half past 2, he said, as there was to be a race, about 12; everybody that could procure a horse was in the saddle to ride to the race only a few hundred yards off. The track was frozen and a harrow was employed so the race did not "come off" till late and another race was got up and detained Mr. Harris until near 5 P.M. I did not go to the race ground.

Twas cold and I cared nothing about the race. After
Mr. Harris came in I joined him and went to his house,
he apologizing for the delay, and was introduced to
his wife, her sister, Miss Armstrong from Nashville,
and his two sisters, all young ladies and rather pretty.
They had been at the race. Capt. Davis, Capt. Burgwin
and Lt. Wickliffe were at the dinner. The race was all
the talk. The ladies had lost and won some gloves and
the gentlemen some watches and money. An incredible
amount of conversation grew out of it. After dinner
the ladies withdrew and the card tables were set out.
A moderate game of ucre was soon laid aside for poker,
several other gentlemen came in and mostly joined in
the game and game slang was added to the jockey slang.
Capt. Burgwin, Lt. Wickliffe, Mr. Ridgeway did not
play. I never play and after a little time they were
called out by messages which I perceived came from
the ladies in an adjoining room and the doors being
open at one moment shew the ladies at a card table. I
was then decidedly alone, so I took my cap after a few
moments and have come away.

Fort Gibson, Sunday 28 Nov. Weather moderated
today and I rode 3 miles to the Arkansas. Left my
horse and crossed in a boat, found the celebrated Wild
Cat [20] (Coacoochee) Seminole chief. He recollected me
but we had no interpreter and I went in pursuit of

---

[20] Coowacoochee, whose English name was Wild Cat, was one of the
most celebrated Seminole chiefs and warriors, and it was largely by his
force and intelligence that the Seminole Indians maintained their resistance
through the years of warfare from 1836 to 1842, during which time the
government was attempting to remove them from Florida. After his arrival
in the West in 1841, however, Wild Cat became of great service to the
Government as a guide and scout and in aiding his tribesmen in establishing themselves in their new home. Wild Cat engaged in trade with the
Comanche and other southwestern Indians, and in 1850 he induced a
number of Creeks and Seminole to remove with him to the Mexican side
of the Rio Grande where he died soon after.

Micco, found him ¼ of a mile off and he returned with me to Coacoochee. Still could not talk but Micco's eyes glistened with delight at seeing me. He was in my camp several weeks in Florida and I treated him kindly.

P.M. Mr. Field (Cherokee half-blood) married a Miss Ridgeway in Philadelphia whose brother is now here – an intelligent young man. He has been in this country two or three years and I presume introduced Mr. Field to his family in Philadelphia. He says a Mr. Bartin now living below Fort Smith was a discharged soldier and became an agent of Harrison & Glasgow in issuing provisions at this place.

Fort Gibson, 29 Nov. Introduced myself to Dr. Powell the Phrenologist just in from a search after Osage sculls; opened a bag of them, one a chief's scull – zealous if not enthusiastic – opposed his doctrine to hear him defend it. He introduced me to Charles Candy a Cherokee half-breed who rode in with him today. Candy looks as well as and something like old Mulanphy (when I saw him 1829) who died worth millions; a larger man Candy is, and his wife is a very large woman. They have gone on to the Council.

Mr. Field introduced me to another Candy (William) a young man of about 25 or 30, very genteely dressed and educated, his manners those of a gentleman like those of Mr. Field. There is a quiet demeanor in some of these educated Cherokees very interesting. Indians are remarkable for a sedate dignity when not engaged in a quarrel.

Chapter II

Cherokee Customs – A Journey to the Capital – An
Indian Home – Cherokee Piety – An Indian Council –
John Ross the Executive – Legislative Committees –
An Indian's Religion – The Home of an Indian Mer-
chant – Sequoyah – Park Hill – An Incident of the
Seminole War – Civilization of the Cherokee – Killing
of Boudinot.

Tallequah, the capital of the Cherokee Nation, Tuesday Nov. 30, 1841. Arrived from Fort Gibson, 3 P.M.
I rode in company with Mr. Drew [21] a partner of Mr.
Field's, a half-breed over 40 years of age, speaking
good English but, as he told me, without any education
but what he has picked up since he grew to manhood.
Said he could read and write. We rode some 18 or 20
miles together and I kept him talking nearly all the
way. He emigrated with his father in 1809 to this country, has traveled to the north since he grew up (Philadelphia, etc.). He says the ancient customs of the
nation are all gone, the green corn and other dances,
marriages of men with but one woman except with the
most wild of the Cherokees. Knows of but one man of
the half-breeds who has two wives, a Mr. Vann who
has two distinct and large families, not living under
the same roof – is wealthy. He says a man wishing to
be married is obliged to procure a license from the
clerk of the Circuit Court. Upon this any judge or

[21] John Drew was a trader who had been associated with Sam Houston
in business ventures in the West.

clergyman may marry the couple; certifies the marriage on the back of the license which is then deposited with the Court. They have a number of preachers among them, some who do not speak English at all.

We passed several good farms, some owned by white men married to Cherokees and others to half-breeds mostly, log houses like those seen among our own border people. The road was good but not made. Country rolling with small streams, brooks occasionally. Mr. Drew said the country along the road was not well watered, said they could not have mills because the streams were in a flood or almost dry; there are two rainy or wet seasons, September and in the spring. The highest water he ever knew was in September. Thinks it will be good travelling the next six weeks or two months. Says that Cherokees mostly use steel corn mills, turned by hand to grind corn. They raise very little wheat. They raise hogs, cattle and horses. I found Mr. Drew modest and sensible.

As we approached Tallequah we met several persons riding out, two women among them, well dressed and covered with shawls, the men well dressed with hats and all are riding good horses. These people, said I, dont look very wild. Mr. Drew was flattered. Presently we met another party and among them I found one of the Vann's, the Treasurer of the Nation, whom I knew in Washington last summer. We shook hands cordially.

As we came in sight of the capital, I saw a number of log houses arranged in order with streets; or one street at all events, was clearly visible but the houses were very small. One house was painted: "The Council sit there" – "The Committee sit there"; (some distance off) "to the left, the principal chief stays" – we saw a number of people. "There are cooks, public cooks we call them" said Mr. Drew, "along those houses, meat etc., is furnished to them and they cook for the public. Everybody can go to the public tables. See there," said he, "you see some eating dinner." I saw some 20 at one table. "The nation pays the expense." We passed the centre of the town, "I live" said Mr. Drew "with a cousin over yonder. You had better go to Mr. Wolfe's on the hill" pointing in the direction I was riding. He politely offered to show me everything and we parted.

I came to Wolfe's and what do I find – one of the neatest and most comfortable log houses I almost ever saw. Mr. Wolfe is a half-breed, a very portly large man (has a large arm chair expressly made for him) speaks very good English, positively better than many of our country farmers in the West and South. His wife (strange) is a Dutch woman. I suppose she speaks English, but I have not heard her open her lips. Two young women, both speaking very good English have been sewing in the room since they gave me dinner, pork ribs, sliced and fried sweet potatoes, good biscuit of fresh flour (wheat) and a cup of tea, sugar and milk, all on a clean table cloth.

Tallequah, 1st December '41. Mr. Wolfe (named Young Wolfe), turns out to be a preacher. I retired early last evening leaving 6 to 8 Cherokees in quiet conversation in the Cherokee language. About half past 9 (I heard the clocks, for there are two in the house) strike 10 soon after the service; I was wakened by the singing of a hymn, after which I heard the prayer. This morning I was present at the service, a clergyman read a psalm or hymn sung, prayer all in Cherokee, all conducted in perfect propriety and the prayer was uttered from the heart. Carlyle himself would have been pleased, separating the heart and es-

sence from the "clothes." All present evidently understood and spoke English.

Tallequah 2nd Dec. Rained last night and continues
to rain. Yesterday John Ross,[22] Prin. Chief came from
his residence (five miles) near 12 o'clock and rode into
the middle of the Council ground and tied his horse
to a tree. Great numbers of the people were standing
around but Indian-like no one approached him. I was
the first to go up and speak to him. We shook hands
and several questions of civility passed and we separated. He walked a short distance and then began a
general greeting. Very many went up and shook hands
with their head chief. It was nearly an hour after his
arrival before he took his place in a sort of pulpit under
a large shed and the Committee and Council and people assembled promiscuously so far as I could observe
to hear the message. Mr. Vann invited me to a seat. I
remarked in an undertone "anywhere, out of the way,"
when he observed in a loud voice "You'll not be in
the way anywhere, Major, take a seat here" pointing
to a log seat immediately in front of the desk. Mr. Ross
took with him Bushyhead,[23] the Chief Justice,.a good
looking rather portly man, some 35 or 40 years of age.

22 John Ross was born in Rossville, Georgia, October 3, 1790, and died
in Washington, D.C., August 1, 1866. He was the son of an immigrant from
Scotland by a Cherokee wife who was herself three-quarters white. John
Ross was one of the most celebrated members of the Cherokee Nation, a
man of great force of character and of strong convictions. At the head of
the majority faction of the tribe his tenacity of purpose, his zeal in the
defense of the rights of the tribe and his undoubted political ambition
involved him in bitterest controversies after the removal of the majority
of the nation from the East in 1839.

23 Rev. Jesse Bushyhead, Chief Justice of the Cherokee Nation who conducted one of the emigrating parties to the West, died July 17, 1844. His brother Isaac was killed August 7, 1843, at the polling place in Saline district by
enemies of the newly established government, who tried to break up the first
general election under the new constitution.

Mr. Ross then read in English from a written paper his message, which was sentence by sentence translated into Cherokee by the Chief Justice – both standing.

The auditors were seated or standing at pleasure with their hats on and some were smoking but all was perfect order and silence. The council shed was merely a roof sustained by uprights. The seats were split logs or hewn logs supported by pins like a common farmers stool, but long, each seat holding 12 or 15.

In the message Mr. Ross gave an account of his mission to Washington from which he has just returned. He dwelt particularly upon his efforts to obtain a new treaty [24] for the Cherokees, concluding his message by detailing almost the whole of a letter to the delegation from President Tyler, dated last August which seems to promise a new treaty with full indemnity to the Cherokees for all their losses and "wrongs." Mr. Ross dwelt with great formality upon the particulars connected with the letter of the President upon the visit of the delegation to the President's house; upon the fact that the letter was signed in their presence, that the letter was countersigned by the Acting Secretary of War, and that the seal of the War Department was appended; thus giving, said Mr. Ross, the highest sanction possible to the promises and pledges in the letter.

Mr. Ross referred very briefly to the fact that a settlement had been obtained of the "claims of the nation" he called them, for expenses of emigration, stating that, as soon after the adjournment of the Council as the papers could be arranged the accounts would

[24] At this period the Cherokee tribe was in a state of unrest growing out of the opposition of many of the members to the Ross government and the unsettled state of their claims for damages caused by their enforced removal west.

be settled. After the message was read, the correspondence of the delegation with the Government at Washington, was read letter by letter. During a part of this,
I was absent as I had seen the letters in Washington,
but I was present at the close and heard the letter of the
President read. It was twice read in order to acquaint
everybody with its contents. I should observe that in
the message in connection with the exposition of the
contents and promises in the letter Mr. Ross recommended the appointment of proper persons in each district to "take evidence" and ascertain the losses of the
Cherokees with a view to lay the result before the commissioners who might be appointed to negotiate the
new treaty.

He (Ross) has received the money, seemingly or
affectedly as from the treasury of the U. S., and he
designed now to press the claims of the Cherokees for
losses in being forced to emigrate against their will.
If he succeeds in this he will satisfy the people, who
will be paid their losses; but a failure or a great delay
in this, may result fatally for him, for it is certain that
many of the Cherokee consider that Ross has been using
up the per capita fund, or the fund, a certain portion
of which is to be paid per capita, to the injury of the
people. They suppose that over 1,800,000 dollars of
that fund remains for distribution and they have no
idea that the claim for expenses of emigration has been
paid out of that fund. Now the fact is, that only about
$900,000 of that fund remained before the late pay-
ment, so that in truth there remains but a little over
$300,000 for distribution and that fund will be still
farther reduced, for there are other payments yet to
be made. An intelligent white man residing here gives
the opinion that Ross will yet fall a victim to these

measures. He assures me the Ridge party is inveterate against the authors of the death of Ridge and Boudinot.[25] He tells me a great number of persons were concerned in those murders, so many as to protect each other for the present. That they intended to kill some others but failed, not finding them. On the death of Ridge and Boudinot, others fled. That in addition to that permanent cause of hatred, there will be the disappointment on the subject of the per capita, if there should be no further appropriation by the United States.

How far the Government is bound to make good a fund which has been depredated upon by contractors and others is a question. The Government was the trustee for the Cherokee people.

P.M. attended a meeting of the Committee of the nation in a log house, earth floor, no windows, but 2 or 3 benches. Could not distinguish the members from spectators – hats on. President Vann [26] in the chair, i.e., standing by the fire behind a box which had been a

---

[25] Major Ridge, his son John Ridge, and Elias Boudinot were murdered on June 22, 1839, directly after the breaking up of the meeting of the tribe at Tahlequah that was engaged in an effort to establish a government for the whole tribe. These men were prominent leaders in the antagonism to the Ross government and their murder aroused the whole nation to the highest pitch of excitement. Ross was charged with complicity in the affair which prevented for many years the union of the tribe and peaceable adjustment to their new environment.

[26] Joseph Vann, the candidate of the Western Cherokee, for chief, was defeated by John Ross in the election of 1843. He had been elected assistant principal chief in 1839, and served until the revision of the government June 26, 1840, when he resigned and the office was filled by Andrew M. Vann, who served until his death in 1842. Joseph Vann was a merchant and did an extensive business in the Cherokee Nation; he was the owner of the *Lucy Walker*, a fine steamboat that was sunk by a boiler explosion on the Ohio River near Louisville, when Mr. Vann was killed. Captain James Vann, another enterprising Cherokee, was the owner of the steamboat, *Franklin*, doing business on Arkansas River.

merchant's box of goods. The Secretary (Clerk) Taylor a young man, wrote something and then read a resolution that the Treasurer of the Nation should pay debts in proportion to the claims (pro rata). The Treasurer (another Vann) hat on, stepped up to the clerk and began objecting to a requirement in the resolution that he should ascertain the amount of the debts. He said he had no mode of doing it. Several spoke by way of remark, but did not rise, nor address the chair. Mr. Vann started another objection that they had proposed a resolution, not a law for appropriation and he appealed to the Constitution which required that no monies should be paid but upon warrants under an appropriation. After some discussion that was remedied and the act made to read in the form of an appropriation. The resolution or act, was written in English, but was read and interpreted into Cherokee.

At length the law was sent over to the Council. I followed it and went into the Council, same kind of a house. The roll was called and a quorum declared present. The act was read. A young member proposed an amendment that all claims for a hundred dollars and under should be paid in full. Spoke of their being many small claims $1 to $5, etc., were held by poor and necessitous people; called them the "common" people, accounts of that kind ought to be paid in full. Those who held large claims could wait another payment.

His talk in English was explained in Cherokee by the Clerk; another member proposed $50 limit. The young man made another speech rising each time. (There was more form in the Council than in the Committee). The Chair then remarked upon there being two motions before the Council and he first put it to vote. "Shall the bill be amended"? There was but one negative voice. Then shall the limit be $100 or $50, each one voted and there were 15 voices for $100. So "the amendment was carried."

I fell in with a portly looking man, near the council room, before the Council met. We talked of sundry matters when he, of his own accord, said he believed they (Committee and Council) were about calling upon John Ross to account for all the monies he had received from General Scott [27] and from the Government. This accorded with what I had heard from Mr. Paradise, who but a moment before had told me that he had heard that it was intended to demand to know from Mr. Ross whether the amount lately received by him was not paid out of the Cherokee fund; and if so, they intended requiring it to be paid to the nation. Paradise thought there would be difficulty, saying that Ross would pay the money as he originally designed, i.e., would disregard any order from the Cherokee Committee and Council on the subject.

Mr. Wolfe told me today that he was among the first of the Cherokees to adopt Christianity, some 19 years ago in Tennessee when he was 30 years of age (now 49). He was converted by a Methodist itinerant from a conference. The Cherokees always believed (he says) in God and in a heaven and hell, he has heard the old people talk about it. The good go to a good place, the bad to a bad place. He says they never had any idea of the shape of the earth. Thought it a great plain. He, himself, came to think it round about 10 years ago.

Tallequah, Monday 6 Dec. a very fine clear morning. Three days ago, I visited John Ross, Principal

---

[27] Gen. Winfield Scott who was ordered to Georgia in 1838 at the head of troops to enforce the removal of the Cherokee.

Chief of the Nation, his brother Lewis Ross, a merchant; and passed the night at Mr. Woosters [28] the missionary who with Mr. Butler was put into the Georgia Penitentiary for non-conformity to the Georgia Laws while in the Cherokee nation east of the Mississippi. Day before yesterday I returned to Mr. Wolfe's to dinner and found Gov. Pierce M. Butler of South Carolina, here, the recently appointed agent for the Cherokees with him, at the invitation of John Ross. I went to Mr. Ross in the afternoon and remained till yesterday midday and then went and dined with Lewis Ross and came here again last evening after dark.

I have seen a number of people and heard much which has left a general impression. It would be difficult to recall the particulars. Lewis Ross the merchant is wealthy and lives in considerable style. His house is of the cottage character, clapboarded and painted, his floor carpetted, his furniture elegant, cane bottomed

---

[28] Rev. Samuel A. Worcester was a missionary who had been teaching and preaching in the Cherokee Nation for many years. Because of the moral support which he and other missionaries were giving to the Cherokee in their efforts to maintain their national integrity they were seized by members of the Georgia Guard on March 12, 1831, and taken before the Georgia Superior Court in Gwinnett County, charged with violation of the state law by remaining among the Indians without securing a permit and subscribing to an oath of allegiance to the State. They were subsequently released but upon their continued refusal to cease their work and leave the State, they were again arrested on July 7, the writ of habeas corpus denied them, carried before the court, tried and convicted; and as punishment were sentenced to serve four years in the penitentiary at hard labor. Upon appeal the United States Supreme Court reversed and set aside the conviction and ordered Doctor Worcester's release from prison. It was some months however, after the judgment of the Supreme Court that the officers of Georgia saw fit to comply with it. Rev. Mr. Worcester went to Indian Territory to continue his service with the Indians. Here he set up the first printing press where he printed hundreds of thousands of pages of tracts, school books, and pamphlets for the benefit of the Indians. He died and was buried at Park Hill. Mr. Worcester's daughter Ann was the mother of The Hon. Alice M. Robertson, herself a pioneer missionary and a member of Congress from Oklahoma.

chairs, of high finish, mahogany sofa, two superior mahogany Boston rocking chairs, mahogany ladies work table with drawers, a very superior Chickering piano on which his unmarried daughter, a young lady of about 17 or 18, just from school at Rawway in New Jersey, plays some waltzes, and sings some songs. She is lively and pretty with rich flowing curls, very fine eyes and beautiful regular ivory teeth.[29] She has two cousins, twins, Misses Nave, 16 about, modest fair looking girls who have not the confidence and presence of mind of Miss Ross whose accomplishments perhaps overawe them. Mrs. Lewis Ross is a portly fine looking woman who has just returned from a 3 year absence superintending the education of her daughter. A married daughter Mrs. Murrill was also there and her husband a white man who seems to be in partnership with Lewis Ross. Mr. Lewis Ross told me he sold as a merchant no ornaments of any consequence, that the Cherokees bought nothing of that kind now, he sold a great proportion of domestics, some ready-made clothing, especially pantaloons and overcoats, and a great many shoes. Of the latter article the Cherokees make a great use almost dispensing with moccasins.

Lewis don't like the missionaries, could tell me nothing about their doctrines. I asked him specifically about some doctrinal points, the fall, infinite sin, man's inability, necessity of grace, expiatory sacrifice, etc. He said he could tell me nothing about how those things were understood by the converts, that he never troubled

[29] This attractive girl was Mary Jane, sometimes called Mollie, who in 1846 married her cousin William P. Ross. Their son Hubbard Ross of Fort Gibson, Oklahoma, is the owner of a handsome oil portrait of his mother painted while she was attending school in the East. Besides this he has some of the mahogany furniture seen by Major Hitchcock, and three large volumes of the quaintly printed music with which she entertained the appreciative officer.

himself about those *little* things. He admitted the missionaries had reformed some intemperate men and improved the manners of others. I endeavored to satisfy him of their singleness and purity of purpose, freedom from selfishness, etc.[30]

Mr. Worcester explained something of the formation of the Cherokee language and the reason of its admitting a syllabic alphabet. (I have seen Guess,[31] the author of the alphabet). Every syllable in the Cherokee language terminates with a vowel sound; hence in any given alphabet, as our own for instance, the number of sounds would be determined by the number of consonants multiplied by the vowels, say $18 \times 6 - 98$ the number of sounds; so that 98 characters would be sufficient for a syllabic alphabet, and the sentence "O. Katy Jay, I see you are a busy bee" would be written "O Kt J. I. c. u. r. a. bz. b.," an ex: given me by Mr. Doremus who saw Mr. Worcester the day before myself and whom I met at this place. Mr. Doremus is a merchant from New York, on a tour of collection I presume.

Last evening Mr. Paradise in the presence of several

[30] "There are believed to be about two thousand professors of the Christian religion, consisting of Baptists, Methodists and Presbyterians; the former comprise much the largest class, and may be considered the first class of Cherokees. For intelligence and general integrity, there are about four thousand others who might be classed among the first. Much the largest class of Cherokee people are half-breeds, or what are known to be the middle class, who are ardent and enterprising, and passionately fond of gaming."—Report of Cherokee Agent Pierce M. Butler, to Commissioner of Indian Affairs, 1842, U. S. House. *Documents*, 27th congress, third session, no. 2.

[31] George Guess or Sequoyah was one of the most remarkable Indians of any tribe; wholly without education, he invented an alphabet for the use of his tribe which could be mastered in a few days' time, and which enabled those who could use it to read and to write readily. It contributed more than any other factor to the advanced position which the Cherokee occupied among the tribes.

gave an account of the Morman faith. He has recently been at Nauvoo in Illinois, spoke of their faith in the inspiration of Joe Smith, that he interpreted the written tables that were said to be found giving a history of the bible; that they were building what they call a temple in Nauvoo but what in fact is a fortification. That they have an organized force of 500 men. Mr. Wolfe, in allusion to their faith in Joe Smith's inspiration said they ought to come and see the Cherokees and consult their conjures. Mr. P. said they ought to be exterminated.

Park Hill [32] overlooks two prairies of moderate extent and the scenery is as beautiful as the eye can desire. Mr. Worcester's place is about a mile from the residence of John Ross who with his brother Lewis and their connections occupy that beautiful section of country. The Illinois river rushes by the borders of the Ross prairie. It is reported by a gentleman from Fort Gibson that commissioners have been appointed for making a treaty with the Cherokees. Gov. Butler went to Fort Gibson yesterday. The gentleman (Mr. Paradise) says it is understood that Capt. Armstrong, Gov. Butler and one other (name unknown), are the Commissioners, Col. Stambaugh, Secretary.

Mr. Bushyhead, a Cherokee clergyman gave at Mr. Ross', a detailed and very graphic account of his mission to the Seminoles in 1837 to effect their peaceable removal. He succeeded in inducing Miccanopy to enter Gen. Jesup's camp, with some other chiefs and persons, in all about 70 and General Jesup told them they must send for their men to deliver up their rifles and also to send for their women and children. These messages

[32] Park Hill about five miles south of Tahlequah, was the home of John Ross, Lewis Ross and Rev. Samuel A. Worcester.

were delivered to Sam Jones, who answered "who ever heard of women and children making a treaty, that is the business of warriors," and he immediately moved toward the South; about that time Coacoochee who had been seized and confined at St. Augustine, made his escape and declared to Sam Jones that the object was not to make a treaty but to get possession of the Indians. He had himself been seized when in General Jesup's power by invitation, as had been Osceola.[33] This decided Jones to reject the invitation and he prepared for a fight. Mr. Bushyhead and his interpreter after great personal exposure finally returned with bad news to the camp of General Jesup at Fort Mellon and the General then seized Miccanopy and the 70. Mr. Bushyhead is a very interesting man, the Chief Justice of the Nation and all he says bears the impress of truth. His account throws the burden of failure upon General Jesup. He had sent for the Seminoles to come in and make a new treaty and yet one of the first speeches he made to Miccanopy was to tax him and his people with faithlessness to their former engagements. This when everybody knew or might have known that the Seminoles were fighting for what they thought was their rights.

Many of the influential people in this Cherokee nation are half-breeds. They are a free minded, free spirited people very little shackled by conventional forms and on any subject they readily hit upon the strong points and take little heed of minor consideration. They seem to be industrious and orderly. I have

---

[33] Osceola, the Seminole Chief, was seized by General Jesup while in a conference with the white officers — an act condemned as inexcusable treachery. The youthful chief brooded until his spirit was broken and he died a prisoner at Fort Moultrie, S. C., in January, 1838.

not yet seen a drunken man since I came into the nation. The laws prohibit the sale of ardent spirits. I have never seen any assembly of people more orderly than this at Tallequah. There are classes of people here, rich and poor, cultivated and uncultivated and they occupy the same relative positions as with us. The habits of life appear simple and natural. Savage customs and manners have disappeared. There are no villages strictly speaking but settlements more or less densely populated occupying favorable positions embracing a circle of many miles under various names, Grand Saline, Beatty's Prairie,[34] Sallisaw, etc. There are many blacksmiths among them but no shoe makers or professed tailors, no arts of any consequence beyond the building of very good log houses with doors and windows, some of the latter with glass and sliding sashes.

P.M. at Rev. Mr. Worcester's. He has told me the particulars connected with the death of Mr. Boudinot stabbed and finished with a hatchet by three persons, some dozen or more being mounted in the vicinity ready for need. Mr. Paradise told me today that Mr.

[34] The Grand Saline was the settlement near where is now Salina, Oklahoma. Colonel Hitchcock wrote his brother that some parts of the Cherokee Nation were more populous than others, owing to peculiar advantages of soil or vicinity to markets, as along some parts of the Arkansas line, where, he said, perhaps two-fifths of the whole nation had made their homes. While the Cherokee were jealous of the encroachments of the whites, "they seek their vicinity and emulate their progress in domestic comforts; . . . Some of the former not merely rivalling but absolutely excelling many of the whites along the border in every convenience that can be found in a merely country life, good dwelling houses, good stables, well cultivated fields, gardens, orchards, with an ample stock of horses, cattle, hogs, poultry, &c." Cherokee Agent Butler reported: "All persons familiar with that portion of the Cherokees bordering on Crawford and Washington counties, in Arkansas, know that they are industrious, intelligent, and neighborly disposed."— Butler's Report, *idem*. The settlement known as Beattie's Prairie adjoined the Arkansas border.

Lynch, and I think he said Adair (leading men in the nation), gave him the opinion that the losses of people on removal would not exceed $600,000. Mr. Fields told me at Fort Gibson that $500,000 would pay them all. This is of importance.

Chapter III

Cherokee Evening Service – Judge Bushyhead – Cherokee Customs – Joseph Vann – Change in Cherokee
Conditions – War on Whiskey – Osage Visitors Astonish the Cherokee – Iniquity of Osage Treaty – Preëminence of Osage Horse Thieves – Cherokee Statistics
– Legislative Discussions – Cherokee Decorum –Punishment – Return to Fort Smith – By Steamboat to
Webber's Falls.

Mr. Wolfe's (Tallequah) 7th Dec. I remained in
Mr. Worcester's last night and attended a Cherokee
monthly meeting for prayer. The service was conducted
in both English and Cherokee. Mr. Foreman, a Cherokee, engaged in translating the bible into Cherokee,
made an excellent prayer in English. It was perfectly
appropriate – simple and natural and earnest. The language pure English, entirely free from border defects.
I have often had occasion to notice that the English of
the half-breeds is free from many prominent defects
among our border people, West and South. It may be
owing to the influence of the missionaries who are better instructed themselves. There might have been 25 or
30 people present last evening. Good order and perfect
decorum prevailed. I have seen no disorder since I
have been in the nation.

Mr. Wolfe yesterday told me of some of the practices of the old nation, that there were old men who were
respected as conjurers. They would sometimes throw a
piece of venison in a fire and pretend to foretell the

result of an expedition for hunting or war and when a man was sick, they would have him carried to the shore of a lake or a river bank and make the relations go into the water and dive seven times and then they would pretend to say whether the sick man would die or recover.

I am writing on one end of a table while Miss Wolfe (18 or 20) is ironing clothes at the other. I don't see, said I, but that you are as industrious as any of our people. She smiled but said nothing.

P.M. Judge Bushyhead assembled the "people" today and read a memorial inviting them to sign it, praying the Hon. Committee and Council to repeal the resolution calling upon the Government of the U. S. for the head right or per capita money. All was order. He explained the object in a speech. He is very fluent and easy, not affectedly an actor. He is truly an interesting man.

I should notice that besides Mr. Foreman's prayer last evening, which was in English, there was a long address in Cherokee from a Cherokee who speaks no English. He is a regular preacher as Mr. Worcester told me, about 40 years of age, full size, good presence, rather hard features. He spoke with great simplicity of manner but with a very earnest tone of voice. Miss Wolfe says her grandmother lived to be over a hundred years old and recollects hearing her speak of the first appearance of the white men among the Indians. They came and gave the Indians axes and the Indians wore them on their necks for ornaments. Says that last year some of the council wanted to make a law prohibiting white men from marrying among the Cherokees, and she thought they would have passed the law but for her father; that he was abused, accused of wishing to have white men marry his daughters; that he told them such a law would put them back to their former state of wildness. Then she remarked that the Cherokee men had better behave better and stop drinking whiskey and then the "Cherokee girls would marry them."

My shirts by that time, which had been ironed and very neatly done up but unrolled over a chair to dry, were ready to put into my saddlebags, and I took them and began rolling them, but Miss Wolfe interposed. "Let me put them up" – "never mind I can do it" – "I'll do it, said she, I've often put up preachers clothes and they are not different from these I reckon" and so she began to put up one, but did not please herself and tried again smiling and saying "Its the first time I suppose that ever an Indian washed your clothes." "I believe it is, said I, but I've been a good deal among Indians but not like the Cherokees."

Tallequah 8 December. Mr. Doremus, two Messrs. Lynde, Mr. West, Dr. Palmer came yesterday from Fort Gibson and continued their journey this morning except Dr. Palmer. A good deal of conversation with Mr. Doremus an intelligent merchant from New York. Talked with Mr. Joseph Vann this morning sitting in the Committee room before the Committee assembled. Mr. Vann the President of the Committee is 45 years of age, came to this country, 10 or 15 years ago; dresses in a frock overcoat wears a kerchief in a turban form on his head, vest, pants and boots, speaks perfect English and is a clear minded sensible man. Says they had no written constitution here before the last emigration and but a few laws. Country was divided into four districts, tis now 8 – had 3 chiefs and committee and council all elective, Sparse population and many had begun to be comfortable. Some of them have sold their improvements to advantage to the last emigrants. Of these many are very poor and are obliged to work hard for a living. No game of any consequence, used to be buffalo and elk. Thinks they were more comfortable East of the Mississippi, but that the mode of removal deprived great numbers of what little property they had, stock, etc., and that they have had no means of supplying themselves here. Can neither get pay for their losses nor the per capita under the treaty of 1835. States that many died in the removal.[35] Many children died but many are left helpless orphans depending upon the charity of those who are frequently scarcely able to take care of themselves. Says they have but a very few insane among them. There are some cases, a law has been proposed to appoint guardians for them. Very few idiots. Sickness is commonly fever and ague. Many can stop the ague but cannot cure it. Has known it last three years, knew a curious case of a man who had a chill regularly every three weeks "to a day"; generally doctor themselves but white physicians sometimes come among them; knows of two now, one having his wife with him boarding at Mr. Stermet's – have no rights. There are a number of blacksmiths in the nation, some shoemakers; leather is brought from the States. The Government furnishes four blacksmiths, a wheelwright and a cartwright, but knows nothing about them. Don't live in their neighborhood, says if they are not useful it is the fault of the Indian Agent. After leaving him and walking around, I was struck with the number of fine horses in sight; many came here on very fine horses, well dressed – the horses, I mean; had good saddles and

---

[35] It was estimated that over four thousand Cherokee out of a total of sixteen thousand removed, died during the migration, in the concentration stockades while awaiting removal, and directly after they reached their new home.

bridles upon them. Every saddle for the most part covered with a good blanket secured by a circingle. The men generally at this season have warm overcoats, some made of blankets, some of thick pilot cloth. Some have overcoats in the form of hunting shirts bound with a belt of all varieties of cloth. The most have pantaloons, some wear buckskin leggings. Have seen as yet but one man with his legs bare; in summer and at home there may be many more.

Have not yet seen a single case of intoxication or disorder, but yesterday I understood there were signs of liquor on the Council ground and the Sheriffs found on search a barrel nearly full and emptied it without ceremony by bursting the head of the barrel and also broke a gallon jug and a quart bottle wasting the liquor contents of each. At night I hear that the owner of the barrel had sought a quarrel with one of the sheriffs who, however, found no difficulty in protecting his dignity. Many expressed sentiments of indignation against the impudent violation of law in bringing whiskey to the council ground.[36]

While sitting with Mr. Vann he shewed me a message from Jno. Ross to the Committee returning a bill with objections, a regular veto message. It was a bill making an appropriation. I took occasion to express the pleasure it gave me to see the regularity with which business was done, and Mr. Vann made some remarks upon the danger of hasty legislation on one side and the inconvenience of too much form on the other.

Some half a dozen Osage Indians made their appearance last evening at the Council ground. Their heads were shaved and ornamented with feathers and they

---

[36] October 25, 1841, the Cherokee National Council enacted stringent laws against the introduction of spirituous liquors.

wore blankets in primitive style. The Cherokees gathered around them and gazed at them with as much curiosity as if they had never seen an Indian. The Osages would hardly have attracted more curiosity in the city of New York. The Osage tribe is out of favor with all their neighbors. They are thieves to a man, wild, ignorant and barbarous, hate work and are half the time in a starving condition. An immense portion of this western country was originally purchased from them under a treaty negotiated by General Clark, the Superintendent at St. Louis, for a very small annuity, some $8,000 I think; yet the Senate at the time very reluctantly assented to the treaty. I have heard General Clark say he offered to take the conditions of the treaty himself, pay the money and own the country and he said at the same time it was the hardest treaty [37] on the Indians he ever made and that if he was to be damned hereafter it would be for making that treaty. It really seemed to weigh upon his conscience and he was the kindest man in the world to any Osages who might visit St. Louis, but then he was kind to everybody.

Gov. Butler, the other day told a story of an Osage Chief who had a son killed in a ball play got up for the amusement of some officers and other gentlemen from Fort Gibson a number of years since. The chief came to Fort Gibson and demanded a hundred dollars as a compensation for the death of his son and in answer

[37] Kappler, Charles J. *Laws and Treaties*, vol. ii, pp. 69, 116. The first treaty negotiated by General Clark at Fort Clark, September 4, 1808, was ratified in Saint Louis, November 10, 1808. By this treaty the Osage ceded to the United States all of the part of the State of Arkansas lying north of Arkansas River and all of the State of Missouri. By the treaty negotiated at Saint Louis, September 25, 1818, for the promise to pay claims of the whites against them not to exceed $4000, the Osage ceded to the United States all their land now included in Sequoyah, Adair, Cherokee and parts of Muskogee and Wagoner counties, in Oklahoma.

to a remonstrance that a hundred dollars was too much he justified the demand by pleading that the deceased was the best horse thief in the nation; an inferior man might be worth no more than 10 or 20 dollars but his son was worth a hundred. This profession of horse stealing was once common all over this western region and still prevails among the Pawnees and other northwest tribes as also among the Comanches.

Someone told me yesterday that there were originally seven clans among the Cherokees, kept distinct in descent through the female line. That no marriages were permitted within a clan. It was the same among the Choctaws. The custom has grown into disuse among the Cherokees and is expressly abrogated by the constitution of the Choctaws.

Tallequah 9th December, Memoranda. On the 2nd November, 1819, at New Town (old Cherokee Nation) a law was passed requiring all whites who chose to marry Cherokee women to be married legally – prohibited their having more than one wife and "recommended that all others should also have but one wife hereafter."

October 23, 1822. A unanimous resolution in Committee and Council (old Nation), refused to meet Committee appointed by the United States to negotiate for their lands in Georgia declaring emphatically that they never would sell "one foot of ground . . . having not more than sufficient for our nation and posterity."

On 12th November, '24, a census was ordered and information in relation to improvements of all sorts; population was 15,560. There were 1277 negroes (610 male and 667 female) grand total Indian 16,837.[38] This

---

[38] The population of the Cherokee country, by the "enumeration of their

memorandum is from a printed document in the hands of Mr. Bushyhead, the clerk of the Council. I was at his elbow and helped him frame a law, as he was puzzled for English.

Yesterday I was in the Council pending a debate upon a motion to repeal a law of the late Council calling upon the United States Government for the per capita money under the treaty of 1835. A memorial had been sent in, praying the repeal, signed or marked by some 250 persons. A counter memorial signed by only about 20 persons was also presented. A good deal of discussion followed. One man (in English) was opposed to the repeal – talked about the sufferings of the people; their want of money due under the treaty; had voted for the law but a few weeks ago; 'twas too soon to repeal it; the council had no right to do it, etc., in a very miscellaneous and broken speech. And then suddenly broke into a new theme, and "I am in favor, said he, of a motion calling upon our principal chief for a settlement with the nation." He was proceeding to remark upon the amount of money unaccounted for, that neither he nor no other person knew anything about it. He was cut off by the Speaker, who remarked that he had deviated from the subject before the Coun-

agent in 1809 was 12,395 Cherokees, half of whom were of mixed-blood; beside 583 negro slaves, and 341 white, total of 13,319. They have since [1820] increased to 14,500 souls."— Morse, Reverend Jedidiah, D.D. *A report to the Secretary of War of the United States, on Indian Affairs, comprising a narrative of a tour performed in the Summer of 1820, under a commission of the President of the United States, for the purpose of ascertaining, for the use of the government, the actual state of the Indian tribes in our country* (New Haven, 1822), 152. The Commission to the Five Civilized Tribes enrolled 37,917 Cherokee by blood, besides Delaware and freedmen enrolled with the tribe (*The Final Rolls of Citizens and Freedmen of the Five Civilized Tribes in Indian Territory, Prepared by the Commission and Commissioner to the Five Civilized Tribes and Approved by the Secretary of the Interior on or prior to March 4, 1907*).

cil. The orator closed then with a very few more remarks. An old gentleman, without rising from his seat,
observed that it was a "wrong doctrine" to say that the
council had no right to repeal a law. They not only had
the right but it was their duty to repeal any law that
was found to be oppressive to the people, as this law
was shown to be by the memorial. Mr. West (6 ft. 8 in.
high and very well read) said that the memorial was
signed by those living in this neighborhood, that his
constituents were in favor of the law when he left
home. That if they were here he supposed they might
still be in favor of it and for his part he did not see
any inconvenience in the law and could not understand
why or how it could affect any further negotiation with
the United States. Still, to accommodate the wishes of
so many he would be in favor of suspending the operation of the law, etc. Some Cherokee speeches were made
and translated, as the English speeches had been, by
the clerk. One large-sized man over 50 dressed in an
overcoat with large pockets, divested his head of a tur-
ban-like kerchief and advanced to the centre of the
room, bowed profoundly to the speaker (all who had
made regular speeches stood in the middle of the floor)
and made some jocular remark I judge, as the reverend
counselors all laughed. He then began his speech, his
right hand thrust into his right coat pocket a long pipe
stem proceeding from the pocket extending along his
arm to his elbow, with his left hand he made graceful
gestures from time to time until he became excited and
then both hands were employed in gesture, his person
for the most part erect or but slightly bending forward.
I asked a man next to me on which side the orator was
and he said for the repeal. I thought the law would be
repealed. A young full blooded Cherokee made a

speech. He had voted for the law, for the benefit of his constituents, had thought it was right and did not regret it. He was now convinced it was an error, "all men sometimes committed errors and the best way was to acknowledge and repair them." He would vote for the repeal. The first speaker in English in a second speech opposed the repeal. The question was taken and carried by but one majority some members being absent, known to be against the repeal. The act for repeal has not yet been sent to the Committee.

Tallequah 10th December '41. Rode over to John Ross' in company with Mr. Wilson. Am promised a written account of sundry matters, I have proposed by written questions; talked with John Ross riding back to the council ground. In the old nation as property began to accumulate, theft became more common. The neighborhood of the whites (this I had from Mr. Wolfe) introduced whiskey and disorder. The condition of the country produced different effects upon different people. Some were willing to move to this country for a quiet and secure life, others set about measures for punishing evil doers. The want of gaols and penitentiaries made summary proceedings and punishment necessary. Some mounted men were employed as light horsemen, who were for a time judges and executioners. They passed from place to place, tried causes and executed judgment; whipping was the common punishment. This was new and esteemed disgraceful and some on whom it has been inflicted fled the Nation and came to this country making two classes of people here the quiet and orderly, and the mischievous and wicked. The light horsemen in time became overbearing, tyrannical, and oppressive; they were displaced by a new organization of the Government Chiefs, two houses for counsel and the appointment of regular judges and sheriffs (about 1827).

Fort Smith Ark. December 13, '41. Arrived after three days ride on horseback in company with Gov. Butler,[39] Mr. Currier (late Lt.) and Mrs. West sister-in-law to Captain Dawson. They reached Tallequah from Fort Gibson the evening of the 10th and the next day I mounted my horse to accompany them to Mr. Ross'. Called at Lewis Ross' and then continued in company to Mackay's, where I concluded to come here for access to the mail having ordered my letters to this place. I have found the papers I expected from Judge Martin and other letters, including one from the Secretary of War with statements in reference to the expenditures for provision in 1837 and other matters. Introduced to Col. Upshaw, Chickasaw agent, by Capt. Rogers at this place. He says the distance hence to Ft. Towson is about 150 miles, good road. From Gibson road almost impassable, swamps.

Steamboat *Exchange* Fort Smith – 15th Dec. 1841. Hurried on board, taking advantage of the opportunity offered by the unexpected arrival of the boat on her way to Gibson. Shall see the river & save myself an unnecessary ride over my former route to Gibson. Off Salisaw, 18th Nov. A.M. passed Steamboat *Trident* and Gov. Butler exchanged boats and has gone down the

---

[39] Pierce M. Butler was born in South Carolina in 1798 and served in the Seventh Infantry at Fort Smith and Fort Gibson. On May 26, 1826, he was married to Miss Miranda Julia du Val in Crawford County, Arkansas. In 1827, he was in charge of construction of the military road from Fort Gibson to Little Rock. Two years afterward he resigned his commission as captain in the army and served as Governor of South Carolina from 1836 to 1838; September 17, 1841, he was appointed agent to the Cherokee Indians, and he made his headquarters at Fort Gibson. In 1843 and in 1846 he was commissioned to negotiate treaties with the Comanche Indians. As colonel of the Palmetto Regiment of South Carolina he served in the Mexican War and was killed August 20, 1847, at the Battle of Churubusco.

river, Capt. Armstrong and Col. Stambaugh being on board.

I go on to Webber's Falls,[40] mouth of the Illinois, where I purpose taking land route to the Council at Tallequah. In a brief interview Gov. Butler understood that instructions for a treaty with the Cherokees, or instructions preparatory to a treaty are on the way to this country, but have not yet been received by Armstrong; and Stambaugh [41] is ordered here as a Seretary, though for what definite purpose he does not know, as I understood Gov. Butler; had but a moment to speak with him as he returned from the *Trident* in a small boat for his baggage.

I have seen one gallows in the Cherokee Nation in the precincts of the capitol Tallequah. A gallows has been pronounced a sign of civilization. I have not heard of a jail or anything like one. Most punishments are whipping and these are said to be very sure in case of crime.

Webber's landing (75 miles from Fort Smith) – 18th December A.M. Landed last night from the *Exchange*. This is apparently a very fine site belonging to the Cherokees. The Illinois enters the Arkansas from the the north about two miles below this place and the Canadian from the South about six. The Arkansas and

---

[40] Webbers Falls, once a water-fall several feet high in the Arkansas River above the mouth of the Illinois River, was so named from the residence nearby of Walter Webber, a leading chief and merchant of the Cherokee tribe who located there in 1829.

[41] William Armstrong of Nashville, Tennessee, succeeded his brother, the late Maj. Francis W. Armstrong, as Choctaw Agent and Acting Superintendent of Indian Affairs for the Western Territory. On December 26, 1843, he was confirmed by the Senate as Superintendent of Indian Affairs for the Western Territory which office he held until his death at Doaksville, near Fort Towson, June 12, 1847. Samuel E. Stambaugh of Pennsylvania, came to Indian Territory in 1832, as secretary of the commission of which Governor Montford Stokes was chairman.

Canadian up near the North Fork make the Cherokee Southern boundary.

Webber's Landing, right bank (South). 'Tis said that all the streams from the North, emptying into the Arkansas are clear. Those from the South turbid. The Arkansas itself is turbid, at times very muddy, like the Missouri. A similar remark I remember hearing made of the upper Mississippi the eastern branches of which are said to be clear, the western muddy. Rock River is beautifully clear. The Des Moines muddy. The Wisconsin is also clear.

Chapter IV

Mackey's Salt Works – Lynching a Soldier – Return to Tahlequah – Sequoyah or George Guess – Invention of Alphabet – Decadence of Cherokee Customs – Education in the Tribe – Frauds on the Creeks – Great International Council at Tahlequah – Attractive Indian Maidens.

At Mr. Wolfe's (Tallequah) Sunday Dec. 19, 1841. I rode yesterday from Webber's Landing after 10 A.M. to John Ross' by 5 P.M. 35 miles along the west bank of the Illinois, but out of sight of the river except in two or three places. The first fourteen miles to Mackay's on the military road is very rough and hilly after leaving the first prairie. At 12 M. I came to Webber's Salt Well,[42] saw a few Cherokees, a woman washing, men idle, no talk except to ask a black woman distances. Webber not at home. Makes salt, obtains water from a well some 30 ft. only deep. Near Webbers I met Dr. Powell the phrenologist, a man in company; shook hands and the Doctor explained that he had left Fort Gibson in the steamboat the day before and hearing of a soldier having been hung near Mackay's had determined to get his head, pointing to a bag swung upon his saddle bow, and he then expatiated upon the evidences that the man had not been murdered but had committed suicide. 'Twas "a perfectly clear case –

---

[42] Walter Webber operated the salt works on the old military road about seven miles north of the present Gore, Oklahoma; it was about one and one-half miles west of the Illinois River on Salt Branch.

slight hope, tendency to morbid feelings, great courage, slender firmness, etc."

I had talked with Major Lear at Fort Smith of the case. The Major about a month ago had sent the man express to Fort Gibson and had but the day before I saw him heard of his having been found hung in his suspenders near Mackay's on the Illinois about 1½ miles off from the military road. The Major seemed quite sure the man must have been murdered. Said he was a very good man and the Major was much affected at the thought of his murder; the more so perhaps as he was sick himself and his wife dying with a cancer and recently his men had given him great trouble in the neighborhood of Fort Smith by getting into a brawl with some citizens and one of his men was killed and another had an arm *cut off*.

Dr. Powell was perfectly sure the hung man had committed suicide. He had measured his position and found from the height of a horse and the man standing in his stirups would just reach the position in which he was found, but the main evidence with him was the phrenological developments. The Doctor said he had addressed two letters to me and left them with Colonel Mason at Fort Gibson, one of them gives me his opinion of John Ross, phrenological opinion, of course.

I rode on, crossed the military road where it crosses the Illinois and then retraced the road I travelled last Saturday week with Governor Butler near Ross' prairie. I came upon the brow of a very high hill which overlooks an extensive country – dismounted and took my glass but the shades of evening were setting in and I descended the hill and winding around the foot of a smaller elevation, soon came in sight of and passed Lewis Ross' house; reached John Ross' residence and continuing on a few hundred yards met John Ross returning home from the council ground. He invited me to turn back and pass the night at his house and I did so.

The council adjourned yesterday. This morning as I left Ross' to come here (5 miles) the Treasurer David Vann was making some payments.

P.M. Guess, Guest, Gist – who invented the Cherokee alphabet lives near John Ross'. Mr. Ross told me last night that he is of mixed blood. That General Taylor of Cincinnati told him in Washington City some years ago that a Virginian, a Mr. Gist had been sent among the Cherokees on some mission where he remained some time and expressed his belief that the Cherokee Guess was a son of Mr. Gist. That Mr. Gist was the father of the present Mrs. Blair wife of the editor of the Globe. Mr. Ross seemed to have no doubt of this. He told me that when Guess or Gist set about inventing letters he was very much ridiculed, but persevered and succeeded.

I have just been talking with Mr. Payne, a young man of mixed blood living at the mouth of the Sallisaw. Payne was educated at the Dwight Mission as he says by Asa Hitchcock, who is a cousin of mine from Brimfield, Massachusetts, now residing in Illinois. Payne speaks English and Cherokee and writes both languages. He says that Gist came to this country with the Chief Jolly in 1818 and used to live down in Illinois Bayou [43] in Arkansas. That when he set about inventing letters he was not only ridiculed but very much abused and that very many ignorant Cherokees feared that he was engaged in league with dark powers for the dis-

[43] This Illinois Bayou courses the present Pope County, Arkansas. It was on this stream that Dwight Mission was first located.

covery of something that would become a great injury
to the nation. Says that Gist had great difficulty in
satisfying the Cherokees. That on one occasion being
distant from the council then in session he wrote a message to one of his pupils at the Council and sent the
written paper declaring first its contents and requiring
the messenger after hearing it read to bear testimony to
it. He did so, certifying to the correspondence between
the reading of the message at the Council and Gist's
account of it at the time he sent it. This he says had a
great effect in relieving the fears of the people.

Mr. Payne says that Gist's grandfather on the
mother's side was part Shawnee and his father a white
man, so that he has very little Cherokee blood in him.
He tells me he is precisely in the same situation. It
pleased him to praise Gist who he says has a very good
head, "can express a great idea in a few words," adding
that he is now and has been for a long time engaged in
writing a history of the Cherokees. He said some of the
old traditions were very interesting. Spoke of the old
habits and customs. The physic dance of March and
the Green Corn dance of September having been laid
aside for a number of years. Can recollect them and
remembers with what reluctance he went to the first,
had begun to think it was of no use but was obliged to
acquiesce in the customs of others. He spoke of the
great peace speeches delivered by the old men at the
Grand Councils of Confederated tribes as being excellent prayers but full of imagery and difficult to trans-
late.

The Council passed a law for the establishment of
schools and the employment of teachers at a salary of
$500 a year with an allowance of $30 a year for the
purchase of books; to which was added over $100 from

the orphan fund for teaching orphans. The particulars with respect to this last item I have not exactly understood.

William Candy spoke of the mode of executing the Creek contract as "scandalous" that cattle were driven a long ways for issue with but little or nothing to eat; were turned over to the Indians on the hoof under an estimate of weight far exceeding their real weight and were in such wretchedly poor condition that many absolutely fell down and died under the drover's hands. That corn on the ear was inaccurately measured by a flour barrel into wagons at Webber's Falls, 40 miles below Fort Gibson and hauled to the place of issue on one of the forks of the Canadian; the oxen feeding on the corn all the way and quantities of it shook off from the ear on the way and the Indians compelled to receive the remainder at the nominal quantity as falsely measured at Webber's Falls. Several persons have told me, especially John Ross, that the agents of the Government were also the agents of the contractors and hence when the Indians complained to the Government agent the contractor's agent would give them no satisfaction. Mr. Ross says that George Hicks conducted a party of Cherokees west [44] and that after coming under the issue of the contractors the beef was so bad that the physican said they had better not eat it; that he complained and the agent said they should take that or go without beef and that many did go without it.

Mr. Wolfe the other day gave me a history of the great Council of Indian tribes held here or five miles from Tallequah in 1839. I used the account to enforce

[44] George Hicks, a Cherokee, conducted a party of 1118 persons who had 56 wagons and teams, 560 riding and wagon horses. They departed September 7, 1838, and arrived at their destination March 14, 1839.

the propriety of adjusting all points of difference between the United States and the Cherokees, the latter
being the controlling power among all the South West
and West tribes. There were *eleven* tribes represented
here in 1839. They elected a principal and a second
chief, the former being John Luna, a Cherokee with
authority to call the tribes together again whenever he
may deem proper or necessary. John Luna keeps the
wampum belt, the symbol of friendship. A Creek
Chief, McIntosh was chosen second Chief – A Cherokee, Vann, was elected the head War Chief of all the
warriors of all the tribes and Young Wolfe was elected
the person through whom all the addresses to the Council were to be made. Wolf had eleven interpreters assigned to him (including one English).

The Council was in session a week, gave great alarm
to General Arbuckle who warned the citizens of Arkansas to be armed, etc.[45] I have presented a contrary view
and assured the Department of War that the Cherokees
must enjoy a pre-eminence in these Councils and by
doing them justice they will keep all the other tribes
quiet.

John Ross' residence in the Cherokee nation January
1st, 1842 – The day is very clear and mild; called over
here from Mr. Wolfe's and made a call on Mr. Lewis
Ross' family. Saw Mrs. Ross, Mrs. Murrill, Miss Ross

---

[45] The council to which Major Hitchcock refers was held near the present
town of Tahlequah and was begun on September 15, 1838. Invitations were
prepared by Governor Stokes who attended the meeting in company with
General Arbuckle and Creek Agent James Logan. It was not General
Arbuckle who became alarmed as Major Hitchcock says, but General Gaines
who ordered out troops from Jefferson Barracks and Fort Leavenworth to
subdue an imaginary uprising. The meeting was called, as the Indians stated
it, to renew the friendship once existing among their forefathers. For an
account of this meeting, see Grant Foreman, *Pioneer Days in the Early
Southwest*, 275.

and the Misses Nave, the twins who are exactly alike and dress alike precisely. They were very tastefully dressed today and appeared to great advantage.

Cattle were poor, range cattle delivered in March on the hoof at a very rough and exaggerated estimate of their weight. The Cherokees in many instances would not receive them and would go off into the woods and subsist themselves. (Wolfe's brother-in-law did this with 15 others). Some would receive the cattle alive and endeavor to save them, but in repeated instances they would be gathered up by the agents of the contractors who would claim them and issue them a second time. England says that one of the Foremans living near Beatty's Prairie who had bought some cattle had fourteen head driven off in that way. Mr. Jones says that the contractors insisted upon issuing two months rations to (Sit-a-wakes) party on their arrival in the country though they were living only in tents and were without the means of taking care of their rations. Numberless statements coincide in representing that most of the Indians knew but little of their rights under the contract and were exposed by their ignorance to impositions – that impositions were practiced; that when they were discovered by some people who understood the subject and complaint made, the contractor's agent would plead accidental error and correct the mistake, but the error was always against the Indians, etc.

Chapter V

At Beattie's Prairie – A One-legged Buffalo Hunter –
Objections to Fort Wayne – Feather Bed and Calico
Curtains – The Opulent Thompsons – Judge Martin's
Wives – The Inquisitive Helderbrand – Unfinished
Fort Wayne – A Twenty-two-hour Ball – Discharged
Soldiers Marry in the Tribe – Complaint of John Ross
– Conspiracy to Kill Ridge and Boudinot – A Massa-
chusetts Missionary.

Thompson's [46] near Fort Wayne (Beatie's Prairie),
60 miles N. E. from Gibson, about the same distance
west of north from Fort Smith, arrived 4th January,
1842. Left Tallequah the 3rd (yesterday) and came to
Price's and thence here today. Price was absent but I
found Mr. Ware, a white man in his stead. In the evening a Mr. Peterson Thomas came in. There was a man
also came in who has been out on a buffalo hunt with
the Osages. There were two hog drovers present. In the
evening I began talking with Thomas and ascertained
that he lived in what is called the Cherokee neutral
ground [47] with about fifteen families.

---

[46] Beattie's Prairie included about a township of fine land which was
densely settled, according to Colonel Arbuckle; it contained Buffington's
store, and the homes of Franklin and James Thompson, each of whom had
over two hundred acres of land fenced and in cultivation, good residences,
and other improvements; the Government was on the point of removing these
improvements to make room for the erection of Fort Wayne, but the post
was abandoned (Arbuckle to Quartermaster-general, July 20, 1840, Q. M. G.,
Hall of Records, Book 21 A 211).

[47] A tract of land in Southeastern Kansas at one time owned by the
Cherokee Nation.

The white man from the buffalo hunt is club-footed
and can use but one foot at all; his left leg dangles
about, a strange condition for a buffalo hunter. Says he
went for the novelty of it. Several Osage villages set
off together to the West, but after passing the Arkansas,
separated into several parties. His party was 49 lodges,
about 14 in a lodge, all rode horses, had eleven packed
horses, carried their skins for lodges, had rifles, but
used bows and arrows for killing buffalo – bow made
of the bois D'arc wood. Saw arrows sent through the
buffalo; thinks he went 350 miles; went out in September and came back in November, the fall hunt. The
Spring hunt is May and June. The Indians plant corn
and when fairly up they go on their spring hunt. All
go, men, women and children, no fences about their
corn, no cattle in the country. They return in July,
gather their corn in the milk and boil it and dry it, (it
shrivels) when it makes excellent soup. In their hunts
they kill some elk and deer but go for the buffalo. They
keep the skins mostly for lodges, scraping off the flesh
and hair with a sort of hoe rather sharp, cut the meat
into think pieces and dry it and pack it in for use. He
saw some signs (the Indians told him) of Comanches
and Pawnees. 6 or 7,000 [6 or 700?] persons started out
with him; travelled in single file and spread out a great
distance, looked well from an eminence in a Prairie.
Women did all the work, pitched and struck the
lodges; for two days they were obliged to pack wood
for fires.

Fort Wayne (at Thompson's Dr. Benj. F.) January
6, 1842. Introduced to a Mr. Blythe who says he lives
on the neutral ground, so called belonging to the
Cherokees. Confirms Thomas' account of the number of
families living there, 14 or 15, some 90 or 100 persons,

says the country is between the State of Missouri and the Osage Indians 50 miles North and South and 20 to 25 East and West, no others but Cherokees living on it. Osages steal their hogs, etc., but have a good settlement. Seems anxious to know whether that country will be repurchased by the United States from the Cherokees. If the United States purchase it, thinks the settlers should be paid for their improvements. Does not wish to be allowed a reserve but if the country is sold would prefer moving out of it. Was anxious to know what would be done with the head right (per capita) money allowed in the treaty of 1835. I told him I knew nothing and could promise nothing but gave my opinion that if the country was sold by the Cherokees, the settlers would be provided for and I also gave an opinion that the per capita allowance would be continued in any new treaty that might be made.

P.M. Such a day as this is enough to make a Saint curse a rainy day in the country. Irving's description does not "begin to" come near its horrors, rain, rain, rain, steady rain, all day, no wind even for variety. An old man walking on the piazza as steadily as it rains, children in abundance running about and every few moments one or two of them squalling. No one to talk with but a man who says he is from New York, and shows his importance by inquiring about the progress of building the exchange, etc., and asking me if I think we shall have war with England. I'll start out after dinner if it rains pitchforks.

Seventh January; went accordingly about four miles to Mr. William Wilson's and passed the night and this morning he gave me a paper addressed to me on the subject of Fort Wayne, urging its removal. Wilson is of mixed blood and has written a long letter in defiance of orthography indeed, but giving some strong reasons why the Government should abandon Fort Wayne. Mrs. Wilson I have heard is a white woman, but I am sorry to say she does but little credit to the whites by her housekeeping which to tell the truth is of a very sluttish character. Her house is dirty and her children dirty and her servants!

They gave me a good bed (feather) with calico curtains, but in the usual fashion in this country, with but one sheet. It is singular that I find this custom everywhere. Mr. Ross gave me a couple of sheets but it was by his special order, knowing the habits in the States. The two Thompsons near Fort Wayne are white men. Wm. F. lives nearly West and his brother nearly North of the Fort separated by a small ravine with running water, the head of which, when not swelled with rains is a large spring opposite James H. Thompson. William has over 300 acres under fence and his brother nearly 200, perhaps half under cultivation. William married a daughter of Judge Martin[48] who had two wives, sisters. The Judge is dead and Mrs. Thompson's mother lives within half of a mile of the Grand Saline, 35 miles from here. One of the widows Martin passed a night at Mr. Wolfe's while I was there, and old Helderbrand, Wolfe's father-in-law was there on a visit. The old man is 87 years of age, very gray where not bald and without a tooth in his head, but his eye is not "dim" and the old man is very garrulous and inquisitive. He seemed least disposed to go to bed of any one in the house and would talk with any one who would talk with him.

---

[48] John Martin died October 17, 1840, at the age of 55 years, 11 months and 27 days (Arkansas *Gazette*, December 2, 1840). He was buried at Fort Gibson and his monument records that he was the chief justice of the first supreme court of the Cherokee Nation.

The night that Mrs. Martin was at Wolfe's I slept in the attic over the room where several others slept including old Helderbrand and the widow. The others appeared to be asleep when in a wakeful moment I overheard the old man asking questions of the widow about her husband, how many wives he had and whether they were sisters. I couldn't hear her answers which were perhaps faint and seemed smothered in bed clothes, but the answer to the last question was doubtless in the affirmative as I heard the old man say "that wouldn't do for me" and he continued his questions, asking if they (wives) were happy, etc. Mrs. Thompson is a good looking rather portly woman, has several children and seems motherly. Her husband is an active man "well to do in the world" and says grace at table.

Fort Wayne [49] stands in the bend of the ravine which separates it from the two Thompsons, on the same general level. There is one two story framed house finished intended for two companies of Dragoons, with a kitchen at each end and the foundation for a similar house for two other companies; but the finished building is occupied as a store house and the men live in very low and rude log huts with dirt floors, etc. These are

[49] In 1838, a military post was ordered to be established on the headwaters of the Illinois River near the Arkansas line; however, before it was completed orders were given in 1839 to locate it further north where temporary quarters were constructed across the line from Maysville, Arkansas, near the Spavinaw Creek, and the post was called Fort Wayne. In 1840 work on the new post was suspended from lack of funds to continue it, but there had been erected a large building and others were in various stages of construction. Orders were afterward given to find a new site for this garrison between Fort Gibson and Fort Leavenworth, and in May, 1842, a site was selected at what afterward became Fort Scott, now in Kansas. The buildings at Fort Wayne, however, were occupied by the Cherokee during their disturbances in the forties, and again during the Civil War.

picketed in. This was done after two Cherokees had
been killed by a couple of soldiers at Maysville (3
miles hence in Arkansas) last July.[50] The Cherokees
after that killing or murder, as the case may have been,
made some threats or loud talking and it was thought
prudent to throw some defence around the men and
property in the Fort. Besides the buildings named there
are frames erected for two story buildings with piazas
for officers quarters. These have been standing uncov-
ered several months, all work being suspended until
the Government can decide upon the question as to the
location permanently of the Fort. The Fort is in the
edge of the timber at the South Western extremity of
what is called Batie's Prairie, out of sight from the
Prairie – The Prairie seems surrounded by settlers who
live in the timber and cultivate in the Prairie. The
Prairie is more elevated than the surrounding country
which perhaps accounts for numberless springs found
all around the edge of it, as if to supply the settlers, at
places most convenient for them. Maysville is a miserable place complained of universally as a grogery,
filled with what are called groceries.

P.M. Rode this morning, 8th January, '42 to see
Moses Daniel, a Cherokee four miles north of this
place, Fort Wayne; found him at home, an intelligent
man, apparently perfectly honest and free spirited.
Speaks what he knows simply as knowing it. I took
down in writing what he stated of the contractors Harrison and Glasgow, as he stated it, read it over to him
and he made one correction and then signed the paper
in my presence. A main fact in his statement is that he

---

[50] On the Fourth of July, soldiers and Indians attended a "frolic" at
Maysville, and the next morning the body of a Cherokee with his throat cut
was found near a house in which soldiers had been entertained, and another
was fatally wounded.

saw a Mr. Cooper, nephew of a principal agent of the same name for the contractors buy tickets or due bills for beef at 1½ cents per pound. I was referred by Daniel to Mr. Lynch and I went at once to see Mr. Lynch and met him on horseback near his house two miles north of Fort Wayne on his way to Maysville. I joined him and explained my business when he at once stated that at his store (Lynch, Buffington, and James Allen Thompson) due bills were purchased from Cherokees for which the contractor paid about $3,000. He told me that at first he refused to buy them, but finding that everybody else was buying them, Mr. Thompson came to an understanding with the contractors agent, that they should be paid three cents per pound for all the beef tickets they could purchase. Mr. Lynch referred me to Mr. Agnew a white man now in Mr. Galespie's store at Maysville and to his partner J. A. Thompson. I asked Lynch if he had any objections to my using what he had stated and he said none at all. I rode with him and he introduced me to Mr. Agnew.

Evening; Lieut. Ewell has been giving me an account of a Cherokee ball which he attended last evening at a Mr. Williams' about two miles from the garrison; he says there were about 40 *ladies* and as many Cherokee *gentlemen* with some *white men*; says the ladies were well dressed and that all behaved well; they danced a certain reel incessantly, more complicated than the old Virginia Reel. He was there but a few hours of the night, but says that the dance began yesterday at 3 P.M. and continued till after 1 P.M. today, 22 hours without intermission except for breakfast this morning, which occupied only about ten minutes. They broke down two fiddlers and ended with a third, negroes, who sung occasionally to their music, keeping time with the foot and apparently enjoying the dance as much as the dancers.

There was a jug of whiskey in one of the rooms, kept under a bed, from which a tumbler was occasionally filled and passed around to those who desired it. The fiddlers "took a chance" at the tumbler and then it was offered to him but he declined. I asked if the Misses Taylor were present and he answered no, that they were above the grade of the party, a nice distinction, no doubt.

Thompson's 10th January '42. Last evening a young man (Cherokee) mentioned the name of Daningburgh and on inquiry I found that he has been a soldier of the 7th Infantry and was discharged at Fort Gibson; was first employed by Harrison and afterwards by the Government as an agent for issues of provision; that he married a Cherokee mixed blood and has a farm in Flint district on the Arkansas line. His farm is partly in the state and partly in the Cherokee Nation, about four or five miles north of the Sallisaw. He has several negroes, part by his wife and part made by himself. This is the second discharged soldier I have heard of, the third I think employed by the Government; Daningburgh, Williams, alias Clark now keeping a store at the Cherokee agency, and Barlin employed by Captain Stevenson and now living in Arkansas below Fort Smith.

Lynch, a day or two since, spoke to me of his leaving the old country in 1837, thinks there were a thousand left that year and were allowed *but* $20 for their expenses, but under a promise that they should participate in the benefits of any after-arrangement that might be made, and he then said that Mr. Ross was paying for those who emigrated with him over $90. Last evening a white-man, a Mr. Eliot, who has a Cherokee family living on Grand River, said he had 10 or 12 children; spoke of his having come over to this country before Mr. Lynch, the year before he thinks, and was allowed but $20 for each one. He brought his family at that rate and "found" his waggons and teams (two of them); and he complained of the arrangement by which Ross' people received so much more and said he wanted to find the man who could tell him whether the money now paying out by Ross was from the Cherokee fund. He abused Mr. Ross with considerable temper, saying that for 20 years since his eldest child was an infant, Mr. Ross has been making trouble in the nation and with the General Government.

Thompson's, 11th January '42. Mr. (Dr.) B. F. Thompson has given me the names of two other discharged soldiers employed by the Government officers as issuing agents of provision to Cherokees – O'Bannan (at McCoy's Keese's) and Lyons at Bushyhead's; that Lyons married a sister of Bushyhead's but was killed by a Creek Indian in some quarrel. That O'Bannan also married a Cherokee woman but has deserted his wife and gone off to Virginia. That both of these were drunkards. That Lyons is said to have boasted of the money he made while agent; he thinks that O'Bannan made no money.

Mr. Thompson says that Cooper, the nephew of the contractor's principal agent, openly and freely bought up as many of the due bills as he could, giving from $1\frac{1}{2}$ to 2 cents a pound for beef; that he had waggon loads of bacon which he sold at 15 cents paying for beef tickets, with bacon at that rate. I asked if he knew where the bacon came from and he said he supposed

it came from Missouri, but when I told him that the
Government had sent a large quantity into the country
which by arrangement fell into the hands of the contractors he supposed it was that bacon, but did not
know till I told him of the fact that the Government
had sent bacon into the country. Mr. Thompson further
states that the beef was mostly driven from Arkansas
and Missouri, was too poor to eat, was kept in a pen
near here for this depot; was turned out by the agents
on the hoof at from ¼ to ½ more than their true
weight according to his judgment; that he saw it done
and there appeared to be no remedy. That the cattle,
after issue, would frequently stray back to the pen
and he heard it said but does not know the fact, that
the agents of the contractors would drive them to another depot to prevent their being recognized and there
issue them again. If these things occurred here among
Cherokees who are comparatively intelligent, what
might have been the conduct of the agents among the
Creeks, Chickasaws, etc.

13th January. Mr. B. F. Thompson and Mr. John
A. Bell, both tell me that Jo Spears was a principal
man in the death of Ridge. Bell says at a Council in
June 1839 the plan was arranged to kill Ridge, Boudinot, himself (Bell) and two or three others. The Council adjourned about the 22nd of June for nine days,
that some 30 men passed along here (Baties Prairie)
and that Foreman, living two miles from the Fort
killed a beef for them (don't know who paid Foreman
for the beef). The party continued on the 10 miles to
Ridge's, so arranging their arrival as to reach his house
just before day of the 22nd of June. Jo Spears and two
others entered the house, one snapped a pistol at Ridge
while in bed, his wife asleep by his side. The snapping

of the pistol waked Ridge, he was seized and dragged out of doors where two men held him while a third stabbed him, others coming up and completing the work of death. They had some difficulty in forcing Ridge, though a light slender man, through the door. His wife did not wake until the confusion and noise at the door awakened her.

After the murder the party returned to Tahlequah, the council ground, where on the 9th day from the adjournment the Council reassembled and the first business that was done was the passing of a bill of indemnity for all offences, the object being without naming the murderers, to excuse them. They then passed a law requiring all those who had subscribed the treaty of '35 to appear before the Council and make a public confession of their having been in the wrong. They granted several days and afterwards added 8 more; but the most would not appear and the Secretary of War, Mr. Poinsett on being advised of the act of outlawry, for it was one, against the principal men of the Ridge party, issued an order to the Council to repeal the law and gave some instructions to General Arbuckle, the military commander in the country to take effectual measures for the protection of the Ridge party. The Council was reassembled and a number of the people, and voted a repeal of the law. Mr. Bell says that for several weeks there were about him some 40 men armed and prepared for defence if any attempts had been made upon his life; but he finally thought it best to move into Arkansas, where he now lives.

Bell is bitter against Mr. John Ross and some of his adherents. Says that Mr. Ross received $23,000 for his place in the old nation, having a poor old house and about 40 acres under cultivation. He says that his brother Lewis has made a large fortune by the aid of John. That he received the contract for supplying provisions to the party emigrating; that he bought off three white men, one at $13,000, one at $18,000 and one at $14,000. Of the latter he paid $6,000 in cash and has been sued on his note for $9,000 but escaped owing to some informality. That Wm. Candy and another made $30,000 each in partnership with Lewis, etc.

P.M. 13th Jan. went out five miles to the Rev. Mr. Butrick's, a missionary from Massachusetts sent from Boston 20 odd (22 or 27) years ago. I found him in his school [51] but recently opened 15 or 18 scholars, the least interesting children I have seen. Mr. Butrick has a fine prospect if he expects to raise them to a high level – they will have to be raised from a great depth. I remarked that I understood he had been a long time with the Cherokees, he said, yes, that he had grown old among them smiling languidly. After a few moments he dismissed his school, being noon and we adjourned to his house adjacent to the school where we (Lieut. Eustis and myself) were introduced to Mrs. Butrick a fit looking old dame for a partner to old Mr. Butrick. She was from the North, she said, but had first come out to Georgia and taught school, then returned on a visit to her friends and afterwards came South again and married Mr. Butrick. Mr. Butrick has never returned to the North. They have no children. Mr. Butrick I have been told has more information of aboriginal customs than perhaps any other man who has ever come into the country. I have seen his name in the

---

[51] Rev. Daniel S. Butrick had been a missionary with the Cherokee since 1818, and his wife since 1826; they both came west with the Indians in 1839 (Report of Secretary of War, November 30, 1843, U. S. Senate. *Documents,* 28th congress, first session, no. 2). He died in the Cherokee Nation; June 8, 1851.

article on Indian languages in the appendix to the 6th volume of the Encyclopedia Americana. He very soon shewed himself a decided Ross man, had known him for many years and had always found him an honest man. I did not doubt it, but expressed some apprehension that the elements of discord yet existed in the nation and alluded to some of them. He immediately assumed the ground that Mr. Ross was and had been the head of the nation and not of a party, and called all others but fragments of the nation. That as they had violated the laws of the nation and separated from the nation they were not entitled to the benefits of the arrangement made by Mr. Ross with General Scott, by which those of the "nation" having waggons, etc., received pay for their use in emigrating to this country, etc. He was very pressing that we should pass the afternoon with him, but we excused ourselves as I wished to see Mr. Foreman by appointment.

Chapter VI

Destitute Cherokee – View of the Grand Saline – Return to Fort Gibson – A Tragedy at the Post – Wickliffe's Infatuation – Captain John Rogers – Gambling at Fort Gibson – Method of Distributing Money Among the Creeks – Indian Conception of the Deity – Affluence of Indian agents – A Challenge and Choice of Weapons – Horse Racing in January – Indian Whiskey Dealers.

Fort Gibson, January 16, 1842. Returned here this evening after an absence of more than six weeks. Gov. Butler has kindly sent my letters from Fort Smith (forwarded from Little Rock).

I left Batie's Prairie the 14th instant (accompanied by Lt. Eustis as far as the Grand Saline), passed a night at the house of a full blood Cherokee, Peter, on Spavinaw, 15 miles from the Prairie and the next night at Widow Martins, one half mile South of the great (Grand) Saline. Today I rode here forty miles (35 from Batie's Prairie to the Saline).

On Spavinaw saw the huts of a considerable number of the poorest Indians of the Cherokee nation. They have sat down along the water course and put up small huts, living miserably I suppose. The Grand Saline so much spoken of disappointed me. There is neither the quantity of water from the Spring, nor the strength in the water, I had been led to expect. There is made however about 15 bushels of salt a day and three times that quantity 'tis said can be made. I fell in today with a son of George Hicks who has been in this country since 1819; is opposed to Ross and spoke with severity of him. Says that the opposing party, if everybody would turn out, would vote him out of office.

Fort Gibson 17th January. Wrote 3 or 4 letters. Dined with Col. Mason; regret to hear the particulars as reported of the death of Robert Wilkins a plain white man, a carpenter who has been living about three miles from the post. The story [52] is that he has been living with a Cherokee woman, perhaps not married; that Lt. Wickliffe, one of the Kentucky family rather famed for acts of violence, found access to the Cherokee woman – that last Saturday week night, Wilkins, returning home made upleasant discoveries and chastised his love, Wickliffe disappearing from the house. The woman, I think the story goes, came to the garrison and Wickliffe arming himself with a pistol and cowhide went to the house in the night and holding a pistol at the breast of the white man, who was in the house began laying on with the green hide – "What are you whipping me for," said the man. Not on my own account said Lt. Wickliffe. I am whipping you because Amanda told me to do it. He came back to the garrison and the next, that is Sunday morning, a week yesterday, he went back with a gun charged, it is said with fifteen buck shot, and approaching the dwelling of Wilkins, saw him going into his house, and shot him in the back, eleven buckshot entering his body scattered from the neck down on the left side. Wilkins says he

---

[52] For a further account of this affair see Grant Foreman, *Pioneer Days in the Early Southwest* (Cleveland, 1926), 174. Lieut. Charles Wickliff was dropped from the army rolls April 12, 1842, but was reinstated as captain March 5, 1847; he was honorably discharged July 22, 1848; served with the Confederate Army as colonel of the Seventh Kentucky Infantry; died April 27, 1862 of wounds received at the Battle of Shiloh.

turned around as he fell and saw Wickliffe turning and walking off with his gun. He was within a few paces when he shot, a building near the dwelling house enabling him to approach unperceived.

The only color of cause that I hear assigned for this, is that Wilkins had threatened Wickliffe's life; but Col. Mason says he was not so dangerous as an old squaw would have been; and at all events the interference seems to have come wholly from Wickliffe and that too on account of a woman said to have been a common strumpet these ten years past, a woman of so bad a character that, Mr. McDermot informs me, her own sister last Spring refused to receive her into her house, where she lives some 15 or 18 miles from here. It is a very bad case.

18th January, Ft. Gibson. Captain Rodgers [53] from the Grand Saline sought me out today. Owns the big Saline, rents it for $1,000 for six months, he furnishing fifty kettles. Seems a fair man – Expresses the belief that a great number of Cherokees died for want of provisions in 1839. Saw no issues himself – heard complaints, but knows no facts. Says he heard it was worse among the Creeks than among the Cherokees – the latter knew enough in some cases to obtain something like justice – refers me to Hill, Jacobs [54] and Bryant, the two first some 5 or 6 miles off on the Verdigris, the other 55 miles up Grand River. He too, has claims – came to this country in 1819 under a treaty of 1817; received some provisions, a little, but in the main

[53] John Rogers owned the buildings and extensive equipment for making salt at these springs located near where is now Salina, Oklahoma; these springs, owned at one time by A. P. Chouteau and later by Sam Houston, were visited by Washington Irving in 1832. For an account of these springs, see Foreman, *op. cit.*, 92, 188, 260.

[54] Seaborn Hill and Eli Jacobs.

had to support himself, that is, a party of about 1,000. Tells me he has a paper which threatens punishment to any one who shall speak evil of John Ross, prepared about January or February a year ago – a Lynch business – not under authority of the Government. Says he will send me the paper. Did not speak well of Mr. Ross, but made no charges against him, except that at one time both Ross and Richard Taylor came to this country and, returning, gave a very good account of it – then changed about – that Taylor even bought stock preparatory to moving here. Condemns the Cherokees for not accepting the terms offered by General Jackson in 1817, the whole of the country now occupied by the Choctaws, Chickasaws, Creeks and Cherokees with a large part of Arkansas and annuity of five per cent upon a half a million of dollars. Captain Rodgers promised to ask Bryant to send me a statement of what he saw of the issues to the Creeks. Thinks he will make the statement cheerfully. These three, Bryant, Jacobs and Hill are the only persons I have heard of as having a knowledge of the issues to Creeks.

Captain Rodgers told me that mills were promised in 1817, renewed in 1833 but never furnished. That Smiths, cartwrights, wheelwrights, have been of no use, paid high wages and have sold their work besides, alleging that no iron but their own was furnished, etc.

19th. Memorandum: – Furnished Dr. Maxwell the outline of a letter to Lt. Wickliffe in answer to one denouncing the Doctor as a liar and a slanderer. The Doctor was worried and came to me and after showing me Wickliffe's letter with other papers, expressed a wish that I would "just put down" what I thought of it. I hesitated at first but finally wrote an answer, which seemed to relieve him. I put him on his compassion for

Wickliffe, a "young man and at best very unfortunate"; corrected Wickliffe's impressions as to facts – told him he need not expect to silence remarks upon his late imputed conduct by assuming a bravado tone, and advising humility; declined all further correspondence with him until a proper tribunal should pass upon his conduct. Very odd, sure enough, that Wickliffe should interfere with a man's domestic arrangements, not satisfied with inducing the woman to visit his own quarters, but intruding to the house of her reputed husband, and when the outraged husband threatens chastisement, he arms himself deliberately and rides three miles and shoots the man in his own door and that too in the back, as Col. Mason says "plumb in the back" and then attempts to browbeat a brother officer on alleged remarks upon his conduct with a view to silence comments upon his infamous and barbarous proceedings.

The weather changed last night from moderate to cold. A strong wind from the South yesterday increased in the night and about 12 midnight, we had rain, lightning and thunder and this morning a cold north wind with some sleet and hail. 'Tis now 2 P.M. cloudy and boisterous, but not freezing cold, though it must freeze tonight. Col. Mason looks to his ice house and prays for cold weather. He says that some years ice is not to be had in sufficient quantities to fill the ice house, or it is bad, not solid and clear.

P.M. moved to a room occupied by Mr. Labatte from New Orleans, a merchant on a collecting tour. He has told me many things of the people here; in the main that they are a set of desperate gamblers. (There is a gaming party now engaged over head). He says that Clark, the acting agent for the Seminoles on $3.00 a day gambles every night and bets hundreds of dollars.

Says that Mr. Poinsett ordered Captain Armstrong to give a contract to Mr. Carter of Tennessee, at 14 cents a ration for issuing provisions to the Seminoles sent here by General Armistead about January or February last.[55] That Carter turned the contract over to a son-in-law or step-son, one West, who was unable to enter upon the execution of the business and he took into partnership a man named Olmstead giving him half the profits ('tis said they made $50.00 a day – McDermot says this, or that he heard so).

Labatte says Olmstead games. I forget what he said of West. Says that Harris, the sutler games, and Dr. Maxwell and Captain Davis; that Fields and Drew (Cherokee merchants) game – (Field has a white wife recently married in Philadelphia). Says that gaming and betting on horseracing has broken the merchants in this country and that Harris must go as the others have gone; that he attends to no business himself and knows nothing of the state of his business. Says he has sold goods to the amount of $8,000 to Harris and came for pay; that last year when in New Orleans, Mr. Harris wrote from New York requesting as a friend that he would insure 2800 of goods shipped to New Orleans; he did so, on an open policy, supposing as a matter of course that the goods were shipped to him; but they were shipped to another merchant of which he was not advised. That the goods were lost and the insurance could not be collected because they were insured as if shipped to him. Labatte took a draft on the paymaster, Col. Rector, in favor of William Armstrong, whose niece Harris married, for $4100.

[55] By 1840 several hundred immigrant Seminole under their chiefs Alligator and Wild Cat were encamped near Fort Gibson where they were content to receive government rations, having little desire to engage in farming.

Labatte says he thinks Harris is broke, that he must owe thirty or forty thousand dollars; has not more than eight or ten thousand in stock; assets, he thinks, will not make the difference. He says Harris bet the other day $500 upon one horse race and 250 upon another. He also referred to the common story of his effecting the settlement with Rains, bribing him to silence about the conduct of Harrison and Glasgow for $13,500.

Labatte explained the mode of paying the annuity to the Creeks and Choctaws. The Creeks were paid by towns, some dozen men of a town receiving the money – that in all some 600 persons receive the money. That many poor people and widows and orphans get nothing. That Roly McIntosh received first $1,000 and Opothle-yaholo the second chief 800; that Benjamin Marshall, the Creek interpreter gets 900. That debts are paid, for injuries by thefts, proved and adjudicated by chiefs, etc., and the balance divided, one half to the McIntosh Creeks and the other half to Opothleyaholo's Creeks, and then, by them divided among the heads of towns. They count it around in piles equal to the number of persons to receive it, dollar by dollar till it is all distributed, having persons to watch the piles.

The Choctaws are paid by heads of families, each family being enrolled in some company. The head of the company hands the roll of his company at the payment to the agent sanctioned by the principal men. The rate is determined to even half dollars, say $4.50 to each individual, the fraction of a bit or two bits, reserved for the general fund, paid I suppose to the Chiefs. Labatte says the Choctaws are properly paid but denounces the mode of payment to the Creeks, their poor get nothing, he says.

Fort Gibson, 20th January, '42. Reminiscences of

what Peterson Thomas told me on my ride from Price's to Batie's Prairie. He told me that the Indians knew nothing of the shape of the earth and likened their notion on the subject to placing a piece of bark on the water and loading it with earth; the earth has bounds, but the water not. Then of the deity: he said they all believed in a good Being presiding over the world, but for the reason that he is good they pay him no worship; saying that as he is good, he needs no prayers or services as inducements to serve us; but that inferior beings may be moved, and hence their ceremonies have reference to those inferior beings. And I think he said especially that they implore the evil being not to harm them.

Ft. Gibson, 21st January. Have been reading the various treaties with the Cherokees. In that of 1819 the 6th Article admits an emigration equal to one third of the whole of the Cherokees. This admission was made over the signatures of John Ross, Lewis Ross, James Brown (now living) among others.

Thos. C. Wilson resides here. He met me on board of a steamboat at Van Buren and introduced himself to me. Wilson remarked in conversation that Captain Armstrong came to this country $20,000 in debt; that he has paid his debts and is now worth $40,000. This in a few years on a salary of $1500, while supporting an expensive family. That, to be sure, he has a corn field at the Agency and can sell corn at fifty cents a bushel, but that would not support his family.

He spoke of Clark, alias Williams, a discharged soldier, employed by Government, worth nothing, at first, ended with setting up a store for himself; of Daningburgh, another discharged soldier, worth nothing at the beginning, at the end of the contract for issues, put into his brother Hino Wilson's hands $3,000 in cash, besides having other means. Of McDaniel not only worth nothing but of such bad character that Hill refused to employ him in his store. He is now worth $10,000. He now lives on Red River. He mentioned several others naming some who were bribed by the contractors, one at $500 and another at $1500.

January 22nd, 1842. At Mr. Seaborn Hill's in the Creek country, about a mile from the ferry, from Gibson, over the Verdigris; came last evening, received politely, invited to remain to supper; passed the evening with the family; his young wife is interesting; far from her white friends. Talked with Hill who is an intelligent trader, about the Contractors; knows but little, but has heard a great deal and can refer to those who do know; seems willing, spoke of his quarrel with Harrison. He had said something of frauds and Harrison collared him (Wilson says Harrison wrung his face – not nose, but the whole lower part of his face, for Harrison is a tremendous man with "a hand as big as all out doors"). Hill challenged – Harrison would not relinquish the choice of a bowie knife, to succeed a fire from a rifle, should the rifle fail at 40 yards. Captain Moore of the Dragoons, Hill's second, then refused to allow Hill to meet Harrison and so an end.

9 P.M. It is Saturday evening. There have been races here today attended by everybody from the commanding officer and his lady down to the veriest blackguards in the country.[56] Two common horses, so far as I can hear and both owned by a professed gambler, Alex-

---

[56] Horse racing had for a long time been a popular form of entertainment at Fort Gibson. A New York paper presents a picture of one of these races: "Fall Campaign in the Far West. Fort Gibson 2d Sept. 1838. Horse racing at the post on Sept. 1, 1838. The course was laid out some years since by Capt. Dawson and Lieut. (now Captain) Moore, of the 7th Infantry;

ander, ran. The Sutler Arnold Harris, bet $500 and, true, he happened to win, but how can a Sutler hope to prosper who is in the habit of betting on all the horse races that are got up regularly here every Saturday and gambling at cards every night, as they say he does.

Among other sights today I saw a knot of whiskey sellers – women whiskey sellers. I stumbled upon a knot of people who did not know me and saw a squaw, not old or ugly either, but rather young and good looking, with her left hand so doubled up as to conceal under a shawl a bottle of whiskey from which she was selling by a small tin cup a gill or two gills at a time – a bit a gill. As she emptied her bottle she would go to a clump

---

and being un-enclosed has suffered much injury by the roads crossing it in many directions, which timber and hay wagons have made.

"Hundreds attended from the adjacent country; and if variety of colors, diversity of costume and contrariety of manner can render a race field an interesting scene for observation, ours can lay claim to that merit. The exhibition of character and feeling is without restraint, and no where else can more enthusiasm be displayed; for a half drunken Indian or half breed gives way to every impulse, and vents his joy or disappointment in yells and execrations. The betting ring is a Babel of Tongues; between the wealthy half-breed with his slaves (who dresses in the latest fashion, and in the most expensive style, rides a fine horse and even sports an equipage for his family) and the unclad Indian, there is a great disparity.

"1. $500.00 purse, one mile out. Lieut Simmons' gelding, 92 lbs. (won). Mr. Nowlands S. F. 3 yr. 83 lbs. Time 2.07½, track sandy and heavy. Won by the gelding. The soldiers expresed their delight at the success of one of their officers by their shouts.

"2. Match for suit of clothes, 600 yards; Mr. Olmstead's Ch. g. Red Fox (won). Mr. Doyle's br. g. The winner equipped himself completely from an over coat to an undershirt, putting into the pocket of the vest a penknife and pencil, so that the bill amounted to $180.

"3. Match for hat, 300 yards; sorrel gelding; Bugler, gr. g. 4. Match for $10.00 one mile; black poney; brown poney; The loser had just returned from the Comanche country, and the owner had used him in chasing buffalo. 4. Match for $40.00, 100 yards; chestnut gelding; Pumpkin Slinger, dun g."
— Account in New York *Spirit of the Times*, copied in Batesville (Arkansas) *News*, November 15, 1838.

of bushes near where an older and uglier squaw merchant had a gallon jug from which the bottle was filled.
I saw two or three others selling also. The day was
very fine and clear for the season. Truly God sends his
sunshine upon the just and the unjust, the godly and the
ungodly.

Sunday 23d January. Bought a horse, saddle and
bridle from Lieut. Wickliffe at 95 and 35 – $130. Lt.
Carleton told me yesterday that as Lt. Wickliffe expected to be surrendered to the Civil authority by Col.
Mason, he would be glad to dispose of a horse and I
sent for the horse and tried him and have bought him.
Paid for him by October's account for 155, he paying
me 25. It made my heart ache to see the young man and
think of his late conduct. He seems mild and placid,
almost timid. How could he be induced to kill Wilkins – to shoot him in the back, Wilkins unarmed!

24th January. Mrs. Baylor (mother of Mrs. West
and Mrs. Dawson) arrived at Fort Gibson last evening
with her young daughter Fanny and with two of Captain Dawson's children. Mrs. West remained at Little
Rock to dispose of some furniture preparatory to her
finally leaving there. Mrs. Baylor has heard from Captain Dawson, who has gone to New York and made a
final settlement of the "miserable business" with the
land company. Mrs. Baylor says he is in very low
spirits and that Mrs. Dawson writes in deep depression
of the hard life in Washington where she is compelled
to dress, go into company and wear smiles when her
heart is ready to break. Mrs. Baylor says the Real
Estate Bank (of Arkansaw) had no right to sell Dawson's negroes, that Dawson supposed them safe under a
mortgage to Dr. Merrill of Natchez who became

Dawson's security when they were purchased. I have heard that Dawson [57] had mortgaged them to the Bank. The family is in great pecuniary embarrassment, but this sort of trouble need never break the heart. Mrs. Baylor has come here to open a boarding house for officers.

I also urged Col. Mason to send a quantity of damaged provisions, of which he says he has a large quantity on hand, as a gratuity to the Seminole band under Coacooche over the Arkansas near the mouth of Grand River. He told me he thought he would do it.

Two or three days ago I spoke to Col. Mason of the gambling carried on here and described some things I had seen and more I had heard of – alluding to the dissipations at the post generally and speaking of the murder by young Wickliffe; expressed an apprehension that the attention of the public might be particularly called to the moral condition and character of the Post. To-day he shewed me the outline of an order [58] he is about to publish prohibiting all card playing and gam-

[57] James L. Dawson enlisted in the army from Maryland in 1819; he served at Fort Gibson in the Seventh Infantry, became a captain in 1833 and resigned in 1835. In March, 1829, Lieutenant Dawson was married at Fort Gibson to Miss Sophia E., daughter of Dr. John W. Baylor, surgeon in the army, formerly of Paris, Kentucky (Arkansas *Gazette*, March 25, 1829). In May 1842, Dawson was appointed agent for the Creeks and later became involved in a controversy with Seaborn Hill who had previously been charged with selling whiskey to the Indians. On July 8, 1844, Dawson and his brother-in-law John Baylor killed Hill on the south side of Arkansas River and then fled to Texas. The Governor of Arkansas made a demand on the Texas authorities for the surrender of Dawson, but he resisted arrest and succeeded in escaping (The Northern Standard [Clarksville, Texas], September 4, 1844, p. 3, col. 4; *ibid.*, March 29, 1845, p. 1, col. 1).

[58] Colonel Mason posted a notice that he was going to remove from the post all persons described as blacklegs, gamblers and loafers, and ordering that no persons from other states should run horse races at the fort, and that all arrivals at McDermott's tavern should register giving their name, business and place of residence; and in June he ordered the tavern closed (Arkansas *Gazette*, July 6, 1842).

bling within the precincts of the Post, announcing his determination to punish any case of violation of the order "without respect to persons." In reading the Act of Congress regulating trade and intercourse with Indians I could not see that the commanding officer or Indian agent has any power to eject persons except those who may be in the Indian country in violation of the provisions of the Act. These relate to trade, to making improvements, to the introduction of whiskey, etc.; but merely being in the country violates no provision of the Act. A gambler cannot, under the Act be ejected; he is not in the country in violation of any provision of the Act. Evening – rain today, sent for my horse to go into the Creek Nation, but the rain increasing yielded to the suggestions of Col. Mason and deferred the trip.

Last night it was warm and a fire in my room: five other persons sleeping in the same room kept me awake till late. Threw off coverlid and two blankets, leaving a sheet and one blanket over me. Mem. – had a bed by myself or I should have gone crazy.

Chapter VII

Frauds on the Creeks – A Creek Pocahontas – Her Death on the Arkansas – Departure from Fort Gibson – Ride over the Prairies – With the Creeks on the Canadian – A Creek Prayer Meeting – A View of the Creeks – Resentment toward the Whites – Opothleyaholo – Black Dirt, the Friendly Seminole – Tukabatchi Square – Interesting Rites – A Populous Creek Settlement.

At Seaborn Hills January 27, 1842. Came over from Gibson day before yesterday; and that day and yesterday I took statements from Benj. Marshall, Barnet and others – the purport of which goes to show that the Indians did not receive their rations by about one-fourth; that no proper supervision was exercised by any government agent and that the contractors issued pretty much as they pleased. I have also taken one or two statements in relation to an 8,000 dollar business in which Captain Page is implicated. By these statements it would appear that in 1836 Page took receipts for $31,900 from Creek Chiefs for annuity for 1837 ordered by General Jesup to be paid in advance; that Page retained $8000 for a certain portion of lower Creeks because they declined sending warriors to Florida; that he subsequently gave three or four different accounts of that money but has never paid it. He has stated that he paid it to four persons whom he has named. He has stated he paid it to one. He has stated that he left it in bank at Columbus. He has stated that he brought it to Ft. Gibson and that it would be paid there. He has stated that they once

sent a common Indian to his tent in the night for the
money and he paid it and would not recollect the Indian again if he were to see him, etc. These all may be
explained, but it seems very odd.

Before leaving Gibson, I saw Mr. Bryant, who lives
on Grand River above Captain Rodgers. He told me
he had claims against the contractors and that if he
were to tell what he knew of them they would not pay
him and he could not "afford" to lose his claim. He
however added in conversation that he sold a number
of cattle, at estimated weights to the contractors who
issued the same cattle for more beef than he sold them
for, and that he offered the contractors $200 if they
would pay him at the rate (in weight) at which they
issued – but they refused to accept his offer.

P.M. rode over today with Mr. Hill to his store on
the other side of the Arkansas. I had heard of Milly
Francis the daughter of the celebrated prophet Francis
who was put to death by order of General Jackson in
1818, when Ambrister and Arbuthnot were executed.
The story is historical that a white man, ·prisoner, was
about to be put to death (burned) under the orders of
Francis, when his daughter Milly interposed and saved
his life. Milly is now over 45 & a widow in this country,
living a mile from the Hills store on the South side
of the Arkansas some 2 or 3 miles from the mouth of
Grand River. She has two sons and a daughter living
of eight children, was dressed something like a white
woman as I saw her today. I had heard of her having
a claim upon eight negroes now among the Seminoles
and I sent for her to learn the character of the title she
could set up. She came in with her eldest boy about 14
or 15. She is fairer than Indian women generally as her
father was of mixed blood.

I took down in pencil Milly's account of her title to the negroes and was perfectly satisfied that she told a true tale. The amount of it is that her father went to England (about 1814) and before going divided some negroes among the children. Her elder sister sent the negroes to Florida, intending to follow with the family. The family did not go – The father came back from England and the war of 1817-18 resulted in his death among other things. Years passed and she, Milly, came to this country among the Creeks. When the Seminoles were sent here and had negroes among them, Milly searched for and found a Negress belonging to her, the only one her father had given her and the one who had been sent to Florida. She picked her out of a number of negroes and *Rose* did not know her until she told her name, when she instantly threw her arms about her mistress, Milly, and declared she was her old mistress. Rose has now seven children, which Milly claims, but says her husband does not belong to her.

After I had taken down her story of her title, I spoke of the story of her having saved the life of a white man and she at once told me the whole story. During the war (1817-18) it was "given out" that if any Indian caught a white man he had the life of the white man in his power, (no chief even could save him). Milly heard a war whoop and going to the place found that two Indians had a young white man tied and perfectly naked; other Indians came around and Milly described the white man doubling himself to screen himself from the gaze of those that were looking at him and at the same time looking anxiously around as if to ask if there was no one to speak for him and save his life.

Milly's eyes were very animated as she gave this account. She is a good looking woman now and must have been a beautiful girl. She was a little girl she said, the size of her daughter now. Seeing the young man and thinking it a "pity" he should be killed she went to her father and urged that it was a pity, etc. The father said, go to the men who have the right over the young man's life. She went to them and began to plead. One of them said he should die for that, he had had two sisters killed. She told him that to kill a white man would not bring back his sisters and that he was but a boy and had not the "head" of a man to guide him – (the meaning of this was that he was not old enough to have engaged in the war upon his own judgment). Milly prevailed on condition that the lad should have his head shaved and live with the Indians. She then went up to him and told him his life should be spared if he would permit his hair to be cut off and live as they did. She said he thrust his head out saying Yes, Yes, cut it all off if you choose. His head was then shaved, all but the scalp lock on the top & he was loosed and dressed. Two years afterwards those who had taken him carried him to St. Marks and sold him for a barrel of whiskey to some Spaniards.

Milly says they were not preparing to burn him, as we have the story published, but were about to shoot him. She says that he came back among them sometime afterwards and offered her marriage, but that she refused him, saying, she did not save his life to marry him. Milly said that on her way to this country everybody appeared to know the story and gave her a great many presents, but that now she is very poor and has to work very hard to get a living.[59]

Riding back with Mr. Hill he showed me a cluster

[59] Major Hitchcock has here given some of the particulars of one of the most interesting and romantic stories in Indian history; a story which he

of log huts where he said a family of Natchez Indians lived – perhaps the only surviving family of that "once powerful tribe." I thought of the story of Attala and my reading it one stormy night in Boston in 1819.

said in one of his letters to the chairman of the House Committee on Indian Affairs, he had read in Drake's *American Indians*.

Hillis Hadjo, called by the whites, Francis the Prophet, was a prominent leader of the Indians in the Florida wars, who lived south of where now stands Tallahassee, Florida. In 1816 he went to England with a British officer and created much enthusiasm, being received by the Prince Regent, George IV, with much ceremony; given a commission as brigadier-general in the British army, and presented with a diamond snuff-box, a gaudy uniform and other presents. In December, he attended a ball given on board a Russian frigate lying off Woolwich, England, on the anniversary of the emperor's birth; a London paper reported: "The double sound of a trumpet announced the arrival of the patriot Francis, who fought so gloriously in our cause in America; he was dressed in a most splendid suit of red and gold, and by his side he wore a tomahawk, mounted in gold, presented to him by the prince regent . . ."— *Niles' Weekly Register*, March 15, 1817, vol. xii, 46; *Idem*, June 13, 1818, vol. xiv, 269.

His mission seems to have been to interest the British in aiding the Indians in their war with the United States; it not only failed but probably brought disaster to the chief. In 1818 General Jackson charged that Francis was inciting the Seminole to hostility, though this is denied; "by hoisting the British flag, several Indians were decoyed on board of some gunboats that ascended the St. Marks river the 31st ult. Among them was a chief, and the prophet Francis, both of whom were hanged."— Milledgeville (Georgia) *Journal*, April 18, 1818, copied in *Niles' Weekly Register*, vol. xiv, 168. On April 27, Jackson caused Ambrister and Arbuthnot, with whom these Indians were associated, to be seized, the first shot, and the other hanged, as enemies of the United States (*Ibid.*, June 13, 1818; Croffut, W. A., *Fifty Years in Camp and Field* (New York, 1919), 154; *Handbook of American Indians*, vol. i, 549; Drake, Samuel G. *The Aboriginal Races of North America* (New York, 1880), 403).

In the summer of 1817, a small party of Seminole surprised and captured while fishing in the Apalachicola River, Capt. Duncan McKrimmon, a member of the Georgia militia; Milly who was yet under sixteen years of age, was playing with her sister on the bank of the river near her father's home, when she heard the whoop of the warriors heralding the arrival of the young prisoner and the fate that awaited him.

After Francis had been hanged, a party of Seminole women and children with some negroes amounting in all to 220, "having surrendered themselves at St. Marks, being in a starving condition, arrived at Fort Gadsden, the last of August. . . . The wife and family of the Prophet Francis are among the prisoners; two of his daughters are very interesting young ladies, and

Hill's – 28th January. Milly, yesterday spoke of living in the old nation near Mr. Hamblins (or Hamleys) somewhere near Apalachicola River, I could not exactly make out the place – and spoke of Miss Hamley

speak very good English, as in fact the whole family do except the mother. The eldest, when her father went on board the *Thomas Shields*, shortly afterward followed, supposing her to be a British vessel. Before she got alongside, however, she discovered the deception, pushed off and made her escape. The youngest and most beautiful is carressed by all the officers for having saved the life of a Georgia militia man, whom her countrymen had taken prisoner and were about to put to death, when this modern Pocahontas, finding entreaties vain, determined to save his life or perish with him; she was successful, and the man was preserved. They all set off tomorrow to join their nation in the neighborhood of Fort Gaines."— *Niles' Weekly Register*, December 12, 1818, vol. iii, 266.

Col. Matthew Arbuckle reported from Fort Gadsden: "Duncan M'Rimmon is here — Milly the Prophet Francis's daughter, says she saved his life, or used such influence as she possessed to that effect, from feeling of humanity alone, and that she would have rendered the same service to any other white man similarly circumstanced — she is therefore not disposed to accept of his offer of matrimony, which has been made as an acknowledgment of gratitude. The donation presented through me (by the citizens of Millidgeville) to Milly, has been delivered, and she manifested a considerable degree of thankfulness of their kindness."— *Niles' Weekly Register*, January 30, 1819, vol. xv, 432. Drake intimates that Milly accepted McCrimmon after he satisfied her that his offer was not prompted solely by gratitude (Drake, *ibid.*, 404; *Handbook of American Indians, idem*). But this conclusion of their romantic affair she denied to Major Hitchcock. She also told him that she was Creek and not Seminole.

The romantic Colonel Hitchcock was so interested in the story of Milly, and so moved by the sad state in which he found her, that he reported her case to the Secretary of War, who transmitted the letter and his own recommendation to the House Committee on Indian Affairs (U. S. House. *Reports,* 27th congress, 3d session, no. 274). Congress thereupon passed an act June 17, 1844 (Statutes 1844, vol. 6, p. 928, ch. cliv.), granting to Milly a pension of ninety-six dollars per annum "as a testimonial of the gratitude and bounty of the United States for the humanity displayed by her in the war of one thousand eight hundred and seventeen and one thousand eight hundred and eighteen, in saving the life of an American citizen who was a prisoner in the hands of her people and about to be put to death by them." The act provided further that a medal be struck and presented to Milly "as an additional testimonial of the gratitude of the United States."

However, after this handsome gesture, there was no one in official Washington sufficiently interested in Milly and her splendid chivalry, to carry the act into effect. It appears from the extensive correspondence in the as a cousin or some connexion. When I came back here I mentioned it to Mr. Hill who told me that the widow 'of Hamblin is living some 20 miles from here on the Verdigris – that Hamblin was a Spaniard and is dead. I told him I knew Mrs. Hamblin who was sent from Apalachicola together with a sister and a little daugh-

---

Hitchcock Collection of manuscripts in the Library of Congress, and in the Office of Indian Affairs, that it was three and one half years before the head of the Indian Department wrote to James Logan the Creek agent to inform Milly of the pension and medal that awaited her. The letter was read to Milly and to the Creek chiefs in council, all of whom received it with much interest and pride.

After almost interminable formalities, correspondence and apparent indifference to the destitution of Milly that the pension was intended to relieve, it was May 1848, wanting one month of four years since the passage of the act, that the Creek agent visited Milly, to have her sign a power of attorney so he could collect the money for her. ". . . I received information that she was laying dangerously ill. I immediately visited her and found her as I was informed in dying circumstances and I regret to say in a most wretched condition. I immediately procured medical aid, and done all that was possible to alleviate her sufferings, having so far succeeded as to restore consciousness. I read your letter to her (she comprehending English perfectly) at which she was so highly elated that I flattered myself she was recovering, but my hopes were fallacious; her desease was consumption; she died on the 19th ulto. being about fifty years old. She died a *Christian*, a devout member of the Baptist Church; has left two sons and a daughter; the youngest of the boys is at present at Col. Johnson's Academy in Kentucky. She informed me that at the time the act was rendered which saved the life of Capt. McCrimmon she never expected any pecuniary reward; her family were rich and she did not request it; she had however become very poor and she was grateful for the notice of her by the Government."— Logan to Medill, June 1, 1848, Office of Indian Affairs.

Milly never received the medal or a dollar of the pension, and subsequent correspondence was concerned with the disposition to be made of them to her heirs. While her last days of poverty and sickness were cheered by the information that the Government had acknowledged its obligation to an Indian maiden for her compassion and fine spirit in saving the life of a white youth, her eyes were never to shine with the joy of looking upon the testimonial of that acknowledgement. And if her bones have not been scattered by a farmer's plow, somewhere between the city limits of Muskogee and the Arkansas River, there is hidden the grave of Oklahoma's Pocahontas; the first resident of Oklahoma, and one of the few women in history to have bestowed upon them a medal authorized by a special act of Congress.

ter to Mobile in 1818 and that I saw them at Mobile Point; that Mrs. Hamblin was a beautiful woman and her daughter a beautiful little girl about 12 years old. Hill said the daughter was dead. Said nothing of the sister.

Last evening my yesterday's adventure was constantly recurring to me and last night kept me awake and full of strange reflections. In 1818, i.e., in the winter of '17 and '18, I was at Mobile Point, commanding a small garrison of about 20 men, myself a young Lieutenant just out from the Military Academy. When the Seminole war broke out Major Peters passed the Point on his way to St. Marks with his company of artillery and was detained 15 days by a head wind. I made a great effort to get orders to join him; and asked for a leave of absence for the purpose. When orders were refused by Captain Scott who then commanded Fort Charlotte at Mobile and Fort Bowyer (Mobile Point) its dependency, I failed and Peters went on without me. About that time November or December, I think, a vessel from Apalachicola or St. Marks bound for New Orleans, left under my charge Hamblin's family – wife, daughter & sister-in-law. They remained with me some days, when to relieve myself of the responsibility, of detaining them, I sent them against their will to Mobile in a small row boat. They were of a friendly party if I mistake not, and had been sent from the Indian country as friends and not as prisoners. Mrs. Hamblin was very beautiful, both in person & features and her little girl, one of the prettiest little things I ever saw. The sister was ordinary in her appearance. I remember them well.

And now, after an interval of some 25 years, I am within 20 miles of one of them.

10 P.M. 28th January '42, at Mr. Hill's; and to-day I was at General Roly McIntosh's and took down a number of statements in regard to issues of provisions and other matters.

Upon a hasty calculation from one of the statements of provision issues to 78 persons for a whole year it would seem that the issues & money together, for there was some money paid, amounted to about $5 for each individual, the government paid the contractors about $45!!!

North Fork,[60] Canadian, Sunday January 30, 1842; thermometer 78, Summer heat, south wind rather high; yesterday, Mr. Hill and myself rode over the Prairie between the Arkansas & Canadian. Left his house at about 8 A.M. and the river at 9. Arrived last evening after a journey of 40 miles. Found Dr. Burt here, whom I saw at Prince's in the Cherokee Nation just on his return from an Osage Buffalo hunt; he turns out to have been a Schoolmaster in the Creek Nation and was thrown out of employment by the arrangement with Col. Johnson[61] who has received the principal portion of the Creek School fund. He is spoken well of, and has a claim for services. I find Chapman is here in charge of Hill's branch store. Mr. Alexander came here (8 miles) today from another branch store up the river.

It is Sunday and everything very quiet. Last evening

---

[60] North Fork Town was a settlement just east of the present Eufaula, Oklahoma, located on an early emigrant trail running to Texas, called the Texas Road. It contained traders' stores and was named from its location near the North Fork of the Canadian River.

[61] Col. Richard M. Johnson of Kentucky, former member of both houses of Congress and Vice President of the United States from 1837 to 1841, had established a school for the education of Indian youth which continued for many years; it was called the Choctaw Academy and was located in Scott County, Kentucky. Appropriations were made by Congress to pay for the board, clothing, and education of boys sent to this school from different tribes.

with Mr. Chapman's permission a part of his house was occupied by a party of Creeks, half-breeds and negroes engaged in prayer and singing psalms.[62] They commenced by singing a hymn in Creek to Creek music. It was rather more plaintive than solemn; after that several hymns in English were sung to Methodist or Baptist tunes; words very simple and apparently made by themselves: "Farewell Father," with a chorus and then "Farewell, Mother" and so on sister, brother, preacher, "I'm bound to go on," was about all I could hear of one hymn. I went into the room just a moment. A negro after I came out made a prayer with considerable energy. The feelings were the same that I have seen exhibited in New York and elsewhere.

Main Canadian (at Mr. Alexander's, L. L.) January 31st, 1842. Rode here yesterday, 9 miles from North Fork. Mr. Alexander has a store here in the interest of Mr. Hill. Hill furnishes the goods and gives Alexander a portion of the profits on sales. Alexander is a white man, 27 or 30 years of age. He has been with the Creek Indians, he tells me about 9 years and came to this country with Opothleyaholo's party in December 1836; two years ago he married a half-breed, a daughter of one Jacobs, and is living very comfortably. His

---

[62] "There is at this time in active progress, a considerable religious excitement among the Creek people, which pervades pretty much the whole of the nation. Their religious exercises and meetings are all conducted in a quiet, decent, orderly manner. They have recently sent for the assistance of some white men (preachers), to aid in the organization of churches, discipline, &c. At the last grand council, they passed some very salutary laws in regard to the sale of ardent spirits in the nation. For this offense, they inflict severe corporeal punishment. The good effects of this law are already visible from the altered habits of many that before the passage of the law were too much given to habits of beastly intoxication."— Report of Creek Indian Agent, June 30, 1842, U. S. House *Documents*, 27 congress, third session, no. 2.

wife, enceinte will soon make him a happy father. Alexander is one of two clerks employed by the Nation, the other being Eli Jacobs for the Indians on Arkansas.

I have today taken Alexander's statement in respect to the issues of provisions and I find he proves directly that Harrison provided false measures for issuing corn and ordered or desired him to use them; that he made trial of them, found.they were false and refused to use them; that this brought him into collision with Major Rains on whose representations he, Alexander, was dismissed from the employment of the Government by Captain Stephenson.[63] This is the second instance in which a faithful agent of the Government was dismissed by Stephenson at the instigation of contractors agents; Irving was the first I discovered.

Several chiefs came in today and through the interpreter David Barnet I explained my business to be that of procuring information; expressly telling them and repeating it, that I made no complaints against any one in or out of the country, that I simply wanted information about their condition, wants, etc. They have taken a couple of days to send for absent chiefs and to confer together.

I find the Creeks here a different people from those on the Arkansas and very different from the Cherokees. The Creeks over on the Arkansas, with Roly McIntosh for their principal chief who is, indeed the acknowledged principal chief of the Creek Nation, embrace most of those Creeks who emigrated under the first

---

[63] James R. Stephenson of Virginia was graduated from the United States Military Academy, July 1, 1822, and afterward saw much service at Fort Jesup, Fort Towson and Fort Gibson with the Seventh Infantry. From December 28, 1830, to July 5, 1839, as captain on commissary duty, he was engaged in subsisting the Indians who were being emigrated from the East.

treaties with the United States. They appear to be more advanced in intelligence, seem less wild, not to say ferocious than these here.

These Indians are quite primitive in their appearance and I am told by white men that some of the towns this way are so hostile to the whites and so much exasperated by cheats put upon them in Georgia and Alabama, that they will not wear pantaloons. Why they make a difference and wear coats and vests I do not see. Opothleyaholo is a principal man over here, I find, though I understand he has resigned as a chief and is no longer a chief. He did the principal talking today merely giving me some of the heads of the subject on which they intend to dilate in a day or two. He is a tall well made Indian over 45, perhaps 50 years of age. Had on a blue frock coat of good cloth, but wore deer skin leggings. Several of the chiefs today were dressed in cloth coats or overcoats & skin leggings, some had turbans on, nearly all had moccasins instead of shoes. Some common Indians had blankets, worn in the usual Indian style.

First February, 1842, Main Canadian: Sun is clear and bright, no wind, merely cool, a fine morning, cocks crowing, 9 A.M. Mr. Chapman told me at the North Fork that there were not more than 300 remaining of Black Dirts party of Seminoles, about 200 having died. There are two under that bed, said he, pointing to the bed, where I had slept the night preceding. I looked towards the bed, when he added "and one under our feet" just before the fire place. Black Dirt when he first came to this country from Florida in 1836 settled on the North Fork and the Chief occupied the house we were then in, and it seems had buried some of his family or friends under the house. That was the friendly party of the Seminoles who separated from the hostiles in 1835, on the death (murder) of Charley Emathla,[64] who was killed by the hostiles for consenting to emigrate.

Twelve miles visited with Mr. Alexander at the "square" of the Tuckebatchee Town, about four miles hence. It is the only Square (place of business) where there is a *"round house,"* in which is preserved the sacred fire. I was not prepared for what I have seen for I supposed the Creeks more removed from their ancient customs than I find they are. I have begun some account of the Creeks, their laws and customs in another note book, but will condense here just a hint of what I saw and heard this morning.

The *square* consists of four shed roofs forming a rectangle 20 paces on a side within. Each roof is closed on three sides to the ground, the fourth or inner side being open for counsellors to sit in, where mats are spread made of cane for seats. The four sheds are separated at their angles four or five paces for entrance and egress, and they are situated so that diagonals of the Square are nearly upon the meridian line and at right angle to it. Three sides of the sheds are closed with mud and are raised about six feet, the open front inside being a corresponding six feet. Each shed is divided into three parts by a partial partition only raised about elbow high to one in a sitting posture. Upon each parti-

[64] Black Dirt or Fuke-lus-te Hadjo and his band of nearly five hundred Seminole were friendly to the whites and separated from the hostiles before the war of 1836 broke out; they went to Tampa Bay and encamped while the warriors of the band served in the army against the hostiles; they were peaceably emigrated to the West where they lived between the Little River, North Fork, and the Canadian rivers. Charley Emarthla, Jumper and other Seminole chiefs were brought from Florida in December, 1832, to the western Creek country to examine it with a view to committing the tribe to removal; they were taken to Fort Gibson where, on March 28, 1833, they entered into a treaty binding the tribe to accept the land shown them. For his efforts to aid the removal of the tribe, Emarthla was killed by Osceola in 1835.

tion there are two earth bowls of about a foot diameter in which live coals are placed during the Council for the grave counsellors to light their pipes by.

One of the sheds is appropriated, or two parts of the three in which it is divided, to the preservation of articles used in the preparation and drinking of the "black drink." The most curious part of the preparation at the Square is at the West angle a few feet from the angle outside – the *Round house*. This is difficult to describe and considerable ingenuity has been employed in its erection. The main structure is supported upon twelve posts or pillars, one end sunk in the ground. They are disposed in a circle about 9 or 10 feet apart, making a space within of about 120 feet circumference in the centre of which, upon the ground is the sacred fire. The roof over this circle is a cone terminating in a point over the fire some 20 odd feet high. The rafters extend down from the apex of the cone beyond the twelve pillars, which are about eight feet high, to within four or five feet of the ground, which space, of four or five feet is closed entirely with earth – between the pillars and the extreme exterior, a space of several feet, are seats of mats, like those of the sheds. The manner of constructing the roof is very remarkable for Indian work. Upon the alternate couples of the twelve pillars are first placed horizontal pieces – then upon the ends of these are placed other horizontal pieces between the other couples of pillars then another series of horizontal pieces resting upon the second set, but drawn within towards the centre of the circle a few inches. Upon these again are other pieces still more drawn in.

There are four tiers of horizontal pieces thus placed upon each other. A. B. C. D. are four of the twelve pillars; pieces are first laid upon A. B. and upon C. D.

then a piece upon these and between B. C., etc. These horizontal pieces are strongly bound together by leather thongs of green hide; it is evident they are of the nature of an arch. They are only carried up to the number of four sufficient for giving a direction and a foundation for the rafters, which are laid upon these extending up to a point in one direction and in the other direction over outside to near the ground. The rafters are strongly bound by thongs and covered with ordinary rived boards for shingles. There is but one small entrance to the house which is next towards the angle of the square adjacent to which the round house stands.

The persons who are appointed to preserve the buildings are obliged every morning to drink a decoction from certain leaves which produces an emetic. The leaves are gathered in season and roasted or dried by a hot fire. I saw a large quantity and put a few in a paper. These are boiled for some time until a thick froth is produced. The froth is removed and the black liquor cooled and drank as an emetic and then the persons may eat, but not before in the morning. Near the Round House is a small house, closed, in which are secured certain plates of brass and other implements used only in the celebration of the Green Corn Dance which is their sacred festival and is held every year in July. Opothleyaholo [65] don't like our missionaries and

---

[65] Opothleyaholo was one of the great men of the Creek tribe; he headed the delegation that went to Washington to protest against the Creek treaty signed in 1825 by McIntosh yielding their land to the government and it was set aside; though he signed the treaty of 1826, his faction of the tribe did not leave Alabama for ten years. In 1836 when some of the Creek towns prepared to join the insurgent Seminole, Opothleyaholo, at the head of the Tukabatchi Indians captured some of the young warriors who had started the revolt and delivered them to the United States authorities. After the death of the nominal chief of the Creek tribe, Opothleyaholo became their leader, and was their chief counsellor and comfort on their sad march to the West under military compulsion. With ten thousand of his followers

says a man will much more surely get to heaven by worshipping the brass plates than in any other way.

Some of the Indians believe the plates [66] came from heaven, sent by the Great Spirit. There are three of them. Others have a tradition that they were presented by some Spanish King. The fire at the Round House is kept alive throughout the Busk and at the green corn dance it is renewed by fire excited by the friction of two sticks.

There appears to be a considerable number of Creeks in this part of the Nation.[67] We passed by a number of houses in our four miles ride this morning. One was a fine double house with a broad piaza; of course, built of logs. Most of the houses are small and are covered, instead of chinked, with earth which is of a red color quite bright, which gives a quite gay appearance to the house as seen through the woods a little distance off. I went to the house of the Principal Chief of the upper towns and was sorry to find it a miserable cabin, without a floor & very small. Mr. Alexander said he was very poor and has been placed at the head of affairs for his honesty, for which he is held in great respect.

P.M. Since writing the above, I have had the Micco or King of the Tuckebatchee town here and have, through a Negro Interpreter heard him tell his faith and custom with respect to the "plates" etc.; and it ap-

---

of the Upper Creeks, he located on the Canadian River. During the Civil War, in one of the most tragic episodes of that conflict, he lead his faction of the tribe to Kansas, where many of them died, including this intrepid leader (*Handbook of American Indians*, vol. ii, 141).

[66] These plates are said to be still in existence in the custody of Tukabatchi Town officers who will not permit them to be seen.

[67] Colonel Hitchcock is here traveling through the fertile region near the present town of Eufaula, where the large number of followers of Opothleyaholo settled in 1836 and 1837. January 31, the day before this entry, Hitchcock was commissioned a lieutenant-colonel.

pears that Mr. Alexander was in error about keeping up the fire all the year, it is only kept up through the ceremonies of the green corn dance, four days; after that it may go out and during the year it may be made from a house fire; but at the green corn dance it is made from friction. I have written of this in the other note book.[68]

---

[68] The next chapter contains the contents of "the other note book" mentioned by Colonel Hitchcock.

Chapter VIII

Creek Migrations – Appalling Death Rate – Constituents of the Creek Confederacy – Form of Government – Creek Traditions – Customs – Immurement of Widows – Treatment of Infants – Marriage – Green Corn Dance or Busk – Sacred Fire – Plates from Heaven – Power of the Medicine Men – Burial Customs – Witches.

Main Canadian, Creek Nation, January 31, 1842. Information by Mr. H. [J] S. Alexander: Does not think the whole Creek Nation exceeds 16,000. When the principal emigration took place in 1836, he thinks there were between 21,000 and 22,000. What is called Opothleyaholo's party came over principally in 1836 and I took (says Mr. Alexander) a census of them at Fort Gibson where they arrived in December. There were then in that party a few over 11,000. There were several emigrations before that year, as far back as 1827 under a treaty made in 1825, and there were one or two parties came over after '36 including those warriors who served in Florida. Roly McIntosh and a large portion of his people who came over in 1827 settled on the Arkansas river. Opothleyaholo and his party came to the Canadian chiefly, though about 4,000 of this party settled on the Arkansas.[69]

---

[69] Because he signed a treaty with the whites in 1825 agreeing to give up the Creek country in violation of laws which he helped to make, the chief William McIntosh was executed by members of Oakfuskee Town. A new treaty was arranged the next year and over twelve hundred of the faction of McIntosh under the leadership of Roley McIntosh, and that many

In the first twelve months after the emigration of 1836 at the lowest calculation there were thirty-five hundred deaths of the emigrants of 1836. I am sure of this because I took the census of the emigrants of 1836 in 1838. The first three years after Opothleyaholo came to the country there was a decrease, but since then there has been an increase. I took the census again, last summer of Opothleyaholo's people and from this I know there has been an increase.

The principal Indians of the Creek Nation are the Creeks properly so called or Muskogees, next the Uchees then the Hitchitees, the Notchez (Natchez), Coowarsarde and Alabamas. These are exclusive of the Seminoles. These all have different languages, but the young people nearly all understand and speak the Creek language. All the Hitchitees speak the Creek, but the Uchees or many of them, do not speak the Creek. There are two small towns of Alabamas, one is called Oakchoyuchee, but they speak the Alabama language, and though originally a separate tribe are now considered Alabamas.[70]

more of the other faction emigrated from the East in 1827, and the next year located near the mouth of the Verdigris River. While a treaty was made with members of the Creek tribe in 1832 and another in 1833, only a few hundred would depart for the West. And it was not until 1836 a disturbance in the Creek Nation, for convenience called a "war," furnished an excuse to send a large number of troops into their country, herd the Indians into parties of one to three thousand each, and hurry them off to the West. More than ten thousand of them under the leadership of Opothleyaholo arrived and camped near Fort Gibson during the following winter; many of them died on this unhappy journey and after their location in their new and strange surroundings; after that winter the most of these people who looked up to Opothleyaholo for guidance, removed to the Canadian River and located near the present town of Eufaula.

70 The Creek Nation is a confederacy forming one of the largest divisions of the Muskhogean family. The English name "Creeks" originated in the shortening of "Ocheese Creek Indians," Ocheese being an old name for the Ocmulgee River, upon which most of the Lower Creeks were living when the

There are but three families of the Natchez Indians remaining. They have a distinct language, but speak Creek, or nearly all of them do. The Hitchitees may number two or three hundred but are much intermixed and have almost become Creeks.

The Uchees are more numerous, may be 800, and preserve their distinctive character more than any other band or tribe. Not many of them speak Creek and they intermarry but rarely with the Creeks.

The whole Creek Nation is composed of two parties, which were designated in the old Nation east of the Mississippi River, as the Upper and Lower Towns. Sometimes called upper Creeks and lower Creeks. They are still to a considerable extent distinct; the upper Creeks are principally on the Canadian and the lower Creeks are on the Arkansas.

These parties have separate head chiefs; at present the principal chief of the lower Creeks is Roly McIntosh, as Tommarthle Micco is of the Upper Creeks.[71]

English first came in contact with them. The Yuchi and the Natchez were incorporated with the Creek Confederacy at a comparatively recent period. The Koasati (spelled by Colonel Hitchcock, Cooarsarde) and Alibamu are closely related and joined the confederacy at a much earlier period.

The Hitchiti tribe, also part of the Creek Confederacy was considered the head or "mother" of a group of lower Creek towns which spoke closely related languages distinct from Muskogee. This group included the Sawokli, Okmulgee, Apalachichola and probably the Chiaha (Bureau of American Ethnology. Bulletin 73, *Early History of the Creek Indians and their Neighbors* by John R. Swanton; *ibid.*, Bulletin 30, *Handbook of American Indians* edited by Frederick Webb Hodge; and Gatschet, Albert S. *A Migration Legend of the Creek Indians* (Philadelphia, 1884), vol. 1).

[71] Before their removal from Alabama, the Creeks were divided into what were known as Upper and Lower Creeks. The Lower Creeks lived near the white settlements on the coast and included a considerable amount of white blood to which classification William McIntosh belonged. The Upper Creeks living farther away from the whites were less progressive but being in the majority prevented the Lower Creeks from effecting the removal of the whole tribe. After they came west the killing by the Upper Creeks of McIntosh made the division between the Upper and Lower

In general Council the two principal chiefs preside seated by the side of each other, but Roly McIntosh takes the right and is considered the senior or head chief of the Nation. For local purposes in the upper Creeks there are four chiefs called Counselling Chiefs one of whom is called the King, who transact the current business of the party subject to the control of the principal Chief whenever the latter thinks proper to interfere, as on important occasions.

After these are the Chiefs of the different towns. The whole nation is divided into towns having separate names. There may be forty-five towns,[72] each of which has a principal chief or king and a sub chief. In each town there are persons called *lawyers,* from four up to forty and even forty-five, according to the population, whose duty it is to execute the laws; they are subject to the views of the Head Chiefs of the Nation who send them on important missions when necessary.

The lower Creeks have two persons in authority called Light Horse, who are a sort of Sheriffs for the collection of debts with other similar duties and are paid each a salary of $150 a year.

There is a general council of the nation once a year in the Spring. All of the Chiefs of every grade are permanently in power unless they resign or from misconduct are deposed. The mode of filling a vacancy is assimilated to an election by the people but upon recommendations made by those already in power, to which the popular voice presents scarcely an obstacle.

The general council for business is composed of the

Creeks more pronounced and it was not until after the Civil War that the tribe was united under one constitution.

[72] These were political and not necessarily geographical divisions; on their removal some of them were wiped out by death or union with other towns. The remainder retained their identity in their new home.

two principal chiefs and the Kings including those of the Towns. These constitute the Aristocratic portion of the government. There is another branch composed of one or two persons elected by each town from among the lawyers with one judge from the upper and one from the lower Creeks which constitute what is called a committee. This has the appearance of a popular branch. Sometimes the number of the Committee is increased on important occasions.

A law generally originates in the Committee; if approved there, it is sent to the principal chiefs for their approval. If approved by the principal chiefs it is a law. But practically the Chiefs make the laws and unmake them. Besides the written laws there are many usages in force which are not written. Their peculiar ceremonies and customs are not written.

The lower Creeks have to some extent abandoned their old customs, but the upper Creeks who are less advanced in civilization, have retained most of their ancient ceremonies and customs.

1st February. Tuckebatchee Micco (who has charge of the Round House and sacred implements of worship) tells me they have a tradition that originally seven persons were sent by the Great Spirit down from heaven upon earth, that they attempted to return and one died, the others came back and from them the country was peopled. "Were they men and women?" "Yes, men and women." "And the one that died?" 'I understood he was a man." "How long ago?" "Don't know." (I have an old negro for an interpreter.)

On a further explanation it appears they think there were people on earth before this visitation from heaven. These messengers from heaven sat down in a *Square* and performed some ceremony; the red men tried to find

out what they were about but could not for some time;
but at length they succeeded and found out something
and were then taught how to make fire and how to worship the great Spirit. They brought certain plates from
heaven and gave them to the Creek Chiefs, (adds that
when Col. Hawkins, the former Indian Agent saw
them, he said they came from the King of England, or
from the British.) But the Indians believe that the
plates came from heaven and that they are to be wor-
shipped. The people from heaven told the Indians how
to make a fire and that, once a year, the fire was to be
extinguished entirely and a new one made, by friction;
and then they must thank the Great Spirit for his blessings and that time only were the plates to be seen. When
the people came from heaven, the Indians had nothing
to use but the bow and arrow. They would go out and
hunt for a living and lived entirely by hunting. After
a while they found some white people and from them
they got knives and other articles. In old time the
Tuckebatchee Indians (town) met the Cowetas (town)
(these were the largest towns of Creeks) and they
smoked a pipe of peace and agreed to be forever friendly. And they have always been friendly, and all the
other Indians are obliged to look up to them.

The next sentence explains without mentioning the
name of McIntosh who was killed, that notwithstand-
ing his death the Cowetas and Tuckebatchees have still
been friendly.[73]

When the Lord first made men (of all colors) they
were all one people, that the Lord offered them a

[73] William McIntosh belonged to Coweta Town, which was regarded as
the head war town of the Lower Creeks and by reason of his standing in
that town he became the head of the Lower Creeks. Tukabahtchi of the
Upper Creeks was the largest town in the Creek confederacy. Opothleyaholo
and other opponents of McIntosh were members of this town and relations

choice, showing a piece of paper first to the red man and he could make nothing of it and let it alone, and the red man going along he found some roots and some bows and arrows and he said these are mine, and so he lived in the woods by roots and hunting.

The white man then looked at the paper and he could use it and he kept it ("and how about the black people?"). There was nothing said about them.

In old time, at the Busk (Green Corn Dance), the warriors would starve seven days and have nothing to do with women and they were more brave and stout people and they fought a great deal. There were but few of that class of people survived to these times.

The first discovery of corn was "in this wise." A woman, supposed to be an angel, died and was buried by the side of a large hill and from her grave a stalk of corn sprung up. It was seen and watched and attended to and finally the ear that was formed was gathered and shelled and then they had corn. (Tobacco grew from the rib of a woman under the same circumstances.)

In old time the men who went to war and killed the most people were made the head chiefs. The nations formerly were constantly engaged in war, but finally they made peace. (He spoke of some particular tribe engaged in war and sent off by Spaniards, the name of the tribe I could not make out).

Before the world comes to an end, there is to be a general peace of all people, whites and red (the blacks they seem to take no account of). After the peace for a time it will rain blood and when trees are cut the sap will be blood, after that it will be seen that the world

between them and the Coweta had been strained by the strife growing out of the killing of McIntosh.

will be coming to an end, and all people will go to one place to die.

The old people used to say that those who are to be saved will go up; that the others will have towns under the earth. (Here he explained, as if anxious to impress it upon me, that this was what the old people have told him.)

There will be but a few that will go up, the good people; the bad people will go below. (I will put a (2) before the answers to questions put by myself.)

(2) "He says he don't know all that." God sent a man to make the earth and after he had made it he said, here is wood, cedar and poplar, etc., for you to use; he said this to the red man, and land to cultivate.

(2) When he sent a man to make the world, the man made it in a day. God told the man he wanted a world made for his red people. After it was made the man asked the red men if that would do, and the red men said yes, and he made nothing more. Here he explained that there are people living in the water and under the ground, as well as upon the ground; that the old people have told him they have heard the drum (alluding to their dances) under the ground.

At first there were none but red men. The Lord said to three of them, now I want to make some white men and he told them to go to the river and wash. At first only one went and he staid a long time in the water and when he came out he was all over white. Then another went and staid but a short time and the water had been a little soiled, so his color was not changed. Then the third went and the water was more soiled, and when he came out he was black.

Here I asked his own belief about these matters and he did not fully explain. But he said, referring to the white paper which the white man took, that if he could have had the chance he would have taken the paper and then perhaps the Indians would have had everything as the whites have. He ended this strain by asking me to explain what it means, that their black people have meetings, alluding to their having become Christians, saying that the Indians didn't know what it meant and didn't like it "and may be you can explain it," said he.

(2) "He don't know that much," but he expects the world is square.

(2) The sun goes round the earth every day. The old people say it is a great way off, for if it came near it would burn everything up.

So much for talking through a nigger. I find that the sacred fire is only continued through the Busk – Green Corn Dance; after that it may go out and during the year may be lighted from common fire. When they are about to make the fire at the Busk, twelve men watch all night and at the crowing of the cock in the morning they commence making the fire. Sometimes it takes them all the morning and until afternoon to make the fire (by friction).

When there are widows or orphans, with no one to take care of them, I (that is, the Micco or King) turn out the people and put up a house for them, and make a fence and plant some corn for them.

Young people are not so orderly and obedient to the old people now as they used to be in the old nation. When we tell them to do anything, they seem to stop and think about it. Formerly they always went at once and did as they were told; that is, before they came to this country.

When we order out the people to make a public

fence (There is a public field for every town, besides each one's own field) if they don't turn out we send and take away their gun, or horse; or something else to punish them.

Main Canadian. February 1st, 1842. James Island, an intelligent half breed Chief of the Creeks, says of the sacred utensils at the Round House, that when the general emigration took place in 1836, a number of people were selected to convey those articles to the west and they went in advance of the Nation. No man was allowed to precede the party in charge of those articles.

He says nearly the whole nation regard these things with reverence. That other towns have other articles used in celebrating the green corn dance; the Cowetas, for instance, have large Conk shells out of which they take the black drink. They have had these shells for a long time and preserve them with great care. "Other towns have their own customs." Mr. Island does not exactly say he believes or disbelieves the story of the plates coming down from heaven. When I put the question distinctly, but as delicately as I could, he simply said the old people have brought down the story, and every town has its customs.

Island and Alexander, have been talking of prophets among the Tuckebatchee town people and have told several anecdotes of their practices. In cases of sickness, they have prescribed *presents* to the Round House, and have assigned as causes of pains the presence of animals within. A case of salivation they said was caused by two rattlesnakes in the mouth and they required five dollars for a prescription.

Main Canadian, 2nd February. Unwritten laws. When a husband dies his female relations have a right to prevent the marriage of the widow for four years.

After the husband is buried the relatives take the
widow from the grave to the nearest branch and im-
merse her in water; if once, she must remain a widow
one year; if twice, two years and so on, but they cannot
exceed four years. If there is no branch near, they perform the ceremony by dashing a bucket of water upon
her, once, twice and so on.

(The Indians count years by moons, twelve moons
making a year). After the immersion she is carried
back to the house where her husband died and is shut
up within the house and kept there four days. A little
girl is appointed to attend her and supply her food, and
no other person is allowed to go near her. In four cases
out of five, the husband is buried in the house where
he dies, under the bed, and the woman is obliged to
sleep in the bed the four nights of her confinement to
the house. A shed or small house is prepared near the
dwelling and after the four days have expired she is
assigned to that house and compelled to live there during the period of her widowhood, one to four years;
during the time she is not allowed to make or receive
visits, no one is allowed to enter the house though they
may talk to her at the door. She is not allowed to wash
her face, or comb her hair or change her dress. The
little girl attendant may "look" her head, whose privilege it is to eat what she finds and she generally avails
herself of the privilege.

At the expiration of the widowhood, the relations of
the deceased husband repair to the house and take possession of the widow and wash her from head to foot
(it is the women relatives who do all this), comb her
hair and dress it and clothe her completely, often with
a great deal of finery and convey her to the Square
where a dance has been appointed for the occasion. She

looks at the dance and joins in it if she chooses and the same relatives, women, select some man who is appointed to pass the night with her and release her, as it is called, from her widowhood. The man must be single and if after the night's acquaintance the parties agree, they live together as man and wife, if not, they separate and are free to do as they please. If a wife dies her female relations take the man to the branch, etc., the same as in the former case except that the widower cannot be retained a widower over four months; and at the expiration of the time the women select a partner for the night as before.

The women have a custom among themselves. When one is visited with what is peculiar to the sex, about once a month, she is obliged to occupy a separate tent or house, to eat from separate dishes, and to live entirely apart from all others until they are passed, and then they are taken and thoroughly washed whether winter or summer and returned to the family. The utensils used by her are laid aside until required for a similar purpose. No man is ever allowed to sit in the seat which has been used by a woman under those circumstances.

At the period of child birth the woman is obliged to leave the house and the child must be born out of the house, winter or summer; and the mother must not enter the house for ten days and must not sleep in the house for two months, and if taken sick in giving birth to a child, she is not allowed to sleep in the house for four months. Before the child is allowed to suckle it is taken to a branch or spring and water thrown upon its tongue several times. Children are often bathed in a creek by the time they are a month old; formerly they used to be rolled in the snow, to make them hardy.

When the child is a boy a physic maker, a sort of priest, is called upon for a preparation which is placed upon the mother's nipple to make the child hardy and brave, and an active ball player.

A young man wishing to marry a girl for whom he has taken a fancy goes to an aunt or some near female connection of his own and tells her his wishes. She then goes to the aunt or some near connection of the girl and makes it known. This connection of the girl then goes to the parents of the girl and tells the story. The girl is not consulted in the case. If the parents are willing, a time for the ceremony of marriage is appointed by the connections. At the time appointed an outer house, a corn crib, is selected near the girl's house and a bowl of Sofkee (boiled corn) is placed under the projecting shed of the crib in sight from the house, and here the girl has the privilege of exerting a veto. The girl is informed of the whole business and if she chooses to allow the man to steal up and take a spoonful of Sofkee without her seeing him, it is a marriage and the party sleeps the first night in the corn crib. This has been the old custom, but is going out of date. After the ceremony, the young man is not allowed to visit the house of his wife by day for the period of a month, but must visit his wife after dark and go away before day. The Sofkee part of the ceremony is now generally dispensed with.

A man having a wife, if he takes to another woman, the wife may assent to it passively, but if she chooses she may whip the woman; but in this case she must move away and yields all her rights to the woman, who becomes the principal wife. In this way the man may take as many women as he pleases and is able to support. The wife in the exercise of her prerogative has a right to the assistance of her female relations and when it is exercised the ceremony is severe and makes a lasting impression. Their object is to disfigure their victim and the wife uses her nails and scratches the face of the new wife and with switches she whips. The severity of this ceremony must exercise a considerable restraint upon both husbands and women, making it necessary to consult the wife in advance in order that her assent may be assured before her rights are encroached upon. Alexander said he knew a case, *saw it*, and heard the language when a wife exercised her right saying as she laid on the lash: "you think it is honey, but I'll make it vinegar before I'm done with you."

Green Corn Dance, (Busk, the Indians call it). The meaning of the word Busk is to fast, at the season of green corn, usually in July, the chiefs of the town meet and have a talk about the Green Corn Dance with the people. At this meeting they give orders for the pots and other utensils, except those which are sacred, to be made. Some of the sacred utensils have been handed down from time immemorial. They meet again in seven days, again four days afterwards, and then again in two days. At these several meetings they give orders for preparations, appoint persons to procure wood, others to procure cane, etc., etc. On the fourth meeting they give out the "broken days" [74] for the Busk; seven from

---

[74] When a council, ball-play, or other important event was scheduled, the chief issued to the principal men or others interested, bundles of sticks, the number in the bundle corresponding with the number of days intervening before the engagement. "I saw a chief take from his pouch a bundle of reeds, about an inch long, very carefully and compactly tied together, draw one out and throw it away. I asked what that meant, and received for an answer, 'He is counting the time.' Each of the reeds tied up in that bundle counted a day; every morning one was thrown away, and so continued until the day arrived for which the reckoning had been made." The sticks distributed by Tecumseh fixing the day for the uprising of the Indians from the Lakes to Florida, were painted red and hence the Creeks speak of the

the day they give notice, or six, not counting the day the notice is given.

All persons on the fifth night are ordered to encamp in the vicinity of the *Square*. On the sixth day all the women, dressed in full costumes loaded with ornaments, dance about three hours in the middle of the day. There are men appointed to watch them and if any one leaves the dance without a good excuse, as sickness or other sufficient cause, they are deprived of their ornaments which are confiscated and they don't return. A certain number of the women are appointed to conduct the dance and these are not allowed to eat during the day until after the dance is over and after they have bathed in the branch or creek. These conductors before the dance are covered with what is called medicine, some sacred preparation and this must be washed off before they can eat. The night of the day on which the women dance, the men and women dance together. This is a friendly familiar dance without particular preparation or ceremony.

The day following, that is, the sixth day, is a sacred day and the men fast all day and during the day they take a medicine prepared from an herb that operates like a powerful emetic. On this day, the sixth, the sacred fire is made in a small house within a corner of the square. The persons appointed for the purpose of making the fire remain all the preceding night in the square and at early dawn they commence a process of friction, by rubbing a piece of cane in decayed wood with great velocity until the wood ignites. Sometimes

uprising in which they engaged in 1811 as the "Red Stick War."—McKenney, Thomas L. *Memoirs, Official and Personal* (New York, 1846), vol. i, 164. When the date of such a public engagement had been determined in council, the issuing of the bundles of sticks was spoken of as "giving out the broken days."

it requires many hours for this purpose. The persons appointed for the purpose then prepare, over the new fire, the medicine (emetic) with which the men cleanse themselves; during the day those only who take the medicine and those having duties there by appointment are allowed to enter the Square. On this day, the sixth, the sacred plates and other holy utensils are taken by persons appointed for the purpose from their place of deposit where they have been preserved, unseen by human eyes, for a twelve month, and they thoroughly scour and clean them and about one o'clock they are brought into the square.

These utensils are regarded as presents from the Great Spirit. They are brought into the Square with great state and ceremony. The persons bearing them are preceded by two men provided with cocoanut shells which they rattle all the time, the men singing all the time and they are followed by others with long reeds from the ends of which white feathers stream in the wind. The whole procession dance into the Square and around it four times and then pass outside and dance around another spot four times and then again enter the Square repeating the dance in and out four times. After this the sacred pieces are delivered over to the King, (the Micco) and the next morning, after fasting all day and all night and dancing all night, they dance the War dance. For this dance, there are two men selected called the head warriors. These two come into the Square just before day, with no dress whatever except a piece of stroud and they are painted and covered with ornaments and with a pouch for their pipe and tobacco. There are a portion of women selected to assist the men in singing the war song for the two men to dance after around the square, or ring, in the centre of the Square.

During the time of the dancing, two separate parties are selected and dressed like the two Warriors except that they have shot pouches and rifles; and effigies are prepared and set up outside of the Square to represent enemies surmounted with scalps, generally representing one woman and two men. The warriors approach in the Indian mode of advancing to battle by stealthily crawling behind such objects as best afford screens (during all this time the two warriors are dancing inside of the Square). There are spies out who discover the approach of the two parties who are about to surround the effigies and they go to the corner of the square and give notice to the two warriors that their friends in two parties are about to surround their enemies, the effigies. As soon as this is done a man rushes out with a drum beating it, and at the tap of the drum the head warriors come out of the Square each with an aid and the whole four take up a position resting upon one knee, the Chiefs with the tomahawks and their aids with rifles presented towards the effigies. While in that position they sing a very solemn war song which is answered in a chorus by their friends, the two parties of warriors. During the singing the women who were appointed to sing in the Square pass to a heap of earth previously thrown up for the purpose and are joined by their female friends for the purpose of welcoming their husbands and brothers returning from war. As soon as the women are assembled the head warriors give orders to advance. They take the lead themselves and scalp the effigies and the two parties meet over the effigies as soon as they are scalped and fire their rifles at will accompanied with an uproar of whooping and yelling. They then pass around the hill where the women are, and while the women sing, the men dance and whoop and yell and load and fire their rifles. After dancing around their women for some time the men enter with firing of guns and rejoicing and dance around the Square four times. They then terminate the ceremony for that day by those who have been dancing going to the branch and bathing. After this they return to the Square and break their fast by eating green corn without limit with every other kind of vegetable, pumpkin, watermelons, etc., but no meat nor salt. This occurs about eight or nine o'clock in the morning and the remaining portion of the day is devoted to rest as also the night following, except some may choose to dance for amusement.

It is a rule that if, before the Green Corn dance, any person has ate green corn or even ate food cooked at the fire, where corn has been roasted or otherwise prepared for food he is not allowed to participate in the dance or Busk. All who participate in the ceremony are required to clear away all the fire and ashes from their domestic hearths and take fire from that which has been made at the Square. All who participate in the Busk and take the medicine are obliged for four days to sleep at the Square every night and are not allowed to be with their wives. On the third day of the Busk the men first dance with the plates and then go out with their rifles to kill deer and return early in the afternoon with meat [75] about two o'clock, but they eat no meat this day, but satiate their appetites with Sofkee, etc.

[75] In modern days since game has disappeared this part of their rites is restricted, the Indians going through the pretense of carrying home game killed by them.

The night is passed in dancing and sleeping at pleasure, the women not being present. On the fourth day the meat is prepared with salt and ate for breakfast. After breakfast the women dance in the Square the men merely looking on. Until this day those who have eaten salt are not allowed to touch those who are engaged in the ceremony, who do not, until the fourth day touch salt themselves.

Towards the close of the day the men and women dance what is called the buffalo dance. The men have the stroud on but no other dress except bushes and other means of assimilating their appearance to those of animals, they bend half forward and while dancing imitate the bellowing of buffaloes. The women have terrapin shells tied below their knees, loaded with peas. Small terrapin shells are secured to pieces of leather in rows three or four in a row, with three or four rows and these leathers are tied below the knee. The night of the fourth day the men and women dance together and disperse and go home except certain persons who are appointed for the purpose and who remain at the Square and sleep there for three or four nights. After dancing around the plates on the third day they are disposed of in their appointed place of safety where they remain carefully protected until required the next year.

During the ceremony of the green corn dance the young men frequently engage in a ball play or other amusements and during the whole ceremony everything wears the appearance of rejoicing and gladness and thanksgiving for the blessings of a plentiful promise of the productions of the earth.

Megillis Hadjo, the prophet of the Tuckebatchee town: The people of the town and of the neighboring towns believe that this man has control over the elements and can make the weather to be pleasant or disagreeable, can make it rain or shine. They think he can see into the future and predict events. In cases of sickness he is frequently called upon to divine and to define the cause. Pains in the bowel, he commonly explained by saying there is a mad dog within the patient; in case of stricture in the bladder there is a mad wolf in the patient; costiveness proceeds from two beavers in the bowels of the patient, who have made a dam in him; if pains are added, a bear is inside fighting with the beaver. His cures are all external applications; he makes a decoction from roots and sings over it half an hour or more with a reed in his hand through which he blows into the mixture at the end of every song four times raising bubbles, and then applies the medicine. In the summer of 1840 there was a great drought in the country threatening the destruction of the crops and the old man was called upon to make it rain. After performing his ceremony for a time he published that he was about to be so successful that the country might be flooded, and he thought it best to desist which he did do. Last winter was very cold and the old man was requested to moderate the weather; the present winter is remarkably mild and the old man explains it by saying that he blew off the cold of last winter so far that it has not come back.

The custom of firing four guns, one at each corner of a grave, has for its object to send the spirit of the deceased off. This custom is still prevalent.

At a burial everything of the nature of personal property is buried with the body of the deceased; formerly horses were killed and buried, a dog and the like. The clothing is still buried with the dead. The dead have no shoes or moccasins on when buried, but are buried in stockings or barefooted. Their friends don't wish to hear them walking about. The face of the dead is painted red and black, ear bobs are put on, etc., and their friends frequently throw tokens in the grave. The dead are buried with a handkerchief in each hand. If a man dies from drunkenness, a bottle of whiskey is buried with him, as they say that, dying from liquor, he will want a dram when he awakes in the other world.

The friends of the dead, men and women, meet for four successive mornings after the burial and cry. When a chief dies his friends take the black drink (vomit) eight successive mornings and live on gruel, or white sofkee [76] made without salt. All those who are engaged in the burial of a dead body are obliged to wash their hands in the same bucket of water before they can touch anything. They think that to touch a child or anything a child eats from before purification, the child will be always sickly. It is a common belief that the relations of the dead only must bury the dead; that if any other person, not a relative touches a dead body it is believed that person will be the next to die. In consequence of this when sickness prevailed to a great extent and great numbers died in 1837 and 1838, there were many that died and were not buried, but their bones yet whiten upon the surface of the ground in various parts of the nation.

The Indians believe in witches and wizards and that they can take the form of owls and can fly about at night and at day return home in the form of women and

---

[76] Sofki, Sofkey. A thin sour corn gruel, prepared by the Creek and other Indians formerly of the Gulf region, from corn, water and lye. The Cherokee know it as konahena.

men; that they can take the heart and the spirit out of living men and cause their death; that they can cripple people by shooting through a reed or out of their mouth a rag or blood into the legs of people. Formerly the Indians have knocked old women regarded as witches on the head and threw them in the water, but now there is a law against it; but even last year an old woman was killed for a witch just over the Creek (near the Main Canadian).

There are clans among the Creeks named wind, bear, potato, tiger, aligator, owl, beaver, eagle or bird and a great many others. These are blood connections and custom forbids intermarriage in the same clan. The men marry and bring their wives into the clan, the women marry and go out of the clan, but the man may go to the clan into which he marries. This is a Creek custom. (The Cherokees and Choctaws have both abolished this custom.)

There are people who affect to think they can make it rain and they go to a place of shallow water and roll and wallow in the muddy water every morning for four mornings in succession. They have a pot of medicine in one hand and a buffalo tail in the other, shaking the tail and singing all the time for an hour or more; during these days these people take black drink every morning.[77]

---

[77] For extended accounts of these interesting rites and customs, see Bureau of American Ethnology, 42d Annual Report, *Social Organization and Social Usages of the Indians of the Creek Confederacy*, by John R. Swanton; *ibid.*, *Religious Beliefs and Medical Practices of the Creek Indians* by John R. Swanton; Schoolcraft, Henry R. *Information respecting the Indian Tribes of the United States* (Philadelphia, 1855), part v, 251, ff.; *Handbook of American Indians*, vol. ii, 608.

Chapter IX

A Creek Husband of Five Sisters – Complaint of Creeks – Bitterness toward the Whites – Mode of Frauds on the Indians – Bee Trees and Wax Candles – Early Creek Laws – Departs from the Creeks – A Primitive Home – Edwards's Settlement – Camp Holmes – Jesse Chisholm – An Indian Ball Play.

Second February at Alexander's. Last night there was a heavy rain with lightning and thunder, and this morning dense clouds are floating above and around me, very black in the horizon. A creek that I forded yesterday is said to be rising rapidly and threatens to be swimming. There is a Mr. Taylor about a mile hence married to a half-breed & keeping a small store. He is from New York and was a cadet at West Point some 7 or 8 years ago and was at the Academy, I understand, two years. Mr. Hill brought him to this country as a clerk and he has married in the nation to the great distress of his father, Mr. Hill tells me, who has written letters to Mr. Hill about him.

We passed a family yesterday which Mr. Alexander told me was very large – the man having married five sisters. The sisters were an orphan family which fell under the care of the man and he married the sisters as they grew up; he married the two last but a short time ago. We stopped at the house; one of the wives came in, a good looking matronly woman. I saw a fine looking little boy at the door with a bow and arrow in his hand and called to the little fellow. The wife called him

forward and patting him on the head (it was clean) I
asked if it was her son; "My sister's" said she, her eyes
brightening however, with as much indication of pride
as if the boy was her own.

Ten A.M. Enehemathla, Okfuskee Town, a chief, says
through Mr. Islands, that his people never received
sufficient provision from the contractors; that towards
the close of the year one of the agents came to him and
said "you have now raised corn and have enough to
live upon, you had better sell your claim for rations."
There was three months rations due, he states and that
he and his people received one dollar and a half each
in money for their claim. Only one dollar and a half
for three months rations! 3 x 30 – 90 rations – 90 x 12½
cents = $11.25! So the Contractors put into their own
pockets $9.75 for each!!!

Alexander's; third February. Yesterday I took sundry statements in writing from Indians, and in the
evening wrote out rather a minute account of the Busk
or Green Corn Dance from the account of Alexander
under the correction of David Barnet the best interpreter in the nation (unless Ben. Marshall is better). Mrs.
Alexander was also present and occasionally made cor-
rections and additions. The Busk is the grand Indian
festival of thanksgiving & rejoicing for the bounties of
Providence. From the commencement of the councilings
and preparations to the end of the ceremony there
is nearly a month, but the actual ceremonies require but
four days, the first is a fast, the second they feast on the
vegetable productions of the earth, the third is a hunt
& the fourth is a feast with meats & salt, etc. I have
written the particulars in another note book, in which
I have also written of other customs, etc.

Third February. Yargee, son of the head warrior of

the Florida warriors showed me a copy of a letter from General Jesup to his father of the 7th of September 1839 promising to take measures to secure "pensions" to the "wives and children" of the "warriors, who have been killed or have died in the Service." [78]

Fourth February. Phil. Greirson a half-breed (Wm. Greirson his uncle interpreter) says he was sick in 1836 when the emigration commenced of his party. That being unable to travel he was left behind with his family of 9 persons and afterwards emigrated himself all the way, selling his last horse to pay his expenses and has never been paid anything; that Dr. Williams mustered his party for emigration. He appealed to Captain Stevenson and proved his case by chiefs, but got no satisfaction. Mato O Hadjo says (Wm. Greirson interpreter) that there were about 50 in his company entitled to rations in 1837; that they received rations while they were well and able to go for them to the depot; but he got sick and after four months had passed he received no more rations. Ar ti ercha Matha la, states there were 50 persons in his company entitled to rations; that in August 1837 the contractors turned out one beef, a large one, and told him it was a months ra-

---

[78] The Creeks who served in the war against the Seminole; Congress afterward provided land bounties for their heirs. Yargee was a son of Big Warrior, the chief of the Upper Creek Towns in Alabama, who headed resistance to the surrender of their lands in 1825 and who died in January or February of that year. One of Yargee's wives was Milla (or Millie McQueen); she was a niece of General Alexander McGillivray the remarkable half-breed Creek who held commissions from the United States, Spain, and France; who was said by Roosevelt to have been "the most gifted man who was ever born on the soil of Alabama" and in the *Miscellanies of Georgia* said to have been "by all odds the foremost man of Indian blood and raising that Anglo-America has ever seen (Chronicles of Oklahoma, vol. vii, 106, *Alexander McGillivray, Emperor of the Creeks,* by Carolyn T. Foreman). Milla's daughter, Muskogee Yargee, on May 7, 1864, was married to Joshua Ross, and lived for many years in Muskogee, Oklahoma.

tions for his camps; and they gave him four bushels of corn for the same camps and for the same time. That after that for three months he got nothing. He had moved upon the Canadian after a promise by the contractor that he should have his rations there; then they broke their word for three months & then he got full rations.

Fourth February. Yesterday I took down five sheets in writing of talk from Opothleyaholo principally, with a few words from Jim Boy.[79] About a dozen have signed the paper approving the talk. There were some forty-odd Indians in and about the room nearly all dressed in Indian costumes; I mean with but very few indications of a disposition to wear clothing from white ingenuity. They conducted themselves with perfect propriety. David Barnet interpreted and he is a very good interpreter. The Chief would express a sentence, Barnet would interpret and then I wrote, but I was obliged to wait for an entire interpretation and then take the sense and put into English. I put each sentence into a paragraph by itself, a sentence sometimes being nearly half a page or perhaps more than half a page. Some of these people as I am informed and believe, will not wear a white man's dress, such is their bitterness of feeling on account of the wrongs inflicted upon them. Most of those I saw yesterday had on a turban, a shirt of calico bound with a bead belt, buck-skin leggings and moccasins; then some had on overcoats, but the most had a blanket over them. They were not painted; the Creeks are dispensing with that old custom except on special occasions.

Evening. Well, Mr. Yargee, the happy husband of

---

79 Jim Boy or Tustennuggee Emarthla, was a celebrated chief of the Creek tribe. On the outbreak of the Seminole War in 1836 Jim Boy headed

five wives has invited me to dine with him tomorrow four miles off but he is pressing a claim for some $5,000 against the Government. How did this full blooded Indian learn to be civil in this particular way, under such circumstances? One would think he had received his education in New York, yet his negro Tom, his interpreter, says he never went to Washington with any of the Creek delegations. I wonder if one or all of his *houries* will be at table and which will be Mrs. Yargee par excellence.

Fourth February. Evening. Modes of fraud upon Indians in the Old Nation, told by Alexander, memoranda: General Is son – Opothleyaholo's son, Robert I. Ware (used Op's son) and again, false bills of sale for negroes – procured bond for sale of land from the owner of the negroes to protect them, all got up for the occasion. White men pretended to have bought the land for the purpose of protecting the Indians, deceiving them through bribed interpreters and then holding the land. Indians were bribed to personate each other and sell what did not belong to them and the real owner was ejected upon these fraudulent proceedings.

These are some of the "difficulties" alluded to by Opothleyaholo as a cause inducing the Indians to agree to emigrate. In 1834 it appears (Mr. Alexander assures me) Opothleyaholo went to Texas to endeavor to purchase a place for his people in a mild climate,[80] but he could not succeed and returned.

Main Canadian, Alexanders, 5th February. Some one told me the other day that the Shawnees and Tuckebatche Creeks were originally one people, that the

seven hundred Creek warriors who enlisted with the United States Army to put down the uprising. The portraits of Opothleyaholo and Jim Boy are included in the McKenney and Hall gallery of Indian paintings.

[80] See Foreman, *op. cit.*, 205; Yoakum, H. *History of Texas*, vol. i, 328.

language of the two are similar. I have tried in vain to trace these tribes but the traditions reach back but a short period and nothing like chronological accuracy appears. I hear of no remarkable epochs even, except one connected with the union of the Tuckebatche and Coweta Creeks,[81] which was effected after the heavenly messengers had presented the former with the sacred brass plates, which must have been some time after the discovery of America or the West Indies in 1492. It is probable that there is not a trace of a tradition going beyond the latter part of the 16th century or perhaps the middle of the 17th, when the English might have made some impression upon the memories of the Creeks.

By the account of the Micco I judge that Col. Hawkins [82] must have seen the plates of brass for he, they say, told them the plates came from a King of England. There are said to be some inscriptions on the plates which may be in English. Mr. Alexander says he has seen the plates but not near enough to see what is inscribed on them, and he thinks the letters must be illegible from the scouring the plates receive preparatory to the celebration of the Busk.

Looking upon these people as knowing nothing of themselves beyond some hundred and fifty years or two hundred at farthest, what a night seems to rest upon

---

[81] These are two of the Muskogee tribes entering into the union that formed the Creek Confederacy, though originally the Tukabahchee were probably not Muskogee (Swanton, John R. *History of the Creek Indians,* Bureau of American Ethnology, Bulletin 73, p. 277).

[82] Benjamin Hawkins was an Indian agent among the Creeks who wrote *A Sketch of the Creek Country in 1798 and 99.* In Adair's time (1759) the plates "consisted of five copper and two brass plates, and were, according to Old Bracket's account, preserved under the 'beloved cabbin in Tuccabatchey Square,' "— Gatschet, Albert S. *A Migration Legend of the Creek Indians* (Philadelphia, 1884), vol. i, 147.

them. Yet this is merely comparative and their traditions are scarcely more contemptible than our own and their confidence of being the original people is about as well sustained as our own. Can any man doubt that if this continent had never had intercourse with Europe, and that some Cherokee Guess had sprung up among the natives, and provided an alphabet for them, etc., that in process of time, their traditions of the heavenly messengers, the brass plates, the origin of corn and potatoes, would have been recorded and handed down with sacred reverence, surviving the plates themselves as much as if they had been of stone?

At Yargee's. Yargee is over at the Square and left word to be sent for if I came and was in a hurry. I say, no I am in no hurry. Yargee has been sent for to council. I see wax candles are used in the Nation. Bee trees are common, honey plenty, and with the wax they make candles. Yargee (or Yarga) says he has relatives in Alabama who wish to come here, but an uncle of his wife's will not let them come, keeping them and a number of negroes; also keeps them to keep (excuse) the negroes. Don't know how many negroes. Yarga's wife Milla, says the relations are her own brothers (two) and sisters (three), two of the sisters have children, and thinks their husbands *dead*. Yarga shows me a letter of May 9th, 1841 signed Wm. H. Durant, telling him the people are well except that "Sophe" lost one of her children "last summer"; though well it seems they "Ain't" very well satisfied and wish to come to this country. The letter is addressed to Milla Yarga to the care of Dr. McDaniel, but there is no place of date in the letter. "Milla," Yarga's eldest wife, can't name the place, but Yarga says near Tuskene, near Pole Cat Springs in Alabama. Negro Tom has come in and in-

terprets and now it appears that one of Yarga's wives
is behind. He thinks the President, if he knew about it
might send them out here under the charge of a conductor; that otherwise Durant will not let them come.

Tom (Yargee) wants a school for his children.
Wishes he had a grist mill. Thinks the wheel-wright
employed by the Government don't "do well"–"seems
like his work don't stand," timber not seasoned; three
miles off.

Sixth February. After dinner with Yarga, not one
of his wives being at table; Opothleyaholo came in.
Yarga had sent for him. I have made notes of what followed in another book. I came back yesterday to Alexanders and soon after reaching here, a negress belonging to Opothleyaholo's wife came (five miles) with the
compliments of her mistress desiring me to buy some
bead moccasins of which she sent some eight or ten
pairs, the work of her own hands. I bought one pair at
seven dollars the negress saying her mistress was disappointed that I had not paid her a visit and sent the
moccasins supposing I might wish to carry back with
me some of the work of the wife of Opothleyaholo. I
think this was the idea, the explanation came through
Alexander for I did not see the woman. Today the
negress has come again with the commencement of a
bead pouch to show from her mistress who had heard
the woman say that I wanted one, and she sends word
that if the weather will allow, she and her family
(three daughters) will visit me tomorrow.

Alexander's 7th February. Yesterday I made an abstract of the laws written, of the Creeks compiled or
digested I suppose I should say in 1826, before emigration; and an abstract of the digest approved here in
General Council in 1840. The first was prepared in

1826. The first written laws Mr. Alexander thinks do not date beyond about 20 years though the year 1817 is entered opposite the law punishing murder. Most of the laws, there are but few altogether, relate to the punishment of the most prominent crimes known as such among all men and the regulation of property rights. They scarcely touch upon the ancient customs and usages of the nation which are for the most part left in full force. Infanticide was formerly not uncommon; it is prohibited by the written laws. An attempt was made in 1840 to abolish a custom giving to the relations of a husband on his death the power of keeping the widow secluded and forbidding her second marriage for a period of four years. They attempted to restrict the period to twelve months, but the people would not listen to it and the Council yielded to the public voice and repealed the law in 1841.

Eleven A.M. *Mrs.*, the widow of John Oponny has sent a bead belt, $10 and two pouches $15 each; but I have politely praised their beauty to the negro woman and declined purchasing either. "I should be proud of them, but it is not convenient to carry them and I must be content with the moccasins as a sample of bead work." Fifteen dollars for a pouch! At this rate an Indian's dress would equal the cost of a Major General's uniform.

At Opothleyaholo's. Caesar, a black man says he was one of General Jesup's interpreters with the Creek Warriors in Florida. When he went to Florida he left $400 in the hands of his wife, living with Billy Walker about Tuskegee; Walker died and he left his property to Ned Hendrick at Montgomery who now has his wife and the $400. Caesar had no opportunity of going for his wife and money on his way to this country. Says he intended the $400 with what he could earn in Florida to buy his wife and that he Hendrick now ask $3,500 for his wife and three children and refuses to pay the $400. Caesar says he sent word to his wife to put the money in the hands of Hendrick and he keeps it.

Caesar says he received $6 and half a beef for his years rations after he came from Florida; received no corn at all, not a grain. Opothleyaholo dilates upon the wrongs inflicted upon his people, baggage thrown out of the wagons and lost – The Florida warriors, few got rations, got a little money; of the main band, rations issued irregularly; when due, not delivered; and when delivered but half issued. Many were left in Alabama, wishes them sent here.

Opothleyaholo says the Cherokee have got sense just like the whites, but the Creeks have no sense and it is best to treat them as we think best. Says the Chickasaws were treated just as the Creeks have been in provisions.

P.M. Returned to Alexander's and in the evening Lydia Carr, the wife of Elijah Carr was waiting for me. She has come from the other side of the North Fork to tell me that she received no provisions except a small issue on her arrival at Fort Gibson and afterwards, when she moved to the North Fork she received one wagon load of *corn in the shuck*. This was for a party of 31, Jackey, wife and eight children, Elijah Carr, wife and three children, her own aunt and four children, an old man and his wife (Davy) and four negroes, in all 31.

She says that "a great many times our people would go after provision and could not get it." "They (the Contractors) didn't get enough for all and we couldn't get any." She says, that those who were first at the depot carried all away, that she had some money and

was obliged to buy provision. She gave at $1.50 a bushel
for corn, but afterwards bought it for $1.00. She says
she suffered a "heap" from sickness the first year, her
brother, his two children, my aunt and all her children
but one. "This man (the man who came with her) lost
four children, one of mine is gone. I just got two."
Twelve deaths from 31!

She tells me of Louvina an old woman and two boys,
nephews, surviving out of six. Two negroes also living,
persons who received no rations at all, according to her
story, and Lydia says the old woman wished to come
here and tell me but had no horse. Lydia says she heard
a great deal of complaint about provisions and says that
the people don't know of my being in the country or I
would hear enough about it. She says a pound of beef
and 3½ pints of corn would have been enough. If
every body had received that, there would have been
no suffering and perhaps but little sickness.

Lydia says she did not start with the "last big drove"
(of Creeks) but overtook the party at Memphis and
arrived at Fort Gibson with Opothleyaholo.

Eighth February A.M. Davy Grason has come in this
morning and tells me a long list of grievances; never
received any provision of any account, got none of no
amount " 't'all," drove a wagon the whole of the way
from the old nation, clear to Fort Gibson and never
received a cent for it. Lost two horses worth a hundred
dollars, made a list of losses in the old Nation and gave
it to the agent when the Indians were sending on their
losses and the agent never has told me what he did with
it and never gave me any satisfaction about it. I have
never received a dollar of the annuity since I came to
the country. Here I asked him the reason and he said he
didn't know, but he has colored blood in him he says,

and some have told him that was the reason, yet Jim Boy a colored mixed is a Chief. Of provision he says, towards the last, "they" gave him six or seven dollars, nothing for his wife. This man lives on the Arkansas. Says he got some beef and a little corn, had to buy corn, got one hog and that was for four months for eight of us in company.

Two P.M. Eighth February. Came to Connor's 15 miles from Alexander's on the road to Little River (Edwards'). Have a negro guide, Hughes; we passed a few miles of as beautiful prairie as I almost ever saw, not excepting that which so fascinated me a few miles south of the Grand Saline on Grand River. We came upon its beauty suddenly by ascending a hill of easy acclivity, from the summit of which I looked off to the right and had every possible variety in view – hills with and without timber valleys, with and without timber, and plains the same. Several of the hills seemed broken off from their connection with a range and presented isolated objects of beauty. There is scarcely anything in nature that gives me so fine a feeling as riding in a lone country, through such a scene.

Connor lives quite alone, his family I mean. I see some eight or ten people about. He has two log houses about ten by twelve feet and ten feet apart with a common roof over the houses and space between. I can place my hand on the roof. There is no window in either house, the door in each opens into the space. The door-way I should say, for there is no door. A fire place in each house is opposite the door way, no piaza; some twenty feet distant there is a single house, I think just ten feet square, higher than the other two, and the roof projects on one side about five feet. This house has a door-way, no door, and a fire place in the side adjacent

instead of opposite. There are one or two small out-
houses, corn cribs perhaps, and store houses. There is a
shed near with a *horse* for a horse and drawing knife
under it. In the space between the two houses is a great
variety of things, some saddles, bridles and lariats
hanging up, and some small articles secured under the
roof upon the rafters. The houses are chinked and
mudded so as to be perfectly impervious even to air.
They are mudded inside and out. A rail fence encloses
the buildings, just outside of which is a small rail fence
pen for horses with a trough in the centre.

A south wind is blowing with great violence, but the
sun shines and it is not very cold. The single house
seems allotted to me and my negro guide; there is no
bed in it and *we* I suppose shall sleep on the "punch-
eon" floor; a froe – two drawing knives – curry-comb,
saw, chissel, two augars, something like an adze, a
gourd are among the articles above referred to.

P.M. I and the nigger have taken dinner together. If
Maj. Downing could say "I and the General" then *I
and the nigger* should be euphoneous. We dined in one
of *the* two houses, no floor of puncheons even, but of
mother earth. We had some meat so fried out of countenance that I could not tell what it was for some time;
but at length I spied some bristles of a well known
domestic animal, the pride and wealth of the great City
of Cincinnati, where more hogs are butchered in the
hog-killing season than I dare to say. We had some
native corn bread, ground before my face, by the way;
the steel corn mill is in the space between the two
houses. There were just four fried eggs and I must
commend the delicacy of the nigger who considerately
left his for me and I left one "for manners." Then we
had a cup of very good coffee with sugar, but there is

no milk in this country. There was a pepper box on the table, I suppose with salt in it. There was a bedstead in the room (house) made by boring a couple of augur holes in one of the logs of the building two or three feet from the floor (ground) in which are placed horizontal pieces projecting two or two and one-half feet; the ends are supported by crotched sticks, driven into the ground and these form the framework. I perceive specimens of pottery here. The Indians use clay and make a number of cooking utensils with it. There is before me a kettle, shall I call it, that will hold at least four gallons.

Tenth February, A.M. Arrived at Edwards' on Little River at its entrance into the Canadian (at Fort or Camp Holmes)[83] last evening, forty miles from Connor's. Mr. Watson says he heard Donnelly who is now in Texas, say that he saw McBride receive from the contractors $300 in silver for making one single issue to the Creeks, and Mr. Edwards says he has known him to lay out a quantity of salt, far less than its stated quantity, and say to the Indians, there is your salt, take it or leave it on the ground.

Eleventh February. Edwards says that when Gov. – then Col. Dodge – made a visit to the Comanche and Kioway Indians with Dragoons in 1834 he passed this place over to false Washita and then *West*.[84] After-

---

[83] Camp Holmes also called Fort Mason, was constructed in 1834 under orders of Brig. Gen. Henry Leavenworth, by Lieut. T. H. Holmes for whom it was named. It was located on the east side of the Little River about one and one-half miles above the mouth and about five miles southeast of the present city of Holdenville, Oklahoma. Edward's trading settlement was on the opposite bank of the Little River between it and Canadian River. See Foreman, *op. cit.*, 114, 129.

[84] This reference is to a celebrated expedition of five hundred members of the Dragoon regiment that left Fort Gibson in the summer of 1834 under command of Brig. Gen. Henry Leavenworth and Col. Henry Dodge; their object was to meet the wild Indians of the prairies and induce some of their

wards some Comanches went to Fort Gibson and held a council; that Gov. Stokes,[85] the Cherokee Agent some eighty years old, was present and wore spectacles; not long after the council three or four of the Indians died and one of the Chiefs said he *saw* the *poison* proceeding from the eyes through the glasses of the governor which killed his people.

Edwards says there are a plenty of buffalo seventy-five miles west of this. They were formerly here and east of this place. I saw the skeleton head of a buffalo twenty miles east, thinking it that of a large ox, until my guide told me it was a buffalo. It was large and its short horns were in the plane of the forehead instead of projecting forward as those of our common cattle do.

Camp Holmes (Little River) Creek Nation, February 12, 1842. Echo Hadjo and others, Creek Chiefs and Head men, present. Mr. Daniel G. Watson explaining. Echo, a chief, says over fifty came up here, soon after arriving in the country. Says he came to this country from Florida, was one of the Florida warriors and that it was about *this season of the year*. Says they have good land, have fields open and raise a plenty of corn; have hogs, horses, and cattle and live very comfortably.

Echo says there is a town of Creeks more than fifty miles farther up the Canadian, and Mr. Watson adds

chiefs to accompany them to Fort Gibson for the purpose of effecting peace with them as a preliminary to the location of the immigrant Indians in the West. On this disastrous expedition many lives including that of General Leavenworth, were lost by fever contracted by the ill-timed exposure of unacclimated men to extraordinary heat and unwholesome water. For an account of this expedition see Foreman, *op. cit.*, 122 ff.

[85] Montford Stokes, a veteran of the Revolutionary War, had served as senator from North Carolina; he was governor of that state when in 1832 he resigned to accept the appointment as member of a commission sent to

that they went down and received their annuity for this year and bought goods with it; and then bought goods on a credit giving an order upon their annuity for next year, so as not to be obliged to go down next year.

P.M. crossed over Little river (Cha na hatcha) this afternoon and saw Mr. Warren's store. Warren trades mostly with Indian hunters of various tribes including Comanches; receives peltries and furs. Saw a considerable quantity of skins. Saw some Seminole women from Black Dirt's town and sent word twelve or fifteen miles that I would be here at Edwards' tomorrow if he wished to say anything to an officer going to Washington.

Fourteenth February. Mr. Edwards says that Jesse Chisholm [86] who trades among the Comanches and has great influence among them can induce them to send a delegation to Washington if the Government wishes; query – cannot this become a means of making peace between the Texans and Comanches?

Edwards denounces the contractors in the severest language. Saw some salt delivered several bushels short, measured it himself at the request of the Indians – heard McBride a bribed agent of the government tell the Indians to take it or go without salt – saw some corn in the shuck issued at two bushels to the barrel when in no possible way would it shell a bushel.

Fort Gibson to adjust differences among the emigrating Indians and aid in their location in the West. He afterward served as agent to the Cherokee, and died at Fort Gibson November 4, 1842, at the age of eighty-two. See Foreman, *op. cit.*, 86, *passim*.

[86] Jesse Chisholm was a celebrated guide, scout, plainsman, hunter, and trader. He was married to Lucinda the half-breed Creek daughter of Edwards the trader at the mouth of Little River near where he resided. Chisholm was often employed on government expeditions as a guide and acted as interpreter in delicate negotiations with the wild Indians many of whose tongues he spoke fluently. His name is often seen in old official letters and reports in connection with these Indians.

Says the chiefs and half breeds were provided for to prevent their making a disturbance, but the ignorant common Indian and the women – widows, ignorant, helpless, and dependent, were left to starve or beg their way as they could, to dig for roots &c. That for eighteen months or two years scarce any children were seen in the nation, i.e. infants; that the suffering and broken health of the women reduced the women past conception.

Twelve M. At the ball-play ground; the Indians preparing the ground by cutting and grubbing over the space. Sun shining, remarkably still and clear, a glorious spring day, not like the middle of February. In the woods, Indian's huts seen in various directions, cocks crowing, a hen cackling. The Creek women pass all their hair back from the forehead and either braid it or secure it with a comb. Some Seminole women are here. Their hair is parted from ear to ear over the head, the line passing about two inches from the brow. All the hair back of the line is bunched behind, but that in front is combed forward and cut a little above the eye brows so as to cover the principal part of the forehead. Indian women are fond of greasing their hair and traders find considerable demand they tell me for pomatum scented. Some of the Indians, I see, are appearing ornamented or decorated with feathers in their turbans and in the belt which secures their frock. A more lovely day cannot be conceived, except that there is no appearance of vegetation. The trees are perfectly leafless and there is not an evergreen in sight. The mistletoe is very common in this country upon trees in damp places and along the margin of streams. The leaf is a little larger than a shilling and feels like velvet. They are placing the pole in the ground, say 25 feet high over which the ball is to be thrown; the party which throws it over the sixteenth time is victor. No, they must hit the pole above a mark some eight feet from the top as I am just told and the game is sometimes twenty.

The players mingle or scatter about as they please. The men on one side of the game and the women on the other aided by a few men. The men use sticks, the women their hands. The Chief throws the ball up nearly vertical, standing near the pole. The game has commenced, all rush to seize the ball, men and women pell mell together. One gets it, his party tries to give him an opportunity of throwing it. The opposite party to embarrass him, rush on him, catch his arm, in the whirl he loses the ball and another rush, a woman gets it. She holds it firmly in one hand and walks towards the pole followed and surrounded by men and women. She is about to throw it, a ball stick is interposed over her, she sees one of her own side a little way off alone and tosses the ball to her. She catches it and instantly throwing it hits the pole, a general scream and one is marked to the women's side. The ball is again taken and thrown up as before and again the play is all life; a man is chased with the ball, he rushes with it in his sticks, arms extended upwards, strikes his foot against an obstacle and stumbles headlong, losing the ball; a loud laugh and a rush after the ball, a woman is near it, the ball is rolling on. She leans forward, thinks she can reach it by throwing herself at length on the ground and falling reaches forward to grasp the ball but misses it and it is seized by another and thus the play proceeds.

Chapter X

Shawnee Indians – In Camp on Boggy River – Comanche Customs – A Delaware Suicide – Chickasaw Medicine men – Marriage Customs – Rendering Bear Oil – Comanche Buffalo Hunters – Fort Washita – On Blue River – A Missionary Sermon – Conference with Chickasaw Chiefs – Chickasaw Customs – Repent Union with Choctaw – At Boggy Depot.

McClure's. Chickasaw Nation on Blue River 16th February, 1842. Left Edwards', Little River the 14th, with Sambo for a guide. Crossed the Canadian at Jesse Chisholms, passed up the Canadian four or five miles to some Shawnee settlements; the Shawnees were sent from Texas; shewed me a paper signed by General Rusk and another commander, recommending them to the Choctaws and other Indians as peaceable sober industrious Indians, but that they could not live in Texas owing to difficulties with other Indians. Shewed me also a paper signed by some Arkansas authority in 1824, a certificate of good character. We rode on about Southwest and camped at Boggy River about thirty miles from the Canadian. Water froze in a cup at the head of my pallet, but the stars shown very brilliantly and I was frequently awake admiring their splendour, as the winds made music through the trees.

The prairies and woodland the day through, had appeared particularly beautiful, one scene especially attracted me. I was on a hill say five miles from Boggy as the sun was declining to the West, and overlooked the whole circle of five miles nearly; part prairie with strips of woods and spots of wood and streams marked by timber waving through the country; the sight bounded by hills south of Boggy, partly bare and in part timbered and in the timber there were Indian's fires; the smoke rolling up made me fancy I saw volcanos. Sambo said the Indians at this season set fire to the hills to start up the bear. I supposed the season May, fresh, and not February when everything was dead and burnt. I had provided buffaloes tongue for camp meat and biscuit made by the kindness of Mrs. Edwards, but the buffalo tongue is very rich, almost like butter and eating that at night and morning without having coffee gave me a headache to ride upon yesterday and for ten of the twenty odd miles from Boggy to this place I suffered considerable; for five, I could but just sit on my horse and two or three times thought seriously of stopping in the woods. I made out to reach here, sun an hour high or so, and this morning am quite well and now take to my other note book and put down what Mr. McClure says.

McClures, 17th February. A number of little things more or less interesting are unnoticed from not having an immediate opportunity. I remember Mr. Payne, a Cherokee half-breed, educated at the Dwight Mission, telling me at Mr. John Ross in the presence of several Cherokees who assented to it, that there is no word in the Cherokee language, answering to our English word *ought*, so much used by the moralists and especially by the translators of Kant and Cousin. To express the meaning of this word they are obliged to use words which signify that "for a man to do so or so will be right." This is curious and possibly might be commented on by Cousin himself, could he be aware of it.

Sambo, my guide, told me the other day of the habit of the Comanches of singing the first thing in the morning lying flat on their backs and patting with one hand below their breast. This is the habit of the Osages, as described to me by Dr. Burt and shows the brotherhood of those tribes. They hunt together even now and the Osages will not plant except to a very small extent. Dr. Burt told me the Osages talk of selling their country, what remains of it, to the U. S. and living altogether with the Comanches.

Mr. Hume told me last evening of a case of suicide among the Delawares living in this vicinity. A man had two sons, who grew up together, hunted together and lived altogether in each other's company. The father was a great hunter and always took the sons with him after they grew up. One sickened and died and the other brother grieved for a day or two and then deliberately shot himself having said that he wanted to go and join his brother, that now he was gone, he did not wish to remain here any longer. Mr. Hume says this occurred last year, while he was living here.

McClure says the Medicine men of the Chickasaws, in case of sickness, sing over their medicine and then order the patient to give a dance. A beef is slaughtered or a hog or both at the pleasure of the medicine man and a due proportion of corn is beat up and all boiled together. Everybody is sent for in the neighborhood and they eat and dance all night for the *benefit* of the sick patient.

Sambo told me that the Comanches make a drum by stretching a skin over a large buffalo horn and use it in their dances. That they dance incessantly, men and women together; the men naked (except a piece of strouding) and painted. The women have stroud petticoats secured around the waist and a short jacket loose, covering the bust. Live on meat altogether and eat it nearly raw, sometimes entirely so. Mr. Watson told me he has heard (far-fetched) of some tribes or bands in the great western prairies who live, men and women, in promiscuous intercourse, the children belonging to the women.

It is a Creek rule by the way, that the women hold the children in case of a separation of man and wife. Perhaps I should say they are *obliged* to hold them, the men not caring to have any trouble with children.

Watson and several white men made statements of the unmarried Creek women which I did not wish to credit, that they are quite free to do as they please. The laws are extremely rigid with the married women and men too, cropping them and cutting off their noses in case of infidelity; but no notice is taken of the indiscretions of a young unmarried woman whose license scarcely affects their character at all. It is mentioned as the result of polygamy, each young woman deeming herself a wife for the time being. If both parties have been single, they are considered as married. If the man. is married he but adds another wife to his family exposing her, however, to a law giving the prior wife a right to whip her.

McClure says the Choctaws he thinks, are limited to one wife and have a great number of half-breeds among them, but that the Chickasaws continue their old customs more generally and many of them have several wives. Captain Wolf, one of the principal men has three wives, one of them a Delaware woman. McClure has seen them all sitting together like so many sisters.

The weather for two days has been excessively boisterous and today is turning very cold. McClure is building a new house and has neglected his old one, which is open at all points – bottom, top, sides and chimney truncated.

Yesterday I saw Captain Wolf who has sent for some chiefs to meet me at Mr. Humphreys, five miles down Blue, next Monday, 'tis Friday today. They have had a council a few weeks since and appointed a delegation to go to Washington to see after the annuity and attend to other business. Perhaps my being here will save them the expense and trouble of sending to Washington.

Most people who speak English among the Indians use the word *sure* on all occasions to give verity to any opinion, assertion, threat, etc. "I thought I should have died, sure"; "I told him it was as I said, sure"; "You do dat, says a negro passing by another negro and if you don't die, sure." This puts me in mind of another negro, my guide from Barrnets to Edwards. He was saying that Jim Boy, a principal Chief of the Creeks had lost his wife one of the "virtuousest women in the Nation" and her relatives had given him another wife the "outrageousest woman in the world." He described the last as having been a common slut on the Arkansas. It was Edwards I think who told me that; no, it was the same negro guide Hughes. The Creeks have a rule that after a man or woman has "had the law"– been punished, he or she is perfectly restored to a good standing; that a woman who has been cropped may lead off the very next dance dressed up in all her finery. The Seminoles have just such a rule as I remember I was told by my interpreter Billy at Tampa Bay. When a debt is paid, there is an end of the matter.

McClure says it is common to get fifteen or twenty gallons of oil from a bear – that thirty gallons have been "bagged"; Indians try up the whole of the meat and oil comes from the fat of every part and leaves nothing but crisp. He says there is no lean about a bear except its legs and that the oil is better than lard for any culinary purpose. Indians take skins from young does entire, and "bag" the oil in them; and McClure prefers the meat of the bear to any other meat.

Sambo told me that the trained horses of the Comanches know so well their duty that when they see a buffalo it is almost impossible to hold them. They are like race horses on the course. The Indians ride them without bridles or reins of any sort, and the horses in the chase will run up nearly abreast of the buffalo but will never pass him; and when an arrow is sent into the buffalo the horses shear off of their own accord, as if they knew as well as their rider what was to be done. Mr. Brooks, living with Mr. McClure went to the Depot on Boggy [87] today and returned. Tells me he saw Mr. Shelton, a clerk in the store of Lewis and Saffran and that Shelton shewed him a list of Indians to whom corn is yet due under the Glasgow and Harrison contract.

18th February. Still at McClure's. The threatening winds of the past few days seem to have died away and we have a clear still cold morning. The Indians have no oaths among them.

Mr. Hume says that the commissioners acting upon the Chickasaw "incompetent" fund, who are Chickasaws themselves,[88] have been collected at Guy's [89] at the Depot where Saffran and Lewis have their store, and

[87] When the Chickasaw arrived in the West much of the provisions furnished them by the government were brought to a distributing point or depot on Boggy River, which became known as Boggy Depot.

[88] In the Chickasaw treaty of May 24, 1834 [Kappler, *op. cit.*, 309] it was provided that a commission of Chickasaw Indians should be created to

there treated with every luxury the country affords free of charge, supplied with whiskey, etc.; and thus induced to recommend the payment of that fund to Saffran and Lewis.

P.M. 19th at Mr. Humphrey's three or four miles from McClure's, west of Blue. I have been west and south of this place by the way of McLaughlin's to the site selected by General Taylor for a new post about to be established.[90]

Three-fourths of a mile southwest of this is a prairie and about south seven miles over the prairie is an elevated point of woodland and just beyond it farther south commences the timber along False Waschitta.

The strip of woodland from the point at which the post is to be established, runs nearly north and in it about a mile from the Post I found some men engaged in building "an agency" or some buildings for the Chickasaw agent. Standing on the point and looking south over Waschitta some hills are seen in the distance which may be on Red River possibly in Texas. I could find no one to tell me. Texas is only about a dozen miles from the new Fort to be. North West I looked into what I am told is the Great Prairie running to the Cross Timber some fifty miles. The point selected for the new post is well situated in every respect provided

manage the affairs of the incompetent Indians; the names of the members of this commission are given in note 132.

[89] William R. Guy came west in 1837 with the Chickasaw as commissary and assistant conductor; he later settled in the Chickasaw country and married a member of the tribe.

[90] Colonel Hitchcock has just visited the place selected by Gen. Zachary Taylor for a post, which the General the next May is going to name Fort Washita. This post was ordered for the protection of the Chickasaw Indians against the wild tribes of the prairies, and roving bands of Kickapoo, Delaware and Shawnee, who infested their new country; and also against raiding parties of Texans in quest of marauding Indians.

good water can be had by digging. There is wood in sight along the Waschitta.

I saw all along the Prairie I rode through today and also in the two miles of woods past McLaughlin's, shell limestone. The whole prairie is underlaid by that stone or it looks like a collection of shells held together by – I forget the technical name – of flint silex. Some of the shells look exactly like small oyster shells, others like cockle and from seeing the same stone at the bottom of a creek deep cut, the bed must have great thickness. This is the first clear case of shell stone that I have seen since I commenced this tour. The kind of stone in the Cherokee Nation, especially about Fort Wayne, is on the surface when seen, broken into regular figures with smooth surfaces. In some cases hills washed by rains are left covered by that kind of stone and at a little distance the hills seem covered with snow, the rock being light colored.

Humphreys, 20th February, Sunday A.M. Mr. Humphreys gave me a good bed last night in a room by myself, with clean neat bed clothes, white pillow cases, ruffled, etc., etc. So upon a good supper I should have slept well, if I had not had dreams, but my dreams were pleasant, peaceful, and I waked from time to time and my thoughts were in harmony. In the night, however, Mr. Humphreys himself sleeping in the next room got up and stumbled over a chair which brought forth a severe anathema; and then a cat got into my room and tried to climb up the logs of which the house is built to my provision sack in which I have some buffalo tongue and which I had purposely hung up, etc.

P.M. I have come away from Captain Colberts, leaving Mr. and Mrs. Humphreys to hear the afternoon sermon of the Reverend Mr. (Blank) missionary, his morning discourse having satisfied me, and I did not care about seeing the same people again.

There were about thirty-five persons present of both sexes and all colors, white, red, black and mixed, of all shades and children crying. Women better dressed than the men. All were attentive and the discourse, prayers, etc., were about equal to the fifth, sixth or tenth rate class of country preachers. He, the parson, told us there was nothing mysterious or difficult about Christianity, the truths we were to believe were few and simple. First that no man can go to heaven without being converted by the spirit of God, which he called the Holy Ghost; that every man whose heart was changed was so changed by the Holy Ghost, the Holy Spirit of God, terms he used to explain each other; that when we have the Spirit of God, we are safe and can "stand as it were upon a high ridge of land" and look into two worlds. We can look with the eyes of the mind, not with our "visual sight," up into heaven and see the blessed engaged in the worship of God; and we turn around "a little" (suiting the action to the word) and look down (holding a bible over towards the fire place as if reading over a precipice) into hell and see the Devils and the condemned spirits of men in anguish unutterable. There I think are about all of the simple truths, easy to be believed which constitute Christianity.

Humphreys. 21st February, 1842. Monday, the day appointed for some chiefs to assemble here. It is near 11 A.M. and only two are here. Captain Alberson, and Sloan Love; Captain Wolf is expected momentarily. Mr. Love is the U. S. interpreter, Alberson is the principal chief of the Chickasaw tribe. Love has been talking of sundry matters showing a dissatisfaction with the country set apart for the Chickasaws by the treaty with the Choctaws and suggesting his intention of calling for another boundary line, saying he would carry the question to the "Department" before it should stop, but first he will examine the country along the Canadian. He has complained of the Indian Agent for using the Chickasaw Blacksmiths and hinting at other complaints against the agent.

I saw a camp of Boluxies yesterday, one or two families, in a bottom on Blue. Mr. Humphreys says they are supposed to have originally gone from the Choctaw nation into Texas and in the late difficulties have removed here; that they can understand the Choctaw language, but their own tongue has so much changed that they can hardly be understood by the Choctaws. Thinking of them, I remembered the name of a Bay on the Gulf of Mexico west of Mobile Bay, which possibly was derived from the ancestors of this little fragment of Indians.

I thought of the Natchez tribe, dwindled to 3 or 4 families, now in the Creek Nation. Of the Shawnees, formerly in Georgia, afterwards on the Miami, a powerful nation scattered all over the West; what a place, thinks I, for an antiquary.

Captain Wolf and Captain Colbert [91] have been in and after a few explanatory remarks (and a dinner) the whole are in talk together to determine on what they will say to me. Sloan Love has made a statement

---

[91] Levi Colbert died in 1834 before the Chickasaw removed west. His brother the venerable George Colbert, died in his western home in 1839. Among those who survived the latter was his son Pitman Colbert of whom Colonel Hitchcock is speaking. He was placed in a school in Maryland in 1803; became an educated man and long a prominent and useful member of the Chickasaw Nation. In the early Creek War Pitman headed a company of Chickasaw against the Creeks. He became a successful merchant and died at Doaksville. His wife was the daughter of Capt. William McGillivray

about the provision issues; the others say they were well supplied. I see how it is: the Contractors found it their interest to satisfy the principal chiefs and head men, who could have had buffalo tongues and sausages with hot rolls for breakfast if they had desired it.

Sloan Love thinks the Census of the Chickasaws taken at Pontotoc in 1832 exhibited 5440 and odd souls; was so told by Mr. Wyatt Mitchell, who was a clerk engaged in taking the census. Thinks that about 300 remained East.

Mr. Humphreys mentioned, in the presence of the chiefs that he supposed the expense of the nineteen months rations for the Chickasaws was $250,000. He little knows that the Chickasaw fund has been charged over $700,000 for the provisions turned over to Harrison and Glasgow, besides what was paid in money to Harrison and Glasgow. Captain Alberson states that last summer some Texans came into the Chickasaw country and killed some Boluxy Indians alleging that they were hostile to Texas; that he saw with his own eyes a number of Texas armed men in search of enemies on this side of Red River and he does not think it right.[92]

Captain Alberson speaks of the military post contemplated on Waschitta, that it may afford some protection, but in a few years the Chickasaws will be west of it. They are now crossing the Waschitta and settling beyond it.

(called by Hitchcock, McGillibray), a celebrated Chickasaw chief who served under Washington as captain of a company of militia; he died at Doaksville at the age of about ninety (Draper Manuscript Collection, .vol. 10 U). Sloan Love and Isaac Alberson mentioned by Hitchcock, were also prominent members of the tribe.

[92] See Report of Chickasaw Agent, U. S. Senate. *Documents*, 27th congress, second session, no. 1, p. 340; this raid of armed Texans caused great indignation, protests, and voluminous correspondence.

Che-cus-sa Nah-nub-be has come in to complain that he emigrated in a party conducted by Mr. Crocket, a brother-in-law of Colonel Upshaw, the Chickasaw Agent; and that on the way Mr. Crocket said his public funds were expended and he borrowed $100 from Nah-nub-be and $150 from his brother and, Nah-nub-be believes, other sums from other Indians; that he has applied to the Agent to have the money returned to him but has not been able to recover it; neither he nor his brother has been paid. Nah-nub-be lives on Blue River but is now "improving" near the mouth of Waschitta on Red River. A letter addressed to Sloan Love would reach him.

Nah-nub-be further states that he with some others went to the old nation in the spring of 1840 and when he left the steamboat (don't know the name) on which he descended the Arkansas, the Captain carried off down the Mississippi, three of their horses. Sloan Love says Nah-nub-be is one of the substantial men of the Chickasaw Nation and his word may be relied upon.

Further said (not noted in its proper place) that Mr. Crocket employed his wagon at the time of the emigration and never paid him, and that Mr. Crocket also employed Kin-high-che's wagon and never paid for it. This was at the Post of Arkansas,[93] where a number of Indians left the boat and travelled by land. Crocket promised pay at Little Rock or at all events at Fort Coffee, $4.00 a day, but has never been paid at all. That Mr. Crocket gave him a paper which he gave to Captain Armstrong and took a receipt for it from Captain Armstrong who told him the account would be

---

[93] Arkansas Post, the first white settlement in the lower Mississippi Valley, was located on the Arkansas River about 73 miles southeast of Little Rock.

paid; and Nah-nub-be afterwards gave Captain Armstrong's receipt for the paper to Col. Upshaw for collection, but Col. Upshaw has told him the paper was lost. (It is not clear about the paper, whether it was an account or not.)

After noting the above I rode over (nearly due East) 15 or 18 miles to the upper depot on Boggy in company with the principal Chief of the Chickasaws, Captain Alberson, and Mr. Sloan Love, a "commissioner" for the management of the funds of the nation, and the U. S. Interpreter. We talked all the way. I asked questions about the usages and customs of the Chickasaws and took occasion to give Captain Alberson an outline of the system of faith preached by the missionaries in the country, he saying that he knew nothing about it. I gave him quite a long and full history according to the gospel.

He had told me that formerly the Indians of his tribe punished certain offences by cropping both ears and nose. Now done away with. A murderer was put to death immediately if to be found and they rarely got out of the way; if not to be found a relative was put to death and that often led to other deaths. The custom of killing relatives is out of date.

A man wishing to marry (Mr. Love told me) used to ask the consent of some near relative of the girl, and when obtained he would send a present of clothes to the girl herself. If they were accepted the marriage was complete. The parties could separate if they mutually agreed to do so and either party was then at liberty to marry again. The children, in all cases and under all circumstances belong to the mother. It was through the mother that the blood was traced and not through the father. The King, for they had a King, must be able to trace his origin through the mother.

Love went on to speak of the national fund and told me of his determination to insist that all right to its benefits should be derived through the mother. Thus a Chickasaw marrying a Choctaw woman would retain his own right during life, but his children have no claim. A Choctaw, marrying a Chickasaw woman, the woman would enjoy her right and her children would inherit it, etc. Love says there is to be considerable difficulty about the disposition of the National fund (to be derived from the sale of their old lands).

There was a wooded country for several miles today on Blue and then we rode several miles in a prairie till we came to the woods on Boggy. The land all of the way is rich, but underlaid with coarse sand, as was seen by the banks of small streams we passed. The timber in the bottoms is very good, large and various in kind.

No sugar maple, Love tells me, but walnut, oak, over cup oak, Bois d'Arc, etc. In the upland the timber is small and scattered. Trees grow to the size of a foot or so in diameter and then rot at the heart, and are blown down and burned by the prairie fires.

The Chickasaws, according to Love, do not like the idea of losing their name and becoming merged in the Choctaw Nation.[94] It was not his understanding that

[94] On January 17, 1837, a compact was entered into at Doaksville in the Choctaw Nation between representatives of that tribe and of the Chickasaw, the latter not yet having removed from the East; by this agreement the Choctaw sold to the Chickasaw the western part of their domain and provided that the two tribes should unite under a common government in which the former by reason of their greater number, should have a corresponding larger representation. Four districts were provided for of which the Chickasaw should constitute one and the Choctaw three. The Chickasaw later removed from the East, but the preponderance of the Choctaw in their

it was to be so, when they bought the Chickasaw District from the Choctaws. Love dislikes the shape of their district and truly it is very inconvenient. It is a long narrow strip along the Canadian from a point near the North Fork running west, and the line makes a bend to the south and so on to the South East down Island Bayou to Red River, the country extending west for quantity. Love says too, that the Texas boundary is not fixed and creates alarm.

Captain Alberson said today that the Chickasaws in times past have been at war with the Creeks and also with the Choctaws and Cherokees.

I asked Love about the language and he said there was a considerable difference between the Choctaw and Chickasaw language. I asked if he could explain in what and he said the names of things. I asked if the structure of the language was the same in each and he said, yes. Then I made him name some things having different names in the different languages, and it occurred to me that the things differently named were those only which have been introduced to the knowledge of the tribes, perhaps from the whites, since their separation. I found that the Sun, Moon, man, had the same names respectively, but horse, pistol, etc., different names. It had not occurred to Love, but he admitted it might be so. But he said the Choctaws had different languages (dialects) among themselves, but all understood each other. He told me there were some families of the Natchez tribe among the Chickasaws [95] but they spoke Chickasaw altogether. Marshall, the Creek, told

national councils soon proved distasteful to the Chickasaw who then labored for a dissolution of the union which was not accomplished until the treaty of June 22, 1855 (Kappler, *op. cit.*, 531).

[95] The Natchez formerly lived on the Mississippi River near the present city of Natchez; they were engaged in several wars with the French and

me there were a few families of Natchez among the Creeks. Love says the few Boluxys speak Choctaw, but can hardly be understood.

Captain Alberson alluded to something he had said last evening of some Creeks having separated from the Chickasaws and called them a name something like that of Coosada. There was no other name given me in the Creek country resembling the one mentioned by Captain Alberson.

It appears that fragments of Indian tribes are scattered in every direction all over the West. The Shawnees were once in Georgia and were driven by war to the North where their great chief Tecumseh attempted to unite all the tribes from the Lakes to the Gulf and make a stand against the whites. Defeated, the Shawnees, Delawares, and some half a dozen other tribes broke into numberless fragments and dispersed West and South. There are 1500 Kickapoos high up on the Canadian. Several of these wandering families have recently been driven out of Texas.

Upper Depot on Boggy February 22, 1842. Mr. Love told me yesterday that he remembered the time (he is about 35) when the Chickasaws were almost as wild as the wild Indians west of the Cross Timbers. After a time they became industrious and ingenious in manufacturing a number of articles particularly articles of cotton cloth; but that since they have been in the receipt of monies for the sale of their lands east of

in 1729 they massacred the latter at Fort Rosalie; the French in retaliation with a strong force of Choctaw allies, attacked the Natchez, killed many of them, sold other hundreds into slavery and dissipated the remainder who sought homes with other tribes. Some of their descendants are now incorporated with the Cherokee and Creeks (*Handbook of American Indians*, vol. ii, 36).

the Mississippi, they have almost entirely given up both industry, and art.

This reminded me of Mr. Hume's telling me at Mc-Clure's, that the nation would be better off five years hence if the government would stop all payments to the people. Mr. Fields the Cherokee merchant told me it would be better for the "common" people among the Cherokees to receive no money under the article of the Cherokee treaty providing for a per capita distribution of an anticipated unexpended balance.

Col. Guy says he was a contractor on board the steamboat Fox, one of Captain Buckner's boats, with Chickasaws, and that on arriving at Fort Coffee, the Captain wished him to certify to 125 tons of baggage. Guy refused and the Captain said he must have a certificate for a hundred at all events, but Col. Guy "ignorantly" gave him a certificate for 75 only. Mr. Humphreys told me he did not think there could by possibility have been over twenty tons!!! There were but 260 persons on board the boat and the baggage, by an estimate on pretty good data, was all carried in about 16 wagons.

Mr. Love says that Pitman Colbert made last year, 100 bales of cotton; Captain Alberson made 9 bales this year, both on Red River.

Col. Guy told me that the people in this vicinity were nearly all of them Chickasaws; that many merely sat down here at first because the Depot for issues was established here, and they have remained without having the spirit to go out and look up better situations. That very few cultivate corn enough for their own use and, depending upon payments anticipated from the Government, they have lived upon credit until that has gone, and a number have been obliged to sell their horses and cattle and other property.

All accounts seem to agree that the Chickasaws are perhaps in a worse condition than either of the other emigrant tribes resulting in part from their dependence upon what seemed in fact a more favorable treaty than that made by any other tribe.

Chapter XI

At Doaksville in Choctaw Nation – Officers from Fort
Towson – Outline Report to Washington – Influence of
Whites – Of Wild Tribes – Evil of Choctaw-Chicka-
saw Union – Wealth of Chickasaw – Whiskey Trade
on Red River – Effect of Annuities on Indians – Half-
breeds the True Civilizers – Significance of Indian
Customs – Indian Cruelty Exaggerated – Humbug of
Government Reports.

Doaksville (at Fort Towson) 23rd, February. Arrived from Boggy Depot, Mr. Love in company, 70 or
75 miles. Left Boggy yesterday morning and lodged
last night at Mr. Walls and came through today. We
travelled down the west side of Boggy yesterday nearly
the whole distance in timber, but occasionally seeing
the Prairie to the West and South. Wall lives five miles
from the crossing place on Boggy. This morning we set
off and rode the five miles, forded Boggy and soon
struck into the Prairie between Boggy and Kiametia
and then travelled over twenty miles to the latter, most
of the distance in a Prairie and nearly due east. Yesterday we travelled nearly south, today we saw the timber
on our right hand which lines Red River, almost the
whole distance from Boggy to Kiametia. We forded
the latter stream and passed the bottom; by the way,
the bottom is on the west side, where the water mark,
up since January, Mr. Love said, was some fifteen feet
high on the trees; tall oaks, sycamores and one large
maple, the first I have seen west of this. From Kiametia

it is eight or nine miles here, a small prairie in timber. The land is good on the whole route; indeed, I have seen no poor land of any extent since I left Fort Gibson.

I saw shell limestone on Blue River; and from there all of the distance to this place the same kind of stone is seen wherever the rock under the soil is exposed, in creeks and sometimes where the road has washed. We passed one slightly elevated range of hills yesterday three miles north of Walls. The beautiful scenery I have seen today is beyond my time or power to describe.

I have to note one or two items. I had not time to note before leaving Boggy. Col. Guy told me of the fate (and conduct) of Hughes, who was the commissary at the issue of corn to McClure, attempting to issue by a false measure. Guy said and so has Mr. Love told me the same story. That he harbored two slaves in the swamp near the "corn cribs" below Walls, he and another white man; that they were taken up by the Choctaws and brought to Fort Towson; but the facts, though sufficiently proved afterwards could not be established at that time and they were discharged. They talked loud and threatened the Choctaws, who tied them up and whipped them in the woods. They then approached Walls premises (one of whose sons had been " 'tis said" engaged in the outrage), and firing miscellaneously among some Choctaws at work in a field, killed an innocent man and wounded one more. The survivors pursued instantly and Hughes has never been heard of since. His companion is said to be in Texas.

Colonel Fulsom, a Chickasaw half-breed, my landlord at this said town of Doaksville, has been in to see his guest and hear and tell the news. He tells me that Mr. Adams has presented a memorial praying a separation of the Union. Mr. Johnson said he had made a motion for it. There is a difference, yet what a tremendous outburst of indignation there was some eighteen or twenty years ago when President Cooper in, not of, South Carolina said "it was time to calculate the value of the Union." This was when Congress imposed a tariff not agreeable to the South.

Twenty-fourth February. Mr. Love did not tell me what the above named Johnson was until after we left Walls coming this way, Johnson going the other. It appears he is the man who issued at Fort Coffee [96] and according to the statement of Crocket, he issued beef cattle for 800 or 900 pounds each which would not have weighed 500. He appeared too young a man to have had charge of issues. When I first saw him at Walls I thought him a young lad, possibly a half-breed Choctaw from Johnson's school and he seemed beardless. When he spoke I saw that he was a forward pert flippant conceited young fop, and heartless too; for when Mr. Love spoke of having had a negro boy drowned and expressed a proper feeling on the subject, Johnson closed the subject by saying there is $400 gone. Love told me he was very inquisitive about what he called a *Council on Blue* referring to Captain Alberson's intercourse with me.

P.M. Dined with Major Fauntleroy [97] today and saw Captain B. L. Beall and other officers of the Second Regiment of Dragoons. There are three companies of that regiment now garrisoning Fort Towson, not a Fort

[96] The Chickasaw came up the Arkansas River by boat and disembarked at Fort Coffee; from here they traveled southwest overland and settled among the Choctaw.

[97] Thomas Turner Fauntleroy of Virginia, as major of the Second Dragoons was in command during part of the construction of Fort Washita. With rank of colonel he resigned from the army May 13, 1861, and became a brigadier of Virginia volunteers in the Confererate Army. He died September 12, 1883.

but some buildings in a rectangle, one side devoted to officers quarters.

Captain Beall [98] told me of the death of Colonel Cummings [99] of the Fourth Infantry, that he died in New York sometime in January. His death by due course, must promote Lt. Col. Vose [100] to be the Colonel of the Fourth Infantry and myself to be the Lieut. Colonel of the Third Regiment of Infantry to which Vose belonged. Now, thank God, I am separated from Colonel Worth, I care less about the promotion, than I do for its effect in changing me from the 8th Infantry to the Third.

Worth will never give an immediate subordinate any authority and permit him to move in anything without his especial leave. No officer, near him, is or can be anything but a cypher unless he will quarrel all the time. If I am promoted to the Third Regiment as I suppose I shall be, I shall have the command of the Regiment as the Colonel (Many) [101] is himself at

[98] Benjamin Lloyd Beall of the District of Columbia became captain of the Second Dragoons June 8, 1836, and saw considerable service in Indian Territory, being stationed at Fort Towson and Fort Washita. He was distinguished for gallantry in the Seminole and Mexican wars.

[99] Alexander Cummings, born in Ireland, became major of the Third Infantry April 20, 1819, and on March 11, 1823, was transferred to the Seventh Infantry; he saw service at Fort Smith and Fort Towson and the establishment of the latter post in May, 1824, was effected under his command. He became colonel of the Fourth Infantry December 1, 1839, and died January 31, 1842.

[100] Josiah H. Vose of Massachusetts became lieutenant-colonel of the Third Infantry April 23, 1830, and afterward saw service at Fort Towson. He was made colonel of the Fourth Infantry, January 31, 1842; he died July 15, 1845.

[101] James B. Many of Delaware became lieutenant in the Engineers in 1798. In 1804 he received the Post of Arkansas from the Spanish commander; in 1806 he was engaged in service on the upper Mississippi. As lieutenant-colonel in the Seventh Infantry, he came to Fort Gibson in 1824 and served here for many years; in 1834 he was in command of this post. He died February 28, 1852.

death's door and for more than twenty years has never drawn his sword. I gain one point and that is *rank* over Major Wharton [102] who was transferred to the First Regiment of Dragoons in 1833, when a transfer was refused to me by General Jackson.

Beall told me also the death of Colonel Rector (Wharton) paymaster, U. S. Army, residing near Van Buren and who came nearer making a quarrel with me as I passed Van Buren, than any other man ever did and without the slightest cause for it. He was a little drunk and asked me twice to drink with him which I declined and he chose to consider my refusal as personal. When sobered the next day, he apologised for his conduct but had lost some of his own self-respect, and from the nature of man and *his* nature in particular he has borne about with him an uncomfortable feeling in regard to me ever since.

Evening. Supped with Colonel Upshaw, the Chickasaw Agent. Mrs. Upshaw had some preserves made from the fruit of the Bois d'Arc. I never eat preserves if I can avoid it and did not taste of these. The fruit appears to me like the sycamore ball except very large, being sometimes five or six inches in diameter.

Col. Upshaw said that the Caddos were reduced he thought to about 250; that 167 were in the Choctaw Nation and that the last annuity due them was paid this year and now they are without a country and without an annuity and are living here by sufferance of the Choctaws.

I am often thinking at night of my report to be made

---

102 Clifton Wharton was born in Pennsylvania and entered the army from the District of Columbia. As captain he was transferred to the Dragoons March 4, 1833, and saw many years of service at Fort Gibson and surrounding country. He was commissioned a major July 4, 1836 and lieutenant-colonel June 30, 1846. He died July 13, 1848.

of my duties in this country and frequently think out a
series of matters to be touched upon and also the language I might use seems to occur easily to me. I shall
have two reports to make, one upon the condition of the
Indians and one upon the provision matters.

Of the condition of the Indians I had thought among
other things of introducing some speculations upon the
probable effects of the occupation of Texas by whites,
extending in a few years between Arkansas and Red
Rivers west of the 100th degree of W. Longitude. The
trade through the country, etc., and so show that the
Indians have no security here unless they advance in
civilization and begin to own farms in fee simple with
a right of sale. The white blood will finally possess the
country but in that case, not by violence, etc.

Then I have to report upon the influence or action
of the wild tribes west of the Chickasaws. The trade
carried on with them,[103] the depredations they commit
upon the people of Texas and upon the peaceful emigrant Indians, and must suggest a treaty to be made at
Washington with a delegation under Jesse Chisholm
from several wild tribes. Recommend, perhaps, that
Lieut. Britton be charged with the important service of
conducting the delegation to and from Washington;
Chisholm is a Cherokee half-breed married to a Creek
woman and resides on the Canadian 100 miles west of
Fort Gibson. Then I must report upon the Shawnees,
Delawares, Kickapoos and Piankashaws, state their
numbers , where they came from, where they have been
living, where they now live and how they live and sug-

---

[103] Enterprising members of the Creek, Choctaw and Chickasaw tribes
engaged in trade with the western Indians. An interesting account of other
Indians within and near the Chickasaw country is contained in Hitchcock's
letter of March 20 to the Secretary of War in the appendix.

gest a plan for their living quietly on the borders of the Creeks and Chickasaws.

I have to speak of the Choctaws and Chickasaws, showing the discontent of the latter under the treaty by which they purchased the right of settlement among the Choctaws. They don't like the condition of that treaty; thought they were procuring a country for themselves. Don't like to part with their name. Don't like the boundary of their district at any rate, want wood and water, the line too crooked. Don't like the Choctaw laws and are overruled in Council. Supposed wealth of the Chickasaws exposes their women to marriage with the Choctaws and this the Chickasaw men don't like. No remedy for all clear – but the line of the district might be changed to advantage. Chickasaw's line on upper Boggy and Blue, now within a Choctaw District – the line might be carried east of this and the eastern Chickasaw district on the Canadian might be thrown back into the Choctaw district.

Some Cadoes in the Choctaw country. A word of the Cross Timber; avoid the affectation of science, but allude to the possibility of this feature of the country having a strong geological interest in the great valley between the Apalachian chain and the Rocky Mountains. Minerals are found in the country. Salines in abundance. Salt plains of twenty or thirty miles square common property by treaties with all the emigrant tribes.[104] Face of the country, wood lost in prairies, rolling, rich. No pine or maple, mostly oak, post oak, red oak, Spanish oak, water oak, over-cup in the bottoms.

[104] Within the present Woodward and Woods counties, Oklahoma, there is a great salt plain that was known in the early days as the Grand Saline, which was frequented by Indians of many tribes who secured their supplies of salt there. In the treaty with the Creeks in 1833 [Kappler, *op.cit.*, 285],

Bois D'arc also mostly in the bottoms, hickory, black jack in the up-country with other wood. All streams big and little lined with timber to a greater or less extent and the small creeks adjacent to the larger streams are all marked in the distance by timber presenting one of the most beautiful features of the country; so also low and damp places and around springs are spots of wood adding to the beauty. From a commanding elevation overlooking an extensive prairie, thus interspersed with timber, with hills, no mountains; in the distance, with fires, sending up volumes of smoke in imitation of volcanoes, etc.

Buffalo recently gone from east[105] of the False Waschitta, saw their places for rolling and pawing the earth, and bones.

Osages wish to sell their country and live with the Comanches. The Comanches wish their aid against the Texans. The Osages will not plant and their game is gone. They are of the same general habits.

Whiskey trade evils: a distillery near the mouth of Waschitta in Texas for the purpose of supplying our Indians, will breed difficulty and then the Texans may complain though themselves the cause of the difficulty. So in Arkansas, the whites supply the liquor to the Cherokees against the laws of the latter, which occasions brawls resulting in death; and then the Governor of Arkansas issues a proclamation and calls under arms 500 militia, as Gov. Yell has recently done.

Trade, debt, effects: nothing made for export of any

---

defining their boundaries in the West, it was cautiously provided that if the salt plains should fall within these boundaries, the President would have the power to permit all other friendly Indians to visit them and carry away salt for their subsistence.

[105] After 1830 buffalo were seldom seen in eastern Oklahoma where they were formerly numerous.

importance except by a few Choctaws and Chickasaws on Red River with slave labor. Half-breeds give the character to the country. The Creeks do nothing but drink whiskey, and make corn for subsistence; have hogs and cattle. The peltries sent in by the traders mostly come from either the wild Indians or the Shawnees, etc. Whiskey might be stopped on the Arkansas and Red River by the military; it would give the Indians more trouble in procuring it.

Change of habits, loss of old customs, not savage or sanguinary, simple and in some cases highly interesting; respect the aged and the dead. Certain punishments have been objectionable and continue so among the Creeks; cropping, no jails or penitentiaries one reason. Don't work a loss of character to undergo a punishment, but just the contrary; hence Indians rarely attempt to elude or escape punishment, even extending to loss of life, as no character survives a crime unpunished; but when avenged by the law, the offender is restored and a cropped woman may lead off the next dance and is all right. This is one principle by which women submit to law in India, that if they do not, they are despised and they had better die.

In recommending a treaty with the wild tribes, a flourish about humanity to Texas; powder is sold to those tribes by traders from our side of mixed blood, prisoners bought; allude to the woman told of by McClure; general peace may be effected and the wandering tribes from the Missouri may cultivate, etc.

Approve of the establishment of a military post on or west of the False Waschitta – might be nearer the Cross Timber, which crosses Red River forty miles west of Waschitta.

I must make a special report upon the sale of claims

of "incompetent" Chickasaws and of orphans claims, should be stopped or regulated. The Government assumed guardianship over both and both are at the mercy of speculators and fare worse under Government protection than those deemed competent to manage their own affairs. I attended preaching on Blue the 20th February and made some notes on superstition.

25th February. I find a book at Col. Fulsom's "The Moral Instructor," etc., I see an extract from "Dr. Belknap's address to the inhabitants of New Hampshire at the close of his history of that state." Pope's Essay on Man is included in the "Moral Instructor" and I find a Hobbes principle in these two lines — "Respecting man, whatever wrong we call, may, must be right as relative to all."

Doaksville,[106] Sunday, February 27th, 1842. I am to report the effect of the payment of annuities. Indians have classes as well as white men; some are prudent and turn their annuity to a good account, others are improvident and of these many trade in advance and owe the full amount of the annuity when paid by the Government. Others spend it for whiskey or otherwise lose the benefit of it. Traders have large claims on the Indians and from the nature of the case, provide for bad debts by a large advance upon their goods. There is some good with the evil of this as the Indian has, though at a high rate, derived some benefit from his annuity and those who are improvident in advance would be likely to squander their money, if received in hand, for articles of less use to them than those they

---

106 Doaksville, the earliest town within Indian Territory, grew up near Fort Towson; it was named for Josiah S. Doaks, a trader who accompanied the Choctaw to the West and set up a store here in 1831. The town which has since passed away, was located within the modern Choctaw County, Oklahoma.

purchase on a credit. If the present system be an evil, I know of no effectual remedy but that of giving intelligence to the Indians; an attempt to restrict the trade, would be likely to produce indirectness in it, resulting in heavier charges by the traders to cover the increased chances of bad debts (see my other book).

I must say a good deal about the half-breeds, the true civilizers after all. It is mostly those who are in power and wealth among the Cherokees and also among the Choctaws and Chickasaws. There are not many among the Creeks and the relative condition of the tribe is distinctly marked by that fact. The full-blood Indian rarely works himself and but few of them make their slaves work. A slave among wild Indians is almost as free as his owner, who scarcely exercises the authority of a master, beyond requiring something like a tax paid in corn or other product of labor. Proceding from this condition, more service is required from the slave until among the half-breeds and the whites who have married natives, they become slaves indeed in all manner of work. Some full-blood Indians are impelled by the example of the whites to efforts formerly unknown among them and have better houses, own more stock, and cultivate larger fields than their ancestors, etc.

I intend to say something of the general character of Indians, sustaining the outline given by Irving and by Hoffman and by Snelling; and I will rap most others by saying that if others have given as accurate delineations as those writers, it has not been my good fortune to meet with their works. Some may have purposely veiled the simple truth exhibiting the "shows" of things "to the desires of the mind"; but if these desires have in some instances produced pictures of noble heroism, disinterestedness, deep wisdom, and almost prophetic in-sight and a wild grandeur of character, they have, on the other hand, required pictures darkened with incidents of treachery, cruelty and what is called savage barbarity.

Neither of these as a general description of Indian character are correct pictures, and if instances of either have occurred they have been exceedingly rare, but the truth inclines much more to the favorable picture than to the reverse. The latter picture is only true in case of war and there are some reasons for it, without supposing a nature more specifically adapted to it than our own.

The want of established government and laws extending over large communities was the true origin of the Indian custom of taking life for life, without being very particular in taking the life of the murderer himself. The surviving friends of a murdered man would take the life of the murderer if convenient, if not, they would sacrifice some near relation. This is only practicing on a contracted scale, the usage of more civilized nations wanting a common law, that of going to war against a people when the individuals of that people, in case of aggression have been beyond reach. The effect of the custom among Indians is to make all who are related, answerable for the conduct of each individual; and there has been the more reason for this in former times from the nature of Indian customs in regard to clans, securing distinctness to the blood of each clan or name, a custom still in force among the Creeks though dispensed with among the Cherokees and abrogated by express law among the Choctaws.

In war the cruelty of Indians has been much exaggerated and admits also of much extenuation. A war with Indians is not a war by two governments according to modern theory but a war of one entire tribe or people against another entire tribe or people, and it is the business of each party to do to the opposite party the greatest possible injury. It must be considered, too, that Indians have no jails or places of confinement for the security of prisoners; and it is contended by many among civilized nations that prisoners may rightfully be put to death, when to secure them dangerously weakens the party into whose power they have fallen. Indians may always be said to be in that condition during war. But they sometimes torture their prisoners! This is not denied and is by no means to be excused and much less sanctioned; but great commanders among nations calling themselves civilized have done the same thing. The celebrated La Pucelle was burned alive by the Duke of Bedford and history furnishes sufficient evidence throughout numberless pages, that this trait is not peculiar to Indian character.

The facts are not always truly stated in regard to Indians. The history of a case in the Seminole War is to the point. The prisoner whom Milly Francis saved, according to the published history was about to be burned alive, but I have the story from Milly herself whom I saw in the Creek Nation. I had the whole story from her own lips and she says those who had taken the prisoner were preparing to *shoot him*, according to custom, one of them having lost some relations in the War.

I am to speak of the tenacity with which Indians hold to promises; their limited range of ideas makes their memory of what they do, hear, see and know very exact and astonishingly retentive. They are said never to forget a benefit or an injury; the truth is they rarely forget anything and a promise from a white man especially a government agent, they never forget.

Evening. Attended the preaching of the Rev. Mr. Kingsbury,[107] morning in Doaksville and afternoon in the Garrison of Fort Towson. Sought an introduction to him at the Garrison and accompanied him home on horseback a mile from Doaksville, 2 from the garrison. I wished to question him about Missionaries, etc., in the Choctaw Nation. I remained to tea and have a lot of Choctaw books and Mr. Kingsbury is to reduce to notes for me his information on points I suggested.

I found a Miss Arme at Mr. Kingsbury's – a fine looking young lady who left Massachusetts last December and has just arrived here to be a teacher, a missionary teacher. I was surprised to hear her enquire for Miss Avery whom I saw at Mr. Worcester's in the Cherokee Nation and that the two young ladies are cousins. They are both young and fine looking women. Miss Arme the best looking of the two.

I saw Major Colbert today, who is said to have made a hundred bales of cotton last year. I find that he employes an overseer a white man, at a salary of $1200 a year and does nothing himself at all.

So, every step of inquiry leads me farther and farther from a very high estimate of Choctaw talent or industry. There is a great deal of humbug in the reports of the government agents about their "astonishing progress," although 'tis certain that they are very far removed from primitive life.

---

[107] Reverend Cyrus Kingsbury was sent by the Presbyterian Missionary Board of Foreign Missions of Boston to the Cherokee Nation in 1816; two years later he went to the Choctaw Nation and remained until the Indians removed to the West, where he joined them in 1836. He died June 27, 1871.

At Doaksville still; 28th February. I told Mr. Kingsbury yesterday that I would wait for his memoranda
upon the Choctaws. He expressed the same opinion
about the effect of the annuity that Col. Fulsom did. It
produces idleness on the whole, though a few intelligent individuals turn it to a good account. Is it not
the same, all the world over? Where the bounties of
nature have relieved a population from the necessity of
labor have they not lived for ages in sloth, with all its
evils, and is not the reliance upon annuities calculated
to produce the same effect? Is not wealth a dangerous
inheritance among ourselves and infinitely less valuable
than habits of industry?

A stranger at table yesterday just from Texas, told
us of a recent murder by Indians on the South bank of
Red River near the mouth of False Waschitta.

I may say something more of the alleged barbarity
of the customs of the Indians. In their peaceful life,
they have put persons to death for the crime, fancied,
of witchcraft. So have our ancestors down to a very
recent date, and they have had the crime of infanticide
among them to a very limited extent. We have a name
for the crime also which would hardly be the case if
we had not the crime itself. But I can deny that human
victims, as a general practice, have been immolated at
the shrine of superstition, as they have been at one
period or another in a great many nations. Both Greeks
and Romans have that crime to answer for and Car-
thage, on a single occasion, when the city was threatened
with destruction in war, devoted to the flames 200
children of noble birth, at one time.

I do not hesitate, therefore, in giving the opinion that
for simplicity and innocence of manners and customs
the wild people of America may challenge comparison

with any other people upon the globe. It must be remembered that they have had no schools, books or teachers of what we proudly call civilization; they have had no artificial means of transmitting the experience and wisdom of one generation to another and yet by some strange influence they have been protected, as I maintain, against the cruelties imposed upon other nations by superstition and have preserved on the whole a wonderful simplicity of faith and manners. Under the general name of heathens, they have commanded a vast deal of sympathy on the supposition that they were very miserable here and devoted to eternal destruction hereafter; and immense efforts have been made to root out their beautiful illusion by which they expect, as the reward of a good life, that their spirits will enjoy unbounded felicity in the land of their forefathers where all the good will be blessed together and to subsitute what? – rather a vile and contemptible fear of hell instead of a hope of heaven.

By the way, I must not forget what Mr. Kingsbury told me yesterday of the law passed in a Cherokee council about the killing of witches. To put a stop to it a grave council took the subject of witches into serious consideration; received testimony which went to prove that the spirits of witches had the power to pass into the bodies of owls and other animals and travel a long distance and do the mischief they have in hand and then return to the human body; and it was therefore solemnly decreed that it should be lawful to put to death the animal in which the spirit of a witch subsisted; but it was forbidden to put a human being to death to kill the spirit of the witch.

This is worth notice as an exceedingly ingenious disposition of the subject. The council did not deny the common faith in witches but rendered it perfectly innocent or innocuous.

Another conversation with and more papers from Colonel Upshaw. His appointment as emigrating agent is dated 9th March 1837 and signed by B. F. Butler, Secretary of War "ad interim." Shows me a petition of the Chickasaw chiefs to the president dated Pontotoc, February 17th, 1837, announcing that a considerable number of Chickasaws will be ready to remove the then approaching Spring, asks the appointment of emigrating agents and the purchase of provisions *by them* for "the number of people now ready to remove," etc.

A letter from the Commissioner of Indian Affairs April 15, 1837, to "Major A. M. M. Upshaw. Superintendent Chickasaw removal," refers to the appointment of the Chiefs, approves of their wishes and says that their plan, "in its general features had been anticipated by the Department" and informs Major Upshaw that "Lieut. Seabright has been dispatched to Cincinnati to contract for the delivery of 1,300,000 Indian rations and it is expected that he will succeed therein." If he succeeds, 200,000 will be delivered at Memphis, Tenn., by the 10th; 100,000 at Little Rock, Ark., by the 20th; and 1,000,000 at Ft. Coffee on the Arkansas River on the 30th of May next," and it is supposed that this will suffice for "the whole tribe on the route and for four months after their arrival west." [108]

---

[108] To provide for the Creek and Chickasaw immigrants in 1837, great quantities of provisions were ordered from New Orleans and other points to be carried up the Arkansas River by steamboat. A scandal developed from the fact that the authorities at Washington took no notice of the corn and hogs being produced by the Creeks already in the West, and supplies were sent much in excess of the requirements of the situation, entailing a loss of a large amount of money. Thousands of barrels and hogsheads of pork, bacon, and flour were carried by a number of boats and unloaded on the river banks at Fort Coffee and Fort Gibson, to stand in the hot sun, the

The commissioner states that as all the expenses are to be paid from the Chickasaw fund, the Chickasaw are to be gratified in their reasonable wishes, and as to baggage they are not to be limited to the quantity allowed by regulations, strictly, but that the Government will not be responsible for more than 2,000 pounds to each 50 persons.

These are important papers. Instead of charging the Chickasaws with 1,300,000 rations costing possibly 130,000 dollars, they have been charged with some 740,000 in rations, besides what has been paid in money to the contractors Harrison and Glasgow. And so far from the plan being adopted at the earnest request of the Chickasaws, it was devised in anticipation of the request and the purchase made for the whole tribe instead of being limited to the number to emigrate as the chiefs requested. And the purchase was moreover not made by the Superintendent as they had also requested, the only person who could have known how much provision was needed; but was made by an individual no ways in communication with the Chickasaws or their Superintendent but who purchased rations for the whole tribe. Again, if 1,300,000 rations would serve for the march for four months; why send some 7 or 8 times that quantity for a year!

hoops to fall off and the brine run out until the meat spoiled; desperate efforts to re-ship them were futile as the water in the river fell so as to stop navigation.

Chapter XII

Progress of Choctaw Students – Departure for Fort Smith – Guest of Greenwood – Description of Indian Home – Chickasaw Dress – Chickasaw against Choctaw – Arrive at McKinney's – Seminole and Creek Union – Chickasaw Overruled.

Doaksville Choctaw Nation, February 28, 1842. Mr. Kingsbury has given me strictly a professional paper, naming the missionary stations in the Choctaw Nation established by the American Board of Foreign Missions with the number of pupils, etc. I wanted him to go more into details about the propects of civilization; grounds of hope or of apprehension, sources of advancement or hindrance. We had some conversation about the probable destiny of the Red race. I had seen on his table a number of the Missionary Herald in which I found some remarks upon the subject. I questioned him closely and could see that he is not sanguine that the race will be preserved, but he added that there will be *a people* in this country needing education and the gospel.

I must remember that yesterday Mr. Kingsbury brought forward a fat chubby Choctaw girl about eleven years of age, a full blood, whom he said he commenced teaching last November at which time she did not know a word of English. The testament was open and she was told to read "anywhere"–"there" said Mrs. Kingsbury pointing to the first chapter of John. The little girl began and read very cleary, that, in the beginning was the word and the word was with God and the word was good, etc. She did not miss a *word* of several verses. She certainly read to astonishment and I could not help thinking that perhaps she understood what she read quite as well "as most country parsons," (Swift).

Little does she know, poor thing, how those verses have been understood and understood and yet misunderstood for ages. In the beginning was the *deed*, says Faust, but was puzzled as much as before.

At Captain Greenwoods March 1st, 1842. I left Doaksville this morning after breakfasting with Colonel Upshaw the agent of the United States with the Chickasaws, and set out for Fort Smith intending to continue my journey. Mr. Love with whom I travelled from Boggy Depot to Doaksville, offered to inform Captain Greenwood of my being in the country, saying he thought Captain Greenwood would wish to see me; and he very plainly hinted, smiling, that he would have some bitter complaints to make against the agent. I told Love, in answer, that I would not send for Greenwood; but if he had anything to say to me and would come to Doaksville, I would hear him. I remained long enough to give him and others an opportunity of seeing me, but it seems now that Greenwood wished to see me when the Agent was not present, or I conclude so. On my way this morning and about two miles from town I was overtaken by young Henry Colbert. There was an elderly woman in company with Colbert, I understand, his mother. We all rode together some few hundred yards. I told Mr. Colbert I was on my way to Fort Smith and at a fork in the road we separated. He (and his mother) had not gone far, before he turned across and called to me. I stopped, he came up to me and said he believed Captain Greenwood wished to see me. I told him I supposed not, or that he would have called at Doaksville. He said he was sure he wished to see me and that he was then going to his house to tell him of my having set out for Fort Smith.

I finally said I would go with him and did so. He took me to the shop of the blacksmith, thinking that possibly Greenwood might be there as some public plows were to be delivered out at that place. He was not there and we rode to Greenwood's house, where I have heard and taken down in writing some rather bitter complaints against the Agent, etc. A number of persons were present. The sale of the claims of incompetent Indians had been severely condemned and in fact pronounced corrupt.

Evening. Thunder storm; at Greenwoods by invitation for the night. One of the Colberts interprets, harps upon the incompetents fund; talks of a portion of it as having been deposited in Banks and when the agent has been applied to about it, he says "it is paid away or something"; the Indians cannot tell how it is their money is gone. Insinuates very strongly a collusion between the agent and the merchants. Thinks Love also implicated and in league with the agent and merchants. Don't think Captain Alberson free from suspicion. I told Captain Greenwood that both Love and Alberson had said very severe things of the agent and wished him removed. It was at once said that they have ascertained how the people are beginning to feel on the subject and are taking steps to protect themselves. I have not told these people the facts that both Love and Alberson evidently wish the removal of the Agent but do not wish to be seen instrumental in his removal. They talked very obscurely, suggesting a variety of things but

pleading all the time extreme delicacy, yet urging me
to see Greenwood, who Love knew would complain of
the agent. Both Love and Alberson said I would hear
nothing but complaints of the Agent if I remained in
the Nation. Now I can see that if the Agent and Love
and Alberson have been in league together for dispos-
ing improperly of Incompetent claims, the two latter,
seeing the effect upon public opinion, may heartily
wish to free themselves from the agent and yet be tram-
melled in making statements to me. Greenwood speaks
out distinctly, but Alberson talked in a circle for some
time, until I distinctly asked him if he wished me to
report his opinion to the President, when he answered
affirmatively.

Greenwood knows of no religious ceremony among
the Chickasaws. Does not know the object of the Spirit
dance (described to me by Alberson). Says a number
of their old dances have gone out of use and they now
dance sometimes after the fiddle. Play ball and dance a
great deal. Does not think much about schools and ex-
presses no opinion for or against them. Knows nothing
of the Deity.

Lives in a double log house with a covered passage,
country chairs, tables, beds, crockery ware, gave me
good strong coffee, chicken fried and baked, fresh pork,
sliced sweet potatoes, good wheat flour biscuit, and corn
bread for dinner. A supper after dark – same, omitting
the chicken and biscuit. No one speaks English, but a
neighbor, who remains to interpret. Yes, a brother of
this neighbor it seems, lives in Greenwood's family and
speaks a little English.

Greenwood knows nothing about thunder and asks
what we know about it, fears it. (Why? I asked) because he has "seen that it has sometimes killed people."

I explained a little – sparks from the cat's back, same as lightning, can be conveyed off safely. Thunder is but noise; when heard long after the lightning is seen, the lightning is a great way off.

All are tolerably well dressed; the fashion among Chickasaws of full blood, much the same as among the Creeks; a turban, shirt, frock with a cape either fringed or ruffled, bead belt, pouch worked with beads (not so common as among the Creeks), leather leggings and either shoes or moccasins, bead gaiters for the leggings, a knife in the belt. Women, frock long, kerchief for the neck, shoes, material of frock various from bed ticking to fine calico, sometimes but rarely black glossy silk. Expression on both men and women rather demure and subdued. The spirit of their ancestors is gone.

Greenwood says the Chickasaws have always had a *king* and other chiefs, perpetual. When they came to this western country their people scattered among the different districts and have done nothing about their government and some of their chiefs have died. As for the Choctaw laws they seem like the white man's laws and the Chickasaws have never been accustomed to them and don't like them.

Describes the proceedings of Choctaws at some of their preachings plainly; their camp meeting, jumping, singing, hallowing, crying. Don't like it. Says General Coffee saw it in the old nation and did not like it himself.

Has attended some of the Choctaw general councils but cannot understand their laws. Greenwood is an old Chickasaw Chief, perhaps sixty years old and destitute of all the culture of the whites. Captain Magilbury is a still older Indian, also an old chief. These people do not like the whites or their ways or anything in imitation of them; it is not from hostility so much as partiality for their old customs, laws and usages.

The old man Greenwood, still harps upon the laws of the Choctaws, can understand their language but cannot understand their laws. I suggested that they must once have been the same people. Were once the same people, he says, but have no tradition of a separation and knows nothing about it. Says the Choctaws are neither honest nor hospitable. When the Chickasaw delegation came to examine the country,[109] the Choctaws trailed off their horses and then made them pay for their recovery, and they would hardly give a traveler a meal of victuals.

(The interpreter "eructs" against the rules laid down by Don Quixote for the Governor of Barataria. It is common with Indians.)

The interpreter, one of the Colberts, a brother of Lemuel not Henry, is very bitter against the merchants for the manner of buying the claims of incompetent Indians, says it is perfect robbery, that they have charged $150 and as high as $200 for a horse not worth over $30.

Second March. This morning a woman came into the room where I was not yet dressed and conferred mysteriously with the old chief, Greenwood, while he was dressing, old chief's wife silently shutting the door leading into the passage. I had just drawn on my pantaloons and had on one boot, when the woman came

---

[109] The Chickasaw Nation sent a party west to explore the country in 1830 and another in 1833; on these occasions the envoys consulted with the Choctaw about buying part of their country, but it was not until the third effort in 1837 that an agreement was reached. During the eighteen years of their union so much dissatisfaction existed on the part of the Chickasaw that the sentiment expressed by Greenwood was likely to have been repeated many times; but that feeling was forgotten when the union was dissolved.

up and handed me a letter, not a word said aloud by anybody. The letter was wrapped in many folds of a newspaper and my first idea was that some one, perhaps at Doaksville had sent me a piece of important newspaper intelligence. But no, Pitman Colbert had written a letter expressing regret that he had not seen me at Doaksville to tell me that their chief, Captain Greenwood would call on me; is glad to hear I have called at the Chief's, where he hopes I will hear how shamefully the Chickasaws have been cheated by "the speculators," particularly the Incompetent Indians. He declares there is not a white man in the country sufficiently friendly with the Chickasaws to tell the truth or say a word for them.

It was Pitman Colbert's wife and son who overtook me yesterday and it was the young man's mother who sent her son to me after we had separated, urging that Captain Greenwood wished to see me. These efforts would not be made if there was not some strong reason for it. Pitman Colbert came to my room last Sunday morning with a message, it now appears from Greenwood; but it happened the Indian Agent, against whom they wish to complain, was present and he left me without communicating the message. Greenwood himself was in on Saturday to see me, but I had gone to Fort Towson.

A black woman, comes in to make up the beds and sweep the floor, bid me good morning smilingly, asked me where I came from. I paid her the compliment of returning the question. Madison, said she, adding that she was raised among the whites. It was plain it did the blackey good, in her tattered dress and dirty as she was, to see a white man. When she pronounced the monosyllable Madison, I asked Mississippi? No – Alabama.

How long have you been among Indians? – five or six years. "I suppose you can speak their language?" "I can *mumble* it a little," said she, and then there was a silence, when she added, that she belonged to Jim Adkins and reckoned I had heard of him. No, I had not. Another long silence. "He lived by the cotton gin" said the girl and she supposed I had been there. I thought she meant Colbert's cotton gin, and it was no strange supposition to imagine I had seen it yesterday, but no, the cotton gin she meant was in "Madison" the only other place in the world out of the Chickasaw Nation, a place which not to know argues, etc.

After breakfast, the old chief Greenwood asks whether the annuity of the nation can be disposed of as the claims of incompetent Indians have been. I explained *no* and while he is talking it occurs to me that some very public rule should be laid down with authority, that no trader shall be permitted to trade with Indians on a credit except upon his own exclusive responsibility; that his having traded on credit, shall not of itself give him a right to enter the Nation for ·the purpose of making collections. That the hazard of such a mode of trade shall be his own entirely. As a general rule, if he trades honestly the Indians will pay. If they refuse payment it is prima facie evidence of extortion and fraud on the part of the trader.

Old Chief wishes if any answer is addressed for the people, that it be addressed to Major Pitman Colbert, otherwise they may never hear of it.

Old Captain Magilbury says he had a paper (commission) from General Washington, it has been sent to the Government asking a pension for him. Wishes to know about it. Sent it a year ago or fourteen months. Saffrans took it on. When Saffrans returned he said that

General Harrison's death prevented his doing anything for him and he left the Commission in Washington.

At McKinney's, 3 P.M., 26 miles from Fort Towson. Left old chief Greenwood after breakfast this morning and have come sixteen miles over hills the last several miles, covered with a growth of pine, not very large. There are hills along here called the Seven Devils. They are sufficient for making a bad road, but not worth the noise I have heard about them. They range east and west nearly and the seven, if there are seven, are embraced within about eight miles. The sun came out very clear today about 11 or 12 and it has been rather warm. The woods have been "vocal with the music of birds." I had noticed flowers in the prairie before reaching Fort Towson. Today saw more but in the woods, having seen no prairie today; buds are putting out from some of the trees.

Am to report of the Seminoles, having seen both them and the Creeks: They want an agent, should not have one, cannot have one without a violation of the rights of the Creeks.[110] It might be proposed to them, if they have had a promise from unauthorized persons, that they should move to the north of the Senecas and there have a country of their own.

There is no obligation on the Government to execute promises made by unauthorized persons, but to salve the feelings of the Seminoles, so and so, they would not move.

[110] The Government engaged in an effort to unite the Creeks and Seminole as one tribe, and when the latter were removed from the East they were located upon the lands of the Creeks under whose government they were expected to live and form a minority part. Though many years before they had been one people, much unhappiness resulted from this ill-advised arrangement; and as in the case of Choctaw and Chickasaw, the plan was abandoned, and the Seminole later located on their own land under their own government.

I asked for a couple of boiled eggs, seeing some eggs for dinner and Miss McKinney a half-breed Choctaw woman gave me four boiled just to my liking. I ate two without hesitation and then took a third; and while devouring that I eyed the fourth with something like the feeling of the Jew in Ivanhoe, when counting the sheckels and, with a similar result I left my respects for those who might sit at table after me. As it was dinner I asked for, I had no right to tea or coffee, and accordingly I had what was either or neither I could not tell which, and no sugar. Some hog meat (how could a jew travel in this country?) and some indifferent corn bread, yes, some butter, I had like to have forgotten. But chiefly I dined on four boiled eggs. Eggs are always fried in these parts when cooked at all.

Let me see. The subjects on which I propose to address the Secretary of War from Fort Smith are: the Comanche treaty, the stock contracts for Creeks, the Seminole agent, the Chickasaw Incompetent Indians and Buckner. And I think I will recommend the removal of Col. Upshaw, on the single ground, officially, of his having lost the confidence of the chiefs of the Chickasaws; and I can suggest that its being immediately done will relieve the agent from the embarrassment of it appearing to be the result of my report.

I thought today for some manner of alluding to the dirt of the Indians, clean dirt and dirty dirt, for there is a difference.

All sorts of sawed boards are called *plank* in this country – rived shingles, not dressed, are called boards; broad, thick, hewn plank for floors are called puncheons. I slept last night on a pallet of blankets & a coverlet made upon some boards raised the usual height of a bed stead – no sheets, or sheet even.

By the way there were two beds in my room at Doaksville & I took the sheet from one and made up a pair for the other. It is odd that in the Cherokee, Creek, Chickasaw and Choctaw nations where sheets are used at all, there is but one sheet to a bed.

26 miles from Towson, 3d Mar. '42. Some calculations may be made to show the enormity of the wrong committed upon the Chickasaws by charging them with some $740,000 worth of provision, in this way: Take the Creeks at whatever number received rations say 12,000 or 14,000 or whatever the number was, and see what their rations cost at the contract price. Then see what, in proportion it would have cost to ration the Chickasaws, 4, 5, or 6,000.

Then admit that the *million* rations costing say $100,-000 were actually purchased by request of the Chickasaws, which is however not the fact, and add that amount $100,000. The result will be if I am not mistaken, not exceeding $350,000, yet it has cost them, or there has been charged to them, considerably over twice that amount. This mode of calculation presupposes that the Creeks were rationed at a reasonable rate, but if one-third was paid more than should have been, a corresponding advance must be made upon the charged expenses of the Chickasaws. And, again finally, if the Creeks received but half of their rations, or even two thirds, so much the worse again. The seven months rations must be added and accounted for which will ease off the ground of complaint to some extent, but not much if the whole arrangement was a mere trick to get rid of the public rations bought by and spoiling on the hands of the Government agents.

Another calculation is this: that 1,000,000 of rations was deemed sufficient for four months, of course 3,000,-

ooo would have sufficed for a year – suppose them to have cost 300,000 leaves an expenditure, unauthorized of about 440,000.

Again, if Hiram Rich would have contracted for rations at less than ten cents,[111] 6,000 Indians for twelve months, could have been provisioned for less than $200,000; add 7/12 for the seven months, 116,666 and the whole 19 months rations would only have cost some $320,000. Suppose honest issuing commissaries had been employed, three of them at $8.00 a day instead of two (see Green Irwin's statement).

It must not be forgotten that this expense cannot be justified on the plea that it was incurred at the request of the Chickasaws who failed to emigrate at the appointed time. The request of the Chickasaws should have been complied in full; and then as the request will show, the expense would not have been incurred for they desired expressly that the Superintendent of their removal who alone could know both the numbers and time for emigration, should purchase their provisions. The Government choosing to depart from that plan assumed the responsibility of all the consequences. But even if the plea be admitted it only covers 1,000,-ooo of rations say $100,000. There is no pretense of defence for the remaining 640,000 dollars expended for rations and charged to the Chickasaws.

The truth is and may as well be stated, the rations were not purchased for the Chickasaws, but for general issue to emigrant Indians; and when it was ascertained that they were likely to spoil on the hands of the Gov-

---

111 A ration for emigrating Indians consisted of one pound of salted pork or one and one-fourth pounds of salted beef, and one and one-fourth pounds of corn meal; this was intended to subsist one Indian for one day and the bids usually offered by contractors ranged from five to fifteen cents per ration.

ernment agents a mode of getting rid of them was adopted resulting in an enormous wrong upon the Chickasaws.

And after all the rations were not issued, but a contract for issues of fresh beef and corn went into effect in a few weeks after the arrival of the Chickasaws at Fort Smith and should by agreement have taken effect; though it appears that for some two months the Indians on Boggy and Blue received no rations. See McClure's statement and Guy's letter to Upshaw as reported by the latter.

Chapter XIII

Choctaw Traditions – Biloxi Wanderers – Bowles's
Purchase in Texas – Arrive at "Old Pusley's" – Drunken
Indians – High Estimate of the Kickapoo – Murders
in Cherokee Nation – Burial Customs – Trading with
the Comanche – Comanche Customs – Arrive at Fort
Smith – Guest of Zachary Taylor – Stand Watie and
Mrs. Ridge – Plots against John Ross – Casual
Steamboating.

At Stanton's fifty miles from Fort Towson, 4 P.M.
Third March. After riding among hills and over a few
all the way from McKinneys, five miles south of Stan-
tons, is a remarkable view from the brow of a hill looking through a gorge between two other hills about a
mile distant and a mile apart. Through this gorge the
eye overlooks woods in variety, a strip of prairie next
as if laid off in fields for cultivation and then a range
of undulating hills at right angles to the line of sight.
I suppose these hills pass for mountains in this country. I have rode through pines nearly all day, some
cedar, not much – scattering small oaks and black jack.

I must not forget that I passed a black dog or a black
wolf crouching in the road and eyeing me intently as I
rode by but without offering to move. I never saw a
black wolf unless this was one. It had a long slender
body, bushy tail, long sharp nose, a black eye, was itself
a deep black and might have been a dog. It was about
a mile from an Indian house. I mus'nt say hut in this
civilized country.

I thought today how I can inoffensively express the opinion that Indians as Indians, cannot live surrounded by a white population; ignorance must give way and if the native resists cultivation, either purposely or by his nature, then farewell to the Indians. They must go. Can they be cultivated?

Mr. Stanton mentions hickory (b&u) post oak (u), black (u) and red (u) oak, pine, black walnut (u), wild cherry (b), in some places "right smart of it" sometimes 2½ to 3 feet through); black locust (b), Bois d'arc (b), there is honey locust (u), but he has not seen it, he says. Scaly bark hickory (b), maple (b), and sugar tree (b). Some birch (b) in the bottoms, cotton wood (b) and sycamore (b). No poplar, chestnut, Piccans (plenty on Red and Arkansas rivers) butternut, beech. There is red and slipery elm (b) and ash (b) and overcup (b) (the largest and most valuable wood for present use in the country. Makes boards and timber for waggons) hackberry (b). (*b* stands for bottoms, *u* upland.)

Kiametia in sight; was swimming this morning from rain last night, but may be forded now. Rapids a few miles below; no mills nearer than twelve miles this side of Doaksville; is 45 miles from the Arkansas line, 50 from Towson, 85 from Fort Smith. Stanton says the best lands in the nation are west on Boggy and Blue. Good land on Red and Arkansas River, some good land on Canadian and Brushy. The hill in sight South is Kiametia Mountain, north are the potato hills; have crossed the Seven Brothers (not Devils) which are parts of the Ozark Mountains.[112] Several have this name, some in Missouri.

---

[112] Early French residents on the Arkansas located themselves as "Aux Arkansas," *i.e.* "On the Arkansas." This was shortened to "Aux-Arcans"

Stanton plants corn last of March or first of April. Very rarely injured by frost. Corn and potatoes are chiefly raised, as much as is needed; very little sent to market (from this section); furnished a good deal for emigrant Indians; corn, fifty cents to $1.00 a bushel consumed at home and by travellers.

Some cotton raised for home use. Speaks of this neighborhood. Everybody has plenty of hogs and a sufficiency of cattle unless it be a few full-blood Indians. His hogs were fattened on mast (wild nuts) as good a fat as from corn, he thinks.

There is a willow oak (something like live oak, very hard) bears an acorn which falls and is good all the season until it sprouts, very good for hogs. Sometimes the oaks or some of them fail. There is a great deal of black jack, furnishes good mast. Very little game, but few deer, a good many bear and several kinds of wolves, black, yellow and brindle wolf, all large and rather fierce. Prairie wolf is a small grey wolf but little larger than a fox. The larger wolves not often seen in packs.

Sand-stone plenty, no lime nearer than the prairies near Towson. "Flint rock" in the hills, potato hills. Valuable iron ore five or six m. this side of Towson; has a well sixteen feet from surface, 6 feet of slate at the bottom.

Stanton's, fourth March. Stanton told me last evening that an old man named Jones who lived in the old nation at a place called Jones's Bluff on the Tombigbee River, has stated to him that immediately after the revolutionary war of '76 there was a division in the Choctaw Nation under two chiefs; that instead of go-

and "Aux-Arcs," and it was applied to the river, and the country and mountains drained by it; Americans then made "Ozark" out of the phrase.

ing into a civil war the parties separated by mutual
agreement one party living in the north west of Mississippi and West Tennessee and the other in East Mississippi and Alabama. That they lived for some short
time thus separated, having a boundary however established. They afterwards by a regular compact changed
the line and the northwest portion took the name of
Chickasaws.

Jones stated also that at about the same time a small
portion of Choctaws became dissatisfied with the Chief
and went south and lived at the Bay of Boluxy for a
time, and then moved west upon Pearl River, and
thence over the Mississippi as far as some villages of
Cadoes. Since the emigration of the Choctaws some of
those Indians under the name of Boluxy's have been
found; their history and almost their language having
been for the most part lost. I saw some of them on Blue
River living in all the destitution of ignorance and
poverty. They are received among the Choctaws from
the affinity of language which still shows itself, more
than from their former connection with the nation
which is scarcely known to either party. The Boluxies
having lived much among the Cadoes have communi-
cated something of their habits and customs; and some
of these, in consequence, have also found a home in the
Choctaw nation, 167 of them having settled in the Nation, having sold their own country. They have permission to settle West of the Chickasaws.

Stanton says that he was in Texas "the second year
(1819) after a crop" had been made under the Austin
settlement and was there 2½ years; knew Bowles, the
Cherokee Chief.[113] States that Bowles made an agree-

---

113 The Cherokee chief known as "The Bowle" left his nation in 1794
with a band of followers, crossed the Mississippi, and located in what is

ment for settlement in Texas between 1815 and 1817 and moved there and had complied with his agreement; and when Austin, Grace and Cole went to Mexico for their own patent he employed them, and paid them for their services in advance, to procure his patent. Stanton says he heard the arrangement made and understood afterwards that the money was paid in advance; that Austin, Grace and Coles when they returned with Austin's patent, brought also a patent for Bowles and he Stanton saw it. The patent described a country north of Nacogdoches, some sixty miles by thirty. He states that after the whites in Texas declared their independence and defeated the Mexicans they attempted to negoiate for the removal of Bowles, who had taken no part in the war. They could not agree about the terms and the Texans went to war with the Cherokees, killed Bowles,[114] plundered his wife and her negroes and drove the whole of them out of the country. Does not know the immediate cause of the war.

I was myself on the Sabine when the battle of San Jacinto was fought. Bowles was then living about thirty miles from Nacogdoches and though he made no movement at all, yet the people were dreadfully alarmed. They were mostly women and children, the men being in the Texas army under Houston. There were speculators in the country buying up land claims and to reduce the price as much as possible they created alarms; and

now Arkansas on the Saint Francis River. From here he later went to Arkansas River and then to Texas.

[114] The Cherokee who had long lived in Texas were suspected of favoring the Mexicans. The Bowle had received a commission from the Mexican government for his efforts in putting down the so-called Fredonian Rebellion in 1827. In 1839 a force of Texans attacked the Cherokee settlements and killed a large number of them including The Bowle and Big Mush, second chief. The remainder were driven from their homes and a number of them crossed the Red River.

finally (Johnathan Mason at their head) so frightened the people that they fled from Nacogadoches and moved over the Sabine where the east bank of the river for miles was lined for several weeks with women and children living in the open air, or under tents made with sheets and bed quilts. Stanton says that Bowles left the Cherokee Nation in consequence of a feud with the Ridges and that they partially settled for a time along here where I am now noting, on the Kiametia.[115]

Sweet gum (b) (large) Linn (b) (large) Mulberry (b) (small) sassafras spice (b) (small).

I am on a high ridge in the midst of mountains. Kiametia mountain is in the S. E. another N. W. I have been riding up it at least twenty-eight miles, 75 miles from Towson.

Arrived at "Old Pusley's" before sundown, 33 miles from Stanton's; Kiametia River – forded the river in deeper water than where I forded some ten days ago 40 miles or more down the river. Have rode through rough country today – hilly and stony. The "divide" between Red and Arkansas rivers in this longitude, I set down as rough. Up about Blue there is scarcely a hill till you pass the Boggy going South.

Evening, dusk. The people here, except a little black boy speak no English. The boy told me Pusley was absent, but he has just come home with several drunken Indians. So, I am to have a pretty night of it. Will they come here? I am in a small room with two beds. I think this must be the sanctorum of travellers. No candle, a pine knot; customs proceed from a greater depth in human nature than written laws. Men obey the former without coercion, would not hold up customs as

[115] Stanton is confused; The Ridge feud developed many years after The Bowle left the tribe.

phantasmagoria, to be gazed at but for a deeper and graver object.

Pity I have not the Indian words in each of their language for our numerals and a few natural objects as the sun, moon, etc., for comparison.

Five A.M. Fifth March. The Indians were drunk and noisy last night 'till after midnight, and this morning I see they are scattered about under their blankets in the corners of the fence and in open places instead of sleeping even under the piaza.

No one came near me. They had a fiddler, whether a negro or not I don't know. I had taken to my bed when the fiddle began. The fiddler must have been a genius, for he played nothing but variations. Two tunes were favorites, one was "coal black Rose," the other I used to hear Dr. Coleman of the army play on the violin and sing words something like these "O Mr. Balkirk, send for the barber, shave these" (I forget the words). One of the Indians was drunk enough to try to talk English, cursing in English. They never swear in Indian. There is no oath in any Indian language that I have ever heard of –"God *dim* you Jone (John) play for me," etc., while some were dancing after the fiddle, others were singing, and now and then a single voice would be heard from some solitary man, evidently flat on his back. These are Choctaws.

On the Poto waiting the ferry-man, 5th March. The traders who have brought the Chickasaws in debt say they relieved their wants; did they not create their wants? If they traded without express authority, would it not be fair to pay the money to the original claimant and leave him to settle with the traders. If the latter have traded fairly the honesty of the Indian will pay him, the chance is equal.

I am to urge the history of Bowles to show the inveterate hostility of the Cherokees, the followers of Bowles, not under the Cherokee government. Of the Shawnees I am to urge their former connection with Tecumseh whose principle it was, that all Indian lands were the common property of all Indian tribes, no portion belonged to any particular tribe. These Shawnees have wandered off without ever falling under the influence of the whites and probably maintain to this day the principles in which they were nurtured. Some probably fought by the side of Tecumseh.

The Delawares are the most enterprising of all the Indians. The Kickapoos have the highest reputation for courage and independence and I heard the opinion in the Choctaw nation, that the whole power of the nation could not subdue the Kickapoos in case of conflict. Stanton has no doubt of their purpose of going to war against Texas and hence, etc. Texas trading policy to be stated: that of establishing trading houses along the boundary for the Indians to visit.

At McKinney's (2nd) 1½ P.M. 5th. 18 miles from Old Pusley's – 10 from the Oporto or Poto as Col. Upshaw spells it. Col. McKinney says he has not heard of a murder on the line between Choctaws and Arkansas. No trading of any consequence; if people want anything they go and get it and come away. Don't stay to drink or gamble. If they want whiskey they carry it off and don't stay and get into drunken frolics.

Hears of murders in the Cherokee Nation frequently, attributes it to the half-breeds and quarteroons, who are almost white. I should assign another cause, the unsettled condition of the Cherokee Nation, which induces a large number of desperate white men to be among them and about them to prey upon them. The business of the Choctaws is settled and everything is quiet.

Fifth March, 1842. Colonel McKinney, a full blood Choctaw, tells me he is 46 years old, recollects having seen once when young, one of the houses in which the bones of the dead were kept. The house was a loft covered in, raised on posts 8 or 10 feet high. When any one died it was the custom to place the body on a scaffold in the yard by the house, and allow it to remain there until the bones were freed from the flesh. During the time the relations would meet and mourn (cry) from time to time (Captain Alberson told me there was a regular meeting for four days and I suppose there were meetings after that of those who *felt grief* and Alberson said he has seen with his own eyes, the maggots fall from the scaffold during the process of putrefaction and seen them picked up by fowls). After a few months great preparations for a feast, the bone picking feast, were made. All of the relations would come in sometimes a hundred miles, to attend the feast, the ceremony was then performed by taking the bones from the scaffold. They were placed in a box and deposited in the house with others.

Colonel McKinney says there are about 400 Choctaws [116] between him and the agency (Fort Coffee) who keep up most of the old customs, but the old custom of mourning and preserving the bones is entirely dispensed with throughout the nation. The 400 set up poles with clothes on the top at the graves. The dead are buried, now, throughout the nation. Some few bury

---

[116] They were the less progressive members of the tribe, belonging to the district headed by Mushalatubbee.

at their houses, under the porch. Says the Choctaws trade but very little on a credit, perhaps to the amount of annuity, but are not embarrassed.

Nearly all their old dances are done with. Says their customs have been different from those of the Chickasaws *altogether*. (This is strange. Have the same language except in some names of things. This corresponds to what Love and others have told me. Very strange-that the language should remain and the customs all vary).

Has been twice among the Comanches. Confirms the account of the Cross timber (a low scraggley timber); confirms Edwards' account of their horses. Common Spanish horses, except a very few, kept carefully for the chase of the buffalo. Never ride the chase horses except in pursuit of the buffalo. The second time he was out, he killed 99 deer and one bear in 17 days besides buffalo's not counted, bought 40 buffalo robes the first time and brought them in and sold them for $4.00 each. Paid three yards domestic for a robe, got a good horse for 1½ yard of strowding [117] bound with tape. Says the Wako, Tawehash and Kiawa, paint their bodies and faces. The Comanches do not paint at all except with the red. Comanche women cut their hair close; the men wear long hair plaited. Sometimes they plait a buffalo mane and add it to their hair, down to the calf of the leg. Men wear the flap, leggings and moccasins, buffalo for a blanket, or strouding sewed together, very long; women wear a leather petticoat, shirt, shoes like a stocking (of skin) up to the knee. Night come, a speaker calls "eya, eya, eya" a long time, don't know what

[117] Strouding or stroud, a coarse cloth about a foot in width, used by the Indians for breech-clout or flap, tied around the body and the ends or flaps hanging down before and behind.

they say. Make their young ones go into the water cold or warm, makes them hardy; more children and more dogs, have some curious dogs without hair except a bunch between the ears and at the end of the tail, great favorites. They take great care of them and cover them with buffalo robe. He says they don't sing in the morning as the Osages do, says the Osages worship in that way. Is sure the Comanches do not, but he heard some sing, because they chose to sing, as anyone might.

The prairie fly he did not find in the Comanche country but found myriads of common house fly; no horse flies but the others are so numerous it is almost impossible · to keep them from your mouth while eating. Didn't notice any difference of soil in or beyond the Cross timber. No level country (he says) but rolling, no high ridges, however; wood in wet places on streams.

He condemns the conduct of the Chickasaw "head people" and agents for selling the funds of the incompetent Indians; calls it scandalous and asks what the agents are sent here for. Condemns the merchants, thinks them swindlers and the agent no better. Ought to be punished, robbery. Says the claims (some) have been sold at the Agency (Fort Coffee) to merchants there. Jones figures; Jones, a Choctaw in business with Berthlett and Hall, [Heald] have three stores, at Forts Coffee, Towson and Boggy. Jones wrote to McKinney telling him to get pay for debts to Choctaws (by Chickasaws) by trading for incompetent claims; that is – trade with him, Jones, and he take the *claims*; was urged to advise his people to that course. He [McKinney] refused, saying the Chickasaws "will have money some day or other" and can pay; will not touch their claims, says they [merchants] charge double price for their goods when their due bills are presented for payment.

Says the Choctaws have claims for Lost Property, horses, etc. (the old story). A delegation headed by Pitchlyn, is now in Washington prosecuting these claims.

McKinney says he is one of the Chiefs (there are four) of the Choctaw Nation (including the Chief of the Chickasaw district). Isaac Fulsom half-breed, Jim Fletcher, half-breed, Johnson McKinney full-blood, Alberson half-breed, are the four chiefs.

Population of the lower and east district on Red River was about 8,000 (largest); are moving west gradually; whole population used to be 20,000 in the old nation. Thinks they lost over one third when they emigrated, are on the increase now. Never wants to move again, to propose it would make war at once.

Asked him how they voted. The candidates take a position and the voters fall in, in a row (not *row* – they are very orderly) and are counted by judges appointed. Lighthorse men are present to keep order.

Inferior court is called when needed. Seldom needed, has not set for nearly a year; that is, one of the three for the district, the other two have each had a case of murder, one man sentenced to be shot.

6th March. Colonel McKinney has a smiling half-breed wife, a good looking embonpoint woman, who appears as happy as the day is long. So if McKinney is not a half-breed himself, as the other three chiefs are, his house comes under the white blood influence through his wife.

McKinney says he has proposed a general council of Indians.[118] The Creeks were willing but wished the

---

[118] A council was held in May of that year on Deep Fork River near

Council to be held where no agent of the United States would be present. McKinney refused to go into a council of that sort.

Fort Smith 7th March 1842. Arrived last evening and made at home at General Taylor's, my old Lt. Col. of the old 8th Infantry, when I was the Adjutant in 1820 at the Bay of St. Louis, sixty miles east of New Orleans. Nothing can be more friendly than his reception of me. (He became President). Captain W. W. S. Bliss is here at Fort Smith, the Assistant Adjutant General to General Taylor, another warm friend.

I rode 35 miles yesterday from ½ past 7 A.M. till ¼ past 4 P.M. stopping ¾ of an hour at Walls for dinner. The distance of stands together from Fort Towson to Fort Smith make 136 miles.

Fort Smith 8th March. I might be flattered if I chose by an order from Washington of the 1st of March, received by General Taylor yesterday directing precisely what I recommended to the Secretary of War by letter from Fort Wayne of the 9th or 10th of Jaunary. Fort Wayne is ordered to be immediately abandoned and a new post established about 100 miles south of Fort Leavenworth.[119] The property at Fort Wayne is even ordered to be disposed of exactly as I recommended, portions sold and some conveyed to Fort Gibson. The saw mill 18 miles from Ft. Wayne, I recommended might be given to the Cherokees in the anticipated treaty with those people. As the treaty is not yet made the saw mill remains on the hands of the Government, but is ordered to be leased. I did not ex-

the present town of Eufaula, Oklahoma; the Creeks were the hosts and they had as guests representatives of eleven other tribes.

[119] The post established in response to Colonel Hitchcock's recommendation, known as Fort Scott, was located in southeastern Kansas. His interesting letter of January 9, referred to in the text is to be seen in the appendix.

pect so complimentary and prompt an action, when I wrote from Fort Wayne and I wrote rather under an idea of expressing my sentiments without distinctly perceiving or expecting they would be especially regarded. The officer who may be ordered to establish the post against his will may report that there is no good site, with wood, etc. It is a prairie country generally but wood can be found within a circle of twenty miles on some of the streams of the Osage River.

12th March (Fort Smith). Since I have returned here I have prepared several reports for the Secretary of War. Sent one prepared in the Creek Nation about the Stock animal contract, and prepared one of the incompetent Indians of the Chickasaws and one of Captain Buckner; and have sent a long communication to Captain Armstrong the Acting Superintendent of Indian Affairs in the South West. This last is a very serious paper and will form a kind of crisis in my examinations into provision frauds.

Steamboat *Rialto* at Fort Smith, 12th March, 1842 P.M. Just ready to shove off; General Taylor, Major Lear, Captain Bliss and others have taken leave of me at the boat, now first for Little Rock, and then as I thought for Washington; but Captain Rodgers has come down from Fort Gibson with a verbal message from Governor Butler that he must see me by all means before I leave here, and Rodgers thinks the Governor found letters from Washington at Gibson of importance and had no time to write to me. I cannot wait on this uncertainty and have requested any letter coming here from Fort Gibson to be sent to Little Rock for me.

Yesterday I went with General Taylor and Captain Alexander over the works going up at Fort Smith and had pointed out to me the old log barracks and store houses put up by the troops many years ago, General Taylor says, before the Choctaw treaty was made; yet a Choctaw claims to have made a settlement at Fort Smith, and wishes pay from the Government of the United States. The Choctaw is named McKinney and speaks English, for which reason he was employed as a sort of clerk or interpreter by the Sutler for the troops and never made any improvement himself of any sort. There is no sign of any improvement except the buildings put up by the troops.

13th March. Saw Mr. Paschal last evening and his wife who was a sister of John Ridge. Saw also the widow of John Ridge who it seems is a white woman. She is now on a visit to Mrs. Paschal. Saw also a brother of Boudinot named Stanwatie.[120] All in Paschal's house, a strong knot of Ross' opponents. Pascal took me to a private room and read sundry letters addressed by him, one to Mr. Poinsett when Secretary of War, gave me a copy he had; it urged the claims of the connections of Ridge and Boudinot who were killed by some of the Ross party in consequence of the treaty of 1835. He insists very strongly that the Government was bound to protect the treaty party and failing to do so is bound now to make reparation for property as it can, for feeling it cannot.

There was a statement of the heads of claim for losses occasioned by the acts of violence complained of.

---

[120] Stand Watie was a noted Cherokee Indian, a half brother of Elias Boudinot, and after his death a leader of the party which had signed the removal treaty of New Echota. On the outbreak of the Civil War he and his party were the first to ally themselves with the South; he was given command of one of two Cherokee regiments which joined the Confederate forces and participated in the battle of Pea Ridge and in other actions. He was one of the principal authorities for the legends and other material collected by Schoolcraft among the Cherokee (*Handbook of American Indians*, vol. ii, 634).

Another letter was addressed to Governor Butler, the Cherokee Agent, urging the same claims and particularly calling the governor's attention to the Cherokee printer who married a sister of Boudinot's, and who was driven out of the nation with great loss.

Paschal is a young man, that is, for meddling in national matters; is a lawyer in Van Buren and a sort of editor, writing considerably for the paper published in Van Buren especially on Indian and frontier affairs. He has the reputation of considerable talent; I do not perceive much depth in him or much information. He is sprightly and writes editorially so to say, filling his sheet with adjectives and aims at poetic personifications, covering over the real subject matter with words. His mind is bent all to one side which he admitted to me was likely to be the case. He married the sister of Ridge who was murdered and his wife, considerably colored by nature with an aboriginal tint, is plainly of a strong masculine spirit. Speaks English very well, quite naturally as if she had no other language. She said but little, but what she did say was uttered with peculiar firmness of muscle about the mouth, a kind of tension, the result of strong feeling. She has very black eyes. Several, two at least, children.

Mrs. Ridge looked dull and subdued and did not make much impression. I confess I do not like to see white women marrying Indians or half-breeds, though I have not the least objection to white men marrying half-breeds.

Governor Butler had told me of Stanwatie and that he had threatened the life of John Ross; that he is of a cool determined character and that Ross will not be allowed to pass out of the Nation to Washington if he meets with Stanwatie. He also told me he had *heard* that Mrs. Paschal had a man's dress and intended to disguise herself with it and kill Ross herself if an opportunity offers. I placed no great reliance upon these stories, especially the last, but thought it best to see Paschal. I took occasion to hint, that the Ridge party would not be lost sight of by the Government in any new treaty that might be made, and after he had puzzled his brain in endeavoring to account for the order from Washington suspending Butler's taking evidence of claims, I thought it best to suggest that perhaps the Government had concluded to send commissioners here to make the treaty who could take the evidence for themselves. This seemed to strike him and it may serve to keep the Ridges still. I had no other purpose than to keep things quiet in the country. Paschal spoke of the treaty of 1835 and denied the right of the Government to pay the expenses of the Ross party, over and above $20.00 a head, in their emigration, from the fund provided in the treaty. This I think correct myself, but I did not tell an important fact in this business, that Congress by special appropriation added over a million to the treaty fund, not called for by the treaty, a sum more than sufficient, I think to cover all extra expenses under General Scott's arrangement with Mr. Ross.[121]

March 14th. Yesterday towards evening we were

---

[121] After the resistance by the Cherokee to removal under the pretended treaty of 1835, Gen. Winfield Scott was ordered in 1838 to assume command of several thousand troops in Georgia, and to collect, concentrate and remove the Indians. After about five thousand had been removed and many were dying in concentration camps, the Cherokee council authorized John Ross to propose to General Scott that if they could wait until autumn when the sickly season was past, they would remove themselves. Accordingly, General Scott agreed to this plan and the estimated cost of removal was fixed at $65.88 per head. The Indians organized in 13 parties of an average of about one thousand, each in charge of a captain, and this tragic emigration was put under way. They traveled and carried their hastily gathered effects in 650 wagons, and on thousands of riding horses and on foot. For

hailed from the shore by Captain Morrison of the Fourth Infantry who was encamped with his company on the bank; we came to, and the *Rialto* was chartered to turn back to Fort Gibson with the company (Lt. Hagens, a young man was with it.)

The passengers continued on the boat and went up the river until about 3 A.M. when we met the *Effort* coming down and were awakened and transferred. We are now going down with the prospect of reaching Little Rock this evening.

There has been a theological discussion this morning among some of the passengers, strangers to me. They seem to have been in conversation about the phrenologist Dr. Powell who came a few miles down in the steamboat yesterday and left us at Ozark. These discussions in the way they are commonly handled are disgusting especially on board of steamboats.

15th March. Dark last night and a fog this morning until after 8 o'clock. Now under way, we hope to reach Little Rock by one or two P.M.

The proclamation of Governor Yell of Arkansas some weeks since calling upon 500 militia, on the event of the murder of Mr. Long by a Cherokee, is universally ridiculed and condemned and on the frontier was not obeyed.

I heard of three murders in Arkansas when I went up the river in November last. I now hear the particulars of a desperate encounter between a Mr. Phillips and a Dr. Menifee, resulting in the death of the latter. Phillips assaulted Menifee. Menifee fired a pistol and

12,883 persons so removed, Ross was paid in all $1,390,876.57 (U. S. House. *Documents*, 27th congress, 3d session, no. 288). There was much controversy over these accounts which were complicated by the fact that several thousand died on the journey.

hit Phillips – the two advanced upon each other. Phillips with a large knife, Menifee with only an empty pistol, a desperate struggle ensued in which Menifee, repeatedly wounded succeeded in breaking the blade of Phillip's knife, after having the blade drawn through his hand two or three times cutting the tendons, etc. Phillips had another knife and with it finally butchered his antagonist. He is now under bail of $20,000.

First contract, 1st February 1838 (as shown by Sutler Chase with Harrison and Glasgow for issues to Chickasaws (not included in those sent to me), no competition.

Second. Secretary Daniel McDonald in New Orleans went to New Orleans as Captain. Governor Yell owned 1/3 Indian (Steamer), gave way to Upshaw.

Third. *DeKalb* 80 tons, more or less, hauled by four loads of a four mule team. Heard Captain Armstrong say he saw it and laughed about it.

Fourth. Will find a statement of Chickasaw and Creek provision delivered to Glasgow and Harrison, 1st and 2nd quarters of 1839. Showing Harrison and Glasgow receipt for the provision turned over to them if not '39 see '40.

The above memoranda were made from and in the presence of Luther Chase, who was formerly a clerk to late Captain R. D. C. Collins. Mr. Chase declined saying anything about Rains and the report of his having been bribed to suppress a letter from Harrison to him. Of the foregoing memoranda hastily made I add that of the first; it now appears that a contract of the 1st of February 1838 was made for issues to the Chickasaws, which is not included in the copies sent to me from the Indian Office. I *suspect*, and am to examine in Washington, that neither that contract, nor the other of the same date for issues to Creeks was ever put upon record. Look well to this.

Chase assures me both contracts were made at the same time, at Fort Coffee by Captain Armstrong and Captain Collins, *without any competition*. He, Chase, was in a steamboat, but the parties making the contracts were on the bank. Chase says a former contract regularly executed had been made at less than eight cents a ration. These contracts give the Government ration and nearly eight cents besides, and closes at over twelve cents for issues beyond the quantity of government rations turned over to Harrison and Glasgow. More yet – Chase assures me the provision for the general *depot* greatly exceeded that purchased for the Chickasaws, yet it appears that of some $950,000 in provision, some 745,000 is *charged* to the Chickasaws and thus attempted to be covered up because the Chickasaw fund appeared to be available.

No. 2. Chase says that McDonald said to him that Buckner [122] owed him money, and in this way that Buckner and McDonald had bought the steamer *In-*

---

[122] A Government agent on October 1, 1837 made a contract with Simeon Buckner of Louisville, Kentucky, by which he agreed to remove the Chickasaw Indians from Memphis to Fort Coffee in steamboats at the rate of $14.50 each. Buckner had six vessels on which to transport the Indians up the Arkansas River, but from fear of the boats, only 3001 would agree to travel by water; and more than 2000 of them insisted on going by land with their horses. By the last of December, 2600 Chickasaw had arrived at Fort Coffee and before the middle of March all of the boat passengers had arrived there. Here they went into camp while they busied themselves in concentrating all their belongings, including between three and four thousand horses and a large quantity of household effects.

Buckner collected pay for the removal of those who went by land as well as those who rode on his steamboats. A Congressional investigation was made of this business, and the House Committee on Public Expenditures reported in March, 1842, that the Chickasaw fund in the hands of the Government had suffered a loss of $122,243.50 through the improper dis-

dian, the latter having one-third; that Buckner said to him that he must relinquish his interest for, said Buckner, the Indians refuse to go in the boat and I wish to give the interest to Upshaw and then the Indians will go in her and Buckner promised to satisfy McDonald. Upshaw was the Superintendent of Removal of the Chickasaws.

No. 3. Chase says that he heard Captain Armstrong say laughingly that the baggage brought in the *DeKalb* was certified at about 80 tons, but that he either had or saw it hauled from the boat in four loads by a team of four mules.

Steamboat *Effort* 15 March 1842, 9 A.M. going down from Little Rock. The above two or three memoranda add from Chase again, who is to send me a statement to Washington of the provision.

He told me yesterday that he considered Ashley the author of Collins' ruin; borrowed $20,000 at one time $16,000 or $17,000 at another; cannot prove it by his own testimony, but thinks the $20,000 loan can be proved by Ashley's admission to another, not named. Says Ashley goaded Collins after he fell under suspicion at Washington, alarming him with the apprehension of being sent to a state prison and urged him to escape to Texas. Collins drank from the first of his duties at Little Rock, but after his deficit was clearly established he gave himself up to liquor. Says, that he, Chase, on the first settlement he, as clerk, made for Collins after he had received funds from the Indian Bureau, found a deficit of about 18,000 dollars and sus-

---

bursement of money in connection with this removal (U. S. House. *Reports,* 27th congress, second session, no. 454). In the appendix are the letters written by Hitchcock to the Secretary of War on March 7, March 8, and April 29, reporting on the condition of the Chikasaw Indians and the frauds committed on them.

pected it was a deficit in his Quartermaster's accounts, which he afterwards ascertained was the fact. Chase says he became alarmed himself and was disposed to leave Collins but was urged to remain and did so for about a year and then left him; but that afterwards whenever Collins sent for him to make up his account Chase would go. On one of these occasions he found a deficit of about $200,000 and on asking Collins for his cash account he said he had none but on being urged he stated from recollection amounts of money due him from sundry persons, 20,000, 15,000, 10,000, etc., making about 100,000. On this occasion when Collins saw his true situation opening before his view he became violently agitated and said among other things "If I have been a damned fool I'll not live till tomorrow morning." Chase appears to have a great regard for the memory of Collins who he says was in the main an honest honorable man of the kindest feelings in the world and that he was ruined by the blackest villainy ever practiced upon an easy nature.

Dr. Desha yesterday in presence of Chase and with Chase's approbation gave me a list of several names of men supposed to have received money from Collins. There is no positive proof they say. Some of the men made some sort of a settlement and can show receipts in full from Collins. Ashley has no such receipt but has a paper showing a balance due him from Collins; but Desha says that Ashley went through the form of selling some wild lands to Collins for some $20,000 and this he regards as a cloak in the settlement. This land he thinks is within the reach of the Government for Collins was known to have come to Little Rock poor. Chase alluded to his having made some money once, but did not explain in what way. I went yesterday and saw the District Attorney Foster who assured me, as did both Desha and Chase that I could do nothing myself here. Chase is now the administrator, Desha having resigned.

I passed the evening in company with Mrs. West and had music.

16th March. Below the Post of Arkansas. From the mouth of Arkansas River to the Post is about 50 miles, to Little Rock from the mouth 275; from Little Rock to Fort Smith (the border of the State) 300 miles; from Fort Smith to Gibson by water 75 miles (by land 58 miles).

When I left Little Rock I took a handful of old (new to me) newspapers which I have looked through to little purpose. Mr. Webster's letter to Mr. Everett on the subject of the Creole is the most important public item unless it be the debate or debates turning upon John Q. Adams and the memorial asking Congress to take measures for a peaceable dissolution of the Union.

Washington City, April, 5, 1842.

My Dear Mother;

I arrived here safely today from New Orleans, from which place I last wrote to you. I came by the way of Mobile, Montgomery, Augusta, Charleston, Wilmington, Norfolk, and Baltimore, with no incident of any particular importance.

I have been very well received by Mr. Spencer, the present Secy. of War, whom I never saw before. I have nothing to desire indeed on that point. My stay here is uncertain. The duties I had in the Southwest were various and I have not made reports except upon a few incidental points, and shall immediately set about my general report. How long it will occupy me I cannot say, but not long I suppose. I do not intend to make one long general report, but shall make special references to the several matters falling under my observation in the Southwest and at the conclusion shall make a reference to the several reports in place of making one long report. By this means I shall communicate all of the information I have obtained, without a set formality – like that of writing a book.

I intend to acquit myself very well, you may easily suppose. One thing is pretty certain – I shall arouse some violent hostility, but that I cannot help, as I must tell the truth as to my discoveries of fraud in the Indian Country.

Lord Ashburton arrived here last evening and is to be presented to the President tomorrow. He must be very uncomfortable, I fear, for I understand he has only 42 servants; how a Lord can manage his domestic affairs with that number exceeds my comprehension. Maybe he thought it politic, coming to a democratic country to be plain in his equipments and attendants &c.

I forget whether I told you I had been promoted. I am now the Lieut. Colonel of the 3d Regiment of Infantry, which is in the northern part of Florida, near Tallahassee.

Your affectionate son,
E. A. HITCHCOCK

Mrs. Lucy C. Hitchcock,
Burlington Vt.

Appendix

Tahlequah, Cherokee Nation, December 21, 1841.
Hon. J. C. Spencer, Secy of War, Sir;[123]

The Cherokee Council has adjourned amicably and the members have dispersed. Five persons including the principal chief, John Ross, have been appointed a delegation to proceed to Washington to negotiate a treaty. The delegation is composed of John Ross, Jesse Bushyhead, David Vann, Capt. Benge, and William Coudy. Jesse Bushyhead, between 35 and 40 years of age – resides near old Fort Wayne, is of mixed blood – the Chief Justice of the Nation – a regular Baptist preacher – speaks English fluently and is considered the best interpreter in the Nation. He is universally respected and beloved. His mere opinion in the Nation has great weight and his persuasion upon almost any subject can win the people to his views. He is a fair minded man and if he can be satisfied the Nation ought to acquiesce. If he is not satisfied, it may suggest a doubt whether some concessions may not be proper.

David Vann has been at Washington recently and is tolerably well known – resides near the Grand Saline on Grand River – is of mixed blood – speaks English – has less talent than Bushyhead and though an honest man is not so open, direct and fair and has far less weight of character, is the Treasurer of the Nation. He will be guided principally by the Principal Chief in whom he has unlimited confidence.

Captain Benge, was at Washington with the late delegation – is of mixed blood, over 45 years of age – speaks English – has less information than either of the others, but is a man of strong and decided character – of considerable sagacity. His influence in the nation is very great, but is mostly confined to the natives or full blood

---

[123] The letters in the appendix were discovered by the editor since the Hitchcock Journal went to press. This letter was found in the "Old Records Division" of the Adjutant General's Office of the War Department. It bears the endorsement "Lt. Col. Hitchcock; report on the condition of the Cherokees, and matters to be considered in the proposed negotiations with the Cherokee Delegation. Postmarked 'Park Hill, C. N. Dec. 31.' "

Cherokees. The united opinion of Bushyhead and Benge, will be entitled to great consideration, for it will be decisive with the nation, even against John Ross, though the latter of the two will be slow in dissenting from him.

Wm. Coudy [124] resides near Fort Gibson; is of mixed blood – is a young man – has been well educated – has a fine though slender person and graceful carriage with the best manners of our eastern cities. He is well known in the Nation, but is without influence from causes not necessary to mention. His talents, capacity for business, facility for writing etc. have given him a place in the delegation for the use and convenience of his seniors more than from expectation of benefit from his counsel.

I have said nothing of Jno. Ross the principal chief of the Nation, who will head the delegation. Much is said of him in the States, and like other conspicuous men he has been variously spoken of, in terms of great praise and great censure. He resides five miles from this place on a beautiful prairie in sight of Park Hill – is of mixed blood between 45 and 50 years of age – is under size and his manners, unless excited, have a dash of diffidence in them – is not of ready speech – speaks English principally and will not trust himself to address his own people in Cherokee – is a man of strong passions and settled purposes which he pursues with untiring zeal; is of undoubted courage unless it be that he fears the defeat of his plans more than the loss of life and would preserve the latter to execute the former. After much attentive observation I am of opinion that John Ross is an honest man and a patriot laboring for the good of his people. In the recent trouble of his nation, including several years, with almost unlimited opportunities he has not enriched himself. It is unfortunate for his reputation that several of his relatives, particularly his brother Lewis, have realized fortunes through his instrumentality, though it is fair to consider that this may have resulted from contracts properly made. It would be stranger if there was not ambition with the patriotism of Jno. Ross, but he seeks the fame of establishing his nation and heaping benefits upon his people. Though not a fluent speaker, even in conversation, he is a clear-minded accurate thinker of very far-reaching views.

---

[124] William Shorey Coodey was a distinguished member of the Cherokee tribe, of scholarly attainments. For an account of him see "A Cherokee Pioneer" by Carolyn Thomas Foreman, *Chronicles of Oklahoma*, (Oklahoma City) vol. VII, 364.

Among the demands that will be presented by the delegation for consideration at Washington are – an absolute fee simple title to this country; – the payment of losses incurred by the Cherokees when driven from their homes east of the Mississippi; and payment to the Nation for their old country.

The delegation will urge these with all their power. The people here look more particularly for indemnification for alleged losses, no doubt real to a considerable extent; but the delegation will regard the *title* as of most importance. It will be necessary for the commissioners who may confer with the delegation to be fully informed and instructed upon this subject. The claim for title will be pressed to the last extremity and some modification of the reservation in the New Echota treaty of '35, in view of the advanced stage of civilization among the Cherokees may be advantageous. As a part of their plan to procure a distinct and independent position, the delegation will desire the U. S. troops to be withdrawn from their nation. They will urge the corruptions introduced into their country mediately or immediately by the garrisons among them and they will aver that troops are not necessary for the preservation of peace or the enforcement of intercourse laws. On this subject I would remark, that so far as the Cherokees are concerned I should find but little difficulty in acceding to their views; but when the subject is regarded in connexion with the general policy and necessity for distributing troops within view of the more wild Indians and especially the necessity for traversing the country with armed men, there should be a decided negative put upon the wishes of the Cherokees in this respect. I would on no account abandon the right of establishing military posts in their country; but in exerting this right the Department may find the strongest reasons for considering the condition and progress of the Cherokees and rendering the presence of troops among them as little onerous as possible. The power to exercise this discretion ought not to be relinquished.

From my present impressions in regard to this country I should be glad to see an order for the immediate withdrawal of the troops from Fort Wayne and for the relinquishment of its site to the nation. Besides, that I do not think the post essential for military purposes, such an order would be regarded as an earnest of the disposition of the Department not to harrass the Cherokees by a needless military occupation of sites that have been previously selected as especially favorable for settlement by their people. The Cherokees may be excused for a feeling of uneasiness at the distribution of troops or posts in this country – with Forts Gibson and Wayne entirely within their country and Fort Smith on the border of it, when, excepting Fort Towson, their is no post among the Choctaws, Creeks, or Chickasaws.

On the subject of losses (of horses, cattle, and other miscellaneous property) the delegation will be prepared with some show of evidence taken by agents in the country here; but, without impugning the honesty of either the delegation or the agents, I am satisfied that the evidence will be of no value and an estimate only can be formed. I have endeavoured to obtain opinions from intelligent Cherokees on 'this subject and while all to whom I have spoken, admit that no satisfactory evidence can be procured of actual losses, no one has estimated the aggregate at a sum exceeding $600,000. I mention this because the claim when presented may very greatly exceed this sum. Whatever may be agreed upon should be distributed by the Cherokee Government upon principles to be determined by themselves. It will be impossible for U. S. agents to distinguish the claimants or ascertain the amounts due them and the attempt to do so would only create dissatisfaction.

The delegation will set forth that the Nation has not been paid for their old country; payment for their improvements and for the expenses of their emigration they will affirm is no payment for their country, assuming that this country in exchange is no adequate compensation. The amount appropriated for carrying into effect the New Echota treaty [125] has been nearly exhausted. The U. S. Commissioners will need to be well prepared for this. Without being thought obtrusive I hope I may express the opinion that the commissioners should assume the necessity for the removal of the Cherokees without discussing the causes for that necessity and then proceed in the manner of an arbitration, scarcely hoping *fully* to satisfy the delegation on this point. As a contracting party, entitled to demand what may satisfy their sense of justice and their fancy and at the same time compensate for alleged wrongs, etc. they will be in danger of exceeding all bounds of reason. On the simple principle of arbitration, the value of this country and the more permanent security and independence of the Cherokees can be fully taken into consideration. The delegation will not be in so good a situation to judge of this

[125] The New Echota Treaty, the fraudulently procured instrument under which Cherokee removal was enforced by the army, was signed on December 29, 1835.

matter as their posterity will enjoy. Their pride has been wounded and some of them and many of their people have suffered irreparable losses in their families attributable in their minds to their removal to this country. The wife and a sister of John Ross himself died at Little Rock on their way to this country and he has now several motherless children under his widowed roof.

The delegation will not, I think, recognize the New Echota treaty in any manner. This will be a matter of both pride and principle. The Cherokees have never recognized that treaty and in the preamble to their constitution they refer to their emigration to this country as compulsory under the "force of circumstances beyond their control." But the people of the country will expect all the benefits provided for them in that treaty to be continued, and particularly an amount for distribution per capita. They have been deluded into the expectation of a large sum under the anticipated distribution.

I do not see how U. S. Commissioners at Washington can meet the proffered evidence of *losses* that will be made, or investigate indeed any *exparte* statement of the delegation. I am therefore of opinion that Commissioners on the part of the United States should be sent here to meet the delegation, where any statement made by the latter, as to the condition, rights or wants of the people may be verified by actual observation. This will save the Cherokees the expense of sending a delegation to Washington.

I have heard Mr. Ross say that he supposed the delegation would be prepared to set off in March; so that if the Dept. should decide upon sending a commission here it will be necessary to act promptly.

I would remark that the contemplated treaty may have important consequences touching other tribes in the South West. There is a constant intercourse between the Cherokees, Creeks, Choctaws and Chickasaws and any extraordinary allowances in a Cherokee treaty would immediately become a subject of inquiry among the other tribes. Great care should therefore be taken not to awaken their cupidity and consequent discontent and jealousy. This can only be done by an adherence to the strict demands of justice. There are many reasons for paying as little money directly to the people as possible. I would suggest that as far as practicable, the amount which may be considered due to the Cherokees should be expended, if the parties can agree, in erecting a National Council house and in building Court houses etc. in the several districts. Some of their own people have expressed the opinion that a distribution of money among the people would not be a benefit; still, the "per capita" looked for under the New Echota treaty must be continued in any new treaty that may be made, for the reason, if for no other, that many of the people have traded upon the faith of its being paid and their due bills are held by the wealthy and influential in the nation.

I must ask your indulgence while I respectfully recommend that if a commission be sent here, it should be composed of three able men – men of sound judgement, capable of patient investigation and deliberation – of dignified personal deportment tempered with conciliating manners. A failure to make a suitable treaty on this occasion will of course place our relations with the Cherokees in a worse condition than if no assurances had been given like those contained in the letter of the President to the late delegation in Wash[n]. That letter has been published far and wide and copies of it sent to all parts of the Nation. It was undoubtedly conceived in a noble spirit and it needs only a commensurate execution to establish not merely present satisfaction but a permanently growing good which I almost dare to hope may realize the wishes of benevolent men among all portions of our own people.

I would add that in my opinion not any of the Indian Agents in this country should be appointed to negociate the treaty – not but that they may be competent men, but their official connection with the Indians renders it improper for them to be engaged in making a treaty the provisions of which they may be required to execute.

At the commencement of this letter I designed only to convey information of the fact that a delegation had been appointed to negociate a treaty; but having insensibly been led into more general statements I will add some further remarks which may possibly be of use, in case U. S. Commissioners shall not be sent here to observe the people and the country for themselves.

The Cherokees number about 18,000 men, women and children. Their country is divided into eight districts, 3 of which, embracing nearly two thirds of their whole population, are adjacent to the Arkansas line. They have a regular constitutional government, strictly republican. Their constitution and laws are printed in English. The people elect a Principal and a Second Chief for a term of four years; and each district elects five persons for a term of two years, two of whom are designated for a committee (answering to our Senate) and three for a council, or lower house. They assemble in October of each year at Tahlequah about 20 miles north east from

Fort Gibson, for the transaction of business. The forms of procedure are assimilated to those of our State Legislatures, and in their late session, under considerable excitement, the regular proceedings were not violated.

The debates are conducted in English or Cherokee at the pleasure of the member addressing the Speaker, but an interpretation follows in either case if desired by any member. The proceedings are recorded in English. There are Superior and Inferior Courts of justice established, with Clerks and sheriffs and their proceedings are recorded – the laws pointing out the cases for appeals. The few crimes known among them are defined and their punishments prescribed, and punishment is said to be almost certain in case of guilt. No criminal is allowed to escape from an informality in the indictment. This is a provision of the constitution itself and has resulted from the comparatively limited grammatical knowledge yet in the country. Theft is almost the only crime that disturbs the public and even this is of rare occurrence owing to the certainty of detection and punishment. The penalty of death is prescribed for murder, but other punishments are almost entirely inflicted with the lash, there being nothing like a penitentiary or even a jail in the country.

Marriage is solemnized by a magistrate or a clergyman. The certificate is duly recorded and the institution is regarded with great respect, its violation bringing upon the culprit punishment sometimes, and always entire loss of character. It was "recommended" by law in 1819 that Cherokees should have but one wife and the recommendation has been firmly established thru custom. Families distinct therefore; parents are respected and children provided for, the former almost universally anxious for the education of the latter. The desire for education is no doubt aided by the fact that among the Cherokees power, comparative wealth and prosperity are distinctly seen to follow the acquisition of knowledge, – a knowledge of reading, writing and arithmetic being certain of sharing in those rewards. The late Council passed a law for establishing eleven public schools under as many teachers at a salary of $500 each; two teachers are to be assigned to each of the three eastern districts and one to each of the remaining districts.

There is not, strictly speaking, a village in the Cherokee Nation, the people being scattered, each head of a family, for the most part, establishing a separate home, having a log house with an enclosure for raising corn etc. Many of these improvements embrace every com-

fort that can be enjoyed in a high stage of advancement in any country life. From the recent occupation of the country by a large portion
of the Cherokees, carpentry and masonry have not been extensively
used; but there are many houses though of logs, that are perfectly
comfortable; double, with a covered passage between them and a
porch front and rear; embracing a second story with floors, planed,
jointed and grooved supported upon dressed joists – with good doors,
with iron hinges and locks – glass windows with moveable sashes –
the interior of the house neatly white-washed and suitably supplied
with needful furniture; good bed-steds with beds; chairs, tables, and
bureaus, with clocks with brass movements; and what is more notice-
able than all these, the whole is kept in perfect order by a regular
system of habitual and unpretending daily industry. In many of these
houses the duties of the day are begun and closed with prayer to the
Universal Father, sometimes in English and sometimes in Cherokee,
with all the evidence of sincere piety that man can give. I have seen
one house furnished with elegantly wrought cane-bottom chairs,
mahogany sofas and rocking chairs, a splendid and rich-toned Chickering piano – ladies mahogany work table, etc.

On the other hand there is a large class who are familiarly spoken
of as "the poor," "the common people," "the ignorant people"; whose
means of living are scanty and who have been great sufferers in their
transition from the east, to the west of the Mississippi where they
have often wanted an axe when they have been compelled hastily to
construct a shelter from an approaching winter, and in the spring
have wanted the common article of a hoe with which to put a little
seed corn into the ground. In their former homes, though accustomed
to live with but few conveniences, they were not accustomed to live
altogether without them. The more wealthy have horses, cattle. hogs,
sheep and poultry and cultivate extensive fields of corn with pumpkins
etc., all of which are shared among the poor with a kindliness and
liberality that have not been learned from the whites. It was but
yesterday I heard of grain having been purposely left in the field for
gleaners, which strongly fixed my attention upon a familiar story in
the Old Testament.

The dress and general deportment of the prosperous correspond
very nearly to those of a white population. Shoes are almost universally in use; cloth coats and pantaloons are extensively worn, and hats
are common though many prefer a shawl turban in place of a hat or

a fancy handkerchief, neatly knotted, surrounding the brow. The common people wear leggings of dressed deer skins and sometimes coats of the same material, while some continue to wear the blanket as their principal covering. The women nearly all dress comfortably well and many would not be singled out in our cities for a departure from our customs or fashions. The merchants in the country inform me that their sales are chiefly *domestics* and that they sell scarcely any ornaments, these latter having been universally dispensed with, as have many of the customs of the "Old Nation." The "physic dance," formerly celebrated in the month of March, and the green-corn dance of September are no longer known in the nation and the race of Conjurers has disappeared almost as completely as the race of witches from Salem.

The Cherokee laws have made ardent spirits a contraband article. I was present during the greater part of the late session of the Council where several hundred Cherokees were engaged in business and I did not witness a single case of intoxication or disorder. On one occasion indications of the presence of liquor induced a search by authority and part of a barrel of whiskey was seized and broken open, and the contents wasted upon the ground.

It is generally known that the Cherokee has become a written language, through the invention of signs by "the philosopher Guess." This man is spoken of in the States as a native Cherokee. He is so by birth and speaks no English at all but his father was a white man said to be from Virginia, of the name of Gist, while his grand-father on the mother's side was a mixed blood Shawnee, his mother being a White-Shawnee-Cherokee mixed blood. He has an extremely interesting, intelligent countenance, full of cheerful animation with an evident vein of good humor – may be 55 or 60 years of age – habitually wears a shawl turban and dresses rudely, as if not caring for the outward man. His walk has been impaired by a rheumatic affection which has contracted one of his limbs. He has been a kind of Silver Smith among the natives and was early fond of exercising a talent for drawing pictures of men and horses and other animals. He invented the Syllabic signs in the "Old Country" and emigrated to this country in 1818. It is a remarkable fact that while engaged in inventing the signs for writing Cherokee he was ridiculed by some for his temerity, while many of the common people took alarm and became apprehensive that he was in league with the powers of darkness for the discovery of something that was to work great mischief to the nation; and nothing was wanting but the power, to make him renounce his discovery and desist from his labor.

I have not introduced this detail to add truisms, but to state that by means of the invention of Guess the Cherokees have been furnished with considerable reading in their native language, including translations of portions of scripture. The entire gospel of Matthew and John and several of Paul's Epistles; and they have a neat little volume of hymns in Cherokee, which they sing with remarkable skill and taste. It is known that in the Old Country (as they call their former country east of the Mississippi) they had a newspaper issued among them printed one half in English and one half in Cherokee.[126] I am informed that a Cherokee can learn to write his language in three days or even a less time. It is a polysyllabic language, each syllable being terminated by an open vowel sound. This latter peculiarity greatly limits the number of possible sounds, all of which Guess represented by 85 signs; and a knowledge of these will enable any one who can speak the Cherokee language, to write it. Though the Missionaries in the Country have been successful in converting many Cherokees to Christianity by the aid of the invention of Cherkee writing, they have failed to make an impression upon the inventor, who is not friendly to their cause.

I have made this detail perhaps of unreasonable length, but I design it to sustain in part the opinion I have formed and have now to express, that the Cherokees are not only indisposed to war against the United States, but they can only be driven into a war by the very last extremity of wrong that can be inflicted upon them. In this fact I trust will be found the strongest appeal that can be made to the sympathy of the United States, and I confidently hope that the noble sentiments of the President in his letter to the Cherokee delegation will be faithfully executed by a competent commission empowered to do these people "justice with liberality." Something is not only due to the Cherokees as a matter of right, but other considerations unite in recommending it as a measure of policy.

The Cherokees are scattered in isolated families in all parts of the nation. They have intelligence enough to know that a war would

---

126 This was the Cherokee Phoenix (Tsa-la-ge Tsi-le-hi-sa-ni-hi) published at New Echota, Georgia. The first issue appeared on Thursday, February 21, 1828; Elias Boudinot was the editor and Issac N. Harris the printer.

drive them from their homes to a mode of life in the woods which their acquired habits of civilized life would not permit them to sustain for three months – to say nothing of the entire absence from among them of magazines and stores of all kinds; and they have also intelligence enough to know that war could not be waged by a neighboring tribe, with the United States, without their being exposed in a greater or less degree to its dangers. Hence they must perceive a policy, in respect to themselves, in preventing other tribes from going to war, and it should be the policy of the United States to add to their motives to this end, an inspiration of the justice of the white man, whose civilization the Cherokee is struggling to emulate.

As I have already intimated there is a constantly increasing intercourse between the Cherokees, Creeks, Choctaws and Chickasaws. Several efforts have been made to establish general Councils among them extending even to other tribes, and these Councils, with more or less of regularity must mark the future history of these people. It is impossible to question for a single moment the ascendency of the Cherokees in these assemblages, and therefore the Government of the United States has only to furnish the proper motives to these people and the peace and quiet of this whole region will be perfectly secured.

To this end, it is only necessary for the government to show a willingness to do them justice by acknowledging and satisfying such reasonable claims as they may present.

In 1839, at a general council within five miles of this place no less than *eleven* tribes were represented. A belt of wampum was acknowledged as a symbol of general peace; and a Cherokee, the then second chief of the nation was elected to preserve the belt and empowered, whenever he might deem it necessary, to call another Council. Another Cherokee, who is now the President of the National Committee, was elected to be the head War Chief of all the warriors of those tribes, while a third Cherokee had been elected a *Speaker,* through whom all addresses to the Council were made. A speech or talk was interpreted by eleven interpreters, one interpretation being into English. By whom that Council was called I do not know, but even if called by the Cherokees themselves, the fact would not alter the aspect of its proceedings in respect to the United States. The ascendency of the Cherokees may be equally seen, whoever called the Council. I am very far from regarding the prospect of these general councils as a source of danger to the peace of the United

States, but directly the reverse. If all the Indians in this quarter were in the condition of the Osages or of the Sac's and Fox's, such councils might possibly prepare the way for spasmodic efforts of a threatening character against the white settlements, under the influence of some real or imagined wrong; but such a result is not to be anticipated when the Councils shall fall under the influence of the Cherokees in their present advanced intelligence and still less if these people can be made to feel that justice will be accorded to them by the United States.

The question has been very much discussed among us as to whether it be possible to civilize the native American. If the present condition of the Cherokees could be safely attributed to an inherent capacity or capability in these people I should at once assume the affirmative of the question and would aver that the condition and character of a considerable number of the Cherokees would put to the blush a large number of our own people. They have among them many well informed, sensible, orderly industrious and pious people, regardful of everything that contributes to domestic peace, happiness and prosperity, and they exhibit fruits accordingly. But from a very early period the Cherokee Nation seems to have been accessible to white men who from various causes moved among them, married and lived among them,[127] and their posterity is now seen in the enjoyment of most of the power and influence in the Nation. Some were brought in by Agents of the U. S. Govt. under contracts for executing treaty stipulations and some for aught I know, may have fled from the violated laws of the States and sought a refuge among the Cherokees. Both of these causes are still in operation and the latter is regarded as a great evil to be remedied in the anticipated treaty.

However the whites originally came into the country, their sons and their sons' sons born among the Cherokees of Cherokee blood have no sympathy with the whites but are devoted in their attachment to the country of their birth. Their number has become so

---

[127] As far back as 1809 half of the total Cherokee population of 12,395 souls were of mixed blood. Besides these there were then in the Cherokee Nation 583 negro slaves and 341 whites. By 1820 the number had increased to 14,500 (Jedidiah Morse, *Report to the Secretary of War of the United States on Indian Affairs; a tour performed in the summer of 1820, under a commission from President of the United States for the purpose of ascertaining for the use of the Government the actual state of Indian tribes in our country, appendix,* 152.

great and they are so completely identified with the natives that if any man could conceive the desire to separate them from those of full blood (Cherokees), it would be impossible to succeed, and hence these people must be met and treated with according to their present actual condition.

I have the honor to be With the highest respect Your obt. Servt. E. A. Hitchcock Maj. 8″ Infy. Spl. Comm.

Fort Wayne Cherokee Nation, January 9, 1842.
Hon. J. C. Spencer, Secy. of War, Sir:[128] In my communication of the 21″ ult I expressed an opinion in favor of the abandonment of this post by the withdrawal of the U. S. troops. My visit here has confirmed the opinion I then expressed, and I would respectfully suggest a few considerations upon the subject.

The first object in establishing Military Posts on the frontier is the preservation of peace – checking and overawing such Indians as may be disposed to commit depredations within the white settlements.

The second object, incidental to the first, is the occupation of such sites as may keep open a communication between the several posts along the frontier.

I remark in the first place, that the Cherokees along this frontier have not the slightest disposition to commit depredations upon the white settlements in Arkansas. They have their own farming improvements as well established as their neighbors, and they understand their true interests too well to jeopardise their safety by committing outrages over the Arkansas line. The Cherokees have justly complained that a Military force has been unnecessarily established in one of the finest portions of their country – in the midst of an orderly industrious and sober community – bringing with ·it a train of evils before comparatively unknown – exposing their women to seduction and even to violence and inviting the location of dram shops immediately upon the State line opposite the post. (The intercourse Act and the Cherokee laws forbid the introduction of whiskey into the Nation). At one of these shops only a few months ago, two Cherokees were murdered by some soldiers, whose trial and acquittal have in no manner removed the impression entertained by every body

---

[128] Adjutant General's Office, Old Records Division, War Department Files. Hitchcock's copy of this letter is to be seen in the Hitchcock Manuscript Collection in the Library of Congress.

that the soldiers were the guilty party. The presence of a garrison here has thus made and not found excitement and difficulty, and its continuance here will not have the slightest influence in preventing outrage in future, but is calculated to invite it. Every disorder on the Arkansas line, from the character and condition of the population, must be local and isolated – as much so as between Missouri and Arkansas; and in every case hitherto the perpetrators have fallen into the hands of the law and have been dealt with by the law – the death of Ridge and Bondinot only excepted, which was purely a Cherokee affair, not likely to occur again; and even in that case the troops were as powerless as the law.

Fort Wayne is not necessary, in the second place, as a point in the communication by troops along this frontier. It is but 80 miles north of Fort Smith (at the entrance of the Arkansas river into the State). Hence to Fort Leavenworth on the Missouri is 215 miles on the whole of which route there is no post. I know that two or three points on this route have been designated for posts in accordance with a theory,[129] which will never be carried into practice, proposing a line of Military posts from Louisiana to Lake Superior, west of the States. Independent of the expense of establishing such a line of posts, the Military peace establishment of the United States will not allow of their occupation by garrisons of sufficient strength to preserve respectability: In small stationary garrisons the tendency is constantly to a relaxation of discipline, neglect and ignorance of drill and other regular duties, followed by loose morality until reputation is preserved chiefly by their being removed from observation. Distant, small, isolated garrisons, long continued at one post have swallowed up more youthful genius, intelligence and general capability than your Department or the country has any knowledge of. It requires some boldness, perhaps, to speak the truth on this subject, but I am not here to communicate complimentary delusions.

---

[129] Legislation had provided for establishing military posts along the western frontier on a road to be run from Baton Rouge, Fort Jesup, Fort Towson, Fort Coffee, and northward along the western line of Arkansas and Missouri to Fort Leavenworth and extending on to the upper Mississippi River. This action resulted in part from hostilities among the southwestern Indians and anticipated complications growing out of the warfare between Texas and Mexico; but it was largely due to the influence of the new state of Arkansas interested for commercial purposes in bringing back to the western border of that state the garrison that had abandoned Fort Smith to establish Fort Gibson.

In view of all the facts upon the subject under consideration I respectfully recommend the abandonment of this place and the establishment of a post in what has been called the neutral ground (now belonging to the Cherokees) between the Osage Indians and the State of Missouri – at some point about 100 miles south of Fort Leavenworth; perhaps near where the Military road crosses the Marmiton would be a good site.

By a glance at the map prepared in the Indian Bureau, you will perceive that the Indians from South to North range in the following order – Choctaws, Cherokees, Senecas, Quapaws – then the Neutral ground for about 50 miles along the Missouri line, west of which are the Osages; above the Neutral ground are a number of small tribes which have never, since their emigration, given any trouble – as Piankeshaws, Weas, Kaskaskias, Peorias, Delawares and Shawnees; The Pottawotomies, one portion of them, are near, are more numerous and feel less friendly. Of these Indians, the Choctaws have never Killed a white man in war and are proud of it; the Cherokees, next in order, without questioning their bravery, have too much intelligence to disturb the peace even under great wrongs inflicted by the whites – while a satisfaction by the Govt. of the U. S. of their just claims will make them all-powerful in preserving the peace of the entire South West. The Senecas and Quapaws are perfectly harmless.

West of the Neutral ground are the Osages, the greatest thieves near the frontier and who have committed more depredations in Missouri than all the other Indians together along the whole line of the two States of Arkansas and Missouri. These are the Indians, and not the Cherokees that require to be over-awed by the presence of a Military force. North of the Osages are the Pottawotomies who are rather a dissatisfied people and are more likely to enter into a hostile combination than any other Indians.

A post on the neutral ground would be at all times ready to chastise Osage marauders and by thus protecting the people of Missouri prevent a border difficulty which has several times been on the point of breaking out. An undisciplined militia has repeatedly been on the point of carrying blood shed among the Osages for thefts committed by them when rendered almost desperate by starvation.[130]

[130] In the autumn of 1837 a body of armed militia of Missouri commanded by S. D. Lucas undertook to drive from their homes about 300 Osage who had long lived in Southwestern Missouri and others who had crossed the line; the Osage had been killing the hogs belonging to the

A post on the neutral ground would also be in a favorable position to act in concert if necessary, with troops from Ft. Leavenworth upon the Pottawotomies without exciting them by being permanently among them. Such a post could be supplied or supply itself as readily as this of Fort Wayne. The Creeks do not inhabit east of Fort Gibson and are more than fifty miles west of the State of Arkansas, as are also the Seminoles. Fort Gibson is admirably located with respect to those Indians.

When the abandonment of Fort Wayne is mentioned I have generally heard it suggested that the Govt. has expended a considerable sum of money in its establishment; but this does not approach the dignity of an argument for its continuance.

If it is useless in itself, it cannot be made to appear otherwise by alleging its cost to the Govt. Besides, the value of the erections here is not to be estimated by their cost, and in my opinion the whole had better be burned than the post continued. The Saw Mill, 15 or 18 miles from the post, might be sold, or it might be given to the Cherokee Govt. in the anticipated treaty: that Govt. might lease it for a revenue, or sell it. The unfinished building here might be sold and the moveable property conveyed to Fort Gibson. There is one frame building, and one only, weather-boarded and covered for use – there are the frames of three others erected and one other frame ready for raising. These will not be entirely sacrificed by a sale or if they are the loss will be nothing in comparison to the evil of maintaining troops at this point. The temporary huts in which the officers and men are quartered have only given the troops an appropriate exercise in building them and will do no harm by being left on the spot.

I have the honor to be Very Respectfully Yo: Obt, Servt, E A Hitchcock Maj. 8 Infy Spl. Comm.

Fort Smith, Arkansas, March 7, 1842, Hon. J. C. Spencer, Secy. of War, Sir:[131] I have the honor to report that in my recent visit to

---

whites to keep their families from starving. Troops sent out from Fort Leavenworth arrested this movement and restored the Indians to their homes. Much excitement and some bloodshed resulted from this and similar disturbances.

[131] This and the following letters are from copies of the originals made by Colonel Hitchcock, now in the Hitchcock Manuscript Collection in the Library of Congress. The original of the next letter, that of March 8, together with the enclosure is in the Office of Indian Affairs, "Chickasaw Emigration File H 1003."

the Chickasaw Indians I heard very great complaint of the purchases made by traders of the claims of Indians deemed incompetent to manage their own business under the 4th article of the treaty of 1834. The transaction has been characterized with very severe expressions, which it is not my purpose to repeat, but I shall furnish such facts as have come to my knowledge.

While I was on Blue river, some 90 miles northwest of Fort Towson, a white man returned from a store at Boggy, to the house where I was, with some very inferior tobacco, saying he had purchased it by the pound at $2 of brandon money. I did not think the tobacco worth, even there, 50 cts. a pound. I do not indeed use the article but am nevertheless something of a judge of it. Upon asking an explanation what was meant by brandon money some due bills were shown to me one of which the following is a correct copy.

> "Four dollars in goods"
> "1111 charged S & Lewis"
> (Signed) "A. P. Shelden."

This is a true copy & the writing exhibits also the size of the small slip of paper on which the due bill was written. There was no date upon the paper – it is not stated to whom the money is due, the initial only of one of the firm is stated and the whole has no other voucher than the signature of a clerk.

It was stated to me that when one of these due bills was presented for payment a deduction of 50 per cent was first made and the goods beside – were sold at double price. I have accurate information that over $8000 of due bills are in circulation and they are familiarly called brandon bills and pass at half their nominal value. The reason assigned for this by the merchants is that they expect to obtain stock at a depreciation for the claims of incompetent Indians purchased by them & for which they have given due bills.

In another part of the nation I saw a principal chief, Capt. Greenwood, who complained formally of the traders for their proceedings in relation to the incompetent Indians, so called, accusing one of the commissioners who sanctioned the proceedings of participating in the purchase of the claims. On this occasion another due bill was exhibited to me for $12 on which $11 had been paid. The orthography & chirography of this due bill were so careless & unworthy of the importance of the business it represented that I purchased the due bill for 50 cts. and enclose it herewith that it may speak for itself.

It appears that the merchants first purchase the claim of an incompetent Indian and give a receipt for it in some form. I have not been able to see any such receipt but am informed that a number of crosses (X) are marked on the back representing ten dollars each. These are erased from time to time by the merchant in discharge of debts or when transfer is made and in this latter case the due bills above described are issued. An incompetent Indian for instance buys a horse from another Indian: the two parties go to the trader who erases from the back of the receipt the price agreed to be paid for the horse, giving the seller due bills for it in such sums as may suit his convenience. When the due bills are presented for payment they are paid as above stated. It is difficult in a condensed form to give any adequate idea of what I have heard on this subject.

It appears that the traders brought the incompetent Indians [132] in debt and then adopted the plan of buying their claims on a speculation to reimburse themselves. To silence the opposition of others having claims, they are said to have assumed the obligations of the indebted Indians, but with an agreement to pay but 50 cts. on the dollar & that in goods.

The 4th art. of the treaty of 1834 requires that the fund of incompetent Indians shall remain as part of the general Chickasaw fund in the hands of the government, until such time as the chiefs in council shall think it advisable to pay it to the claimant, or to those who may rightfully claim under said claimant, and shall so recommend it.

How far this recommendation of the treaty has been complied with I am not informed but I desire to remark that before any payment is obligatory on the part of the U. S. the chiefs referred to in the treaty, *Seven* in number, must recommend it in council – and they

---

[132] In the negotiation of their treaty of 1834 the Chickasaw Indians exhibited a degree of caution and good judgment never excelled by any other Indians. Article four of that treaty provides: "The Chickasaws desire to have within their own direction and control, the means of taking care of themselves. Many of their people are quite competent to manage their affairs, though some are not capable, and might be imposed upon by designing persons; it is therefore agreed that the reservations hereinafter admitted, shall not be permitted to be sold, leased, or disposed of unless it appear by the certificate of at least two of the following persons, to wit: Ish-ta-ho-ta-pa the King, Levi Colbert, George Colbert, Martin Colbert, Isaac Alberson, Henry Love, and Benj. Love, of which five have affixed their names to this treaty, that the party owning or claiming the same, is capable to manage, and to take care of his or her affairs."— Kappler, Charles J., *Indian Affairs, Laws and Treaties*, vol. II, p. 310.

can only recommend its payment to the Incompetent Indians themselves or to those who may *rightfully* claim *under them.*

It may be doubted whether the original intention of the parties in using these words did not point to a right by inheritance, and not a right acquired by purchase; but whether this be the case or not the claim must be of right, to be *judged* of by the U. S. Hence I conceive that if the traders have purchased those claims irregularly and to the prejudice of the Indians, they are not rightfully possessed of them and the order of the chiefs in their favor is no sufficient authority to pay the money.

The mode of transacting the business does not express the facts in the case and if not a fraud upon the Indians who may know the manner by which it has been done, it is a cheat upon the government unless the facts have been fully explained. Whether they have been or not I do not know.

The due bills are in circulation all over the nation and constitute the circulating medium. A bushel of corn meal is bought on Blue river for $4 in due bills when a dollar & a half or two dollars in specie will make the same purchase. I was told that $10 of them have been paid for a bottle of whiskey and as high as $150 for a horse not worth over $30.

I enclose with this letter an original letter from the Chickasaw, Pitman Colbert, an intelligent half breed residing on Red river, where he cultivates cotton exclusively, having made 100 bales of cotton last. year. The tone and manner of the letter are well calculated to arrest attention & to suggest a doubt whether the traders are not now realizing the opinion expressed by the Chickasaws in the 7 art of the treaty of 1816.

I cannot close this letter without expressing my belief that great numbers of persons are interested in fleecing the incompetent Indians – by trading with them and obtaining due bills whose payment depends, they may suppose, upon the sanction of the govt., to the sale of the claims.

The Chickasaws or very many of them are in a deplorable condition as I shall represent in another report – resulting as I conceive in no small degree by the action of the traders in the country who, however, claim to have relieved the distress they have principally occasioned.

If the Chickasaws had been left to themselves they would by this time have had their houses erected ·and fields under cultivation; but the traders have fostered their habits of idleness & dependence and continued if they have not absolutely created the want they allege they have relieved. This is their ground of appeal to the government, but I regard it as an illusion. Where they have sold a dollars worth of bacon they have sold articles of merchandise not wanted by the Indian for many times that amount. They urge the sale of the bacon but say nothing of the ponies &c &c. they have sold if selling it can be called to charge from two to five times the worth of the article.

It will certainly appear very extraordinary that the portion of Indians over whom the Govt. assumed a guardianship should be precisely those fixed upon for a sacrifice.

E. A.`H.

(Enclosure)   Letter to H. from Pitman Colbert.

"Near Doaksville March 1st, 1842," says that at the request of "Chief Capt. Greenwood or Ishteemolitea, I call in at David Folsom to inform you that he would call to see you but you had left, however I understand you have stopt at the chiefs, consequently I hope you will learn how shamefully the Chickasaws have been use up by the speculators, particularly the Incompetent Indians. . . . The Chickasaws have not a friend of a white man in this country. If they have they are fread to speak & demonstrate to the Government."

Fort Smith, Arkansas, March 8, 1842.
Hon. J. C. Spencer, Secy. of War.   Sir:

I have the honor to report that recently while in the neighborhood of the blue and boggy rivers in the Chickasaw district of the Choctaw Nation I fell in company with Mr. R. J. Humphreys, an intelligent white man, who married a daughter of John McClish a Chickasaw half-breed now deceased. Mr. Humphrey has in his possession a memorandum book kept by his father-in-law during the emigration of himself and family in 1837 to this country, exhibiting a number of particulars whose authenticity cannot be doubted by any one who has access to the book.

Mr. McClish had the immediate charge of a portion of Chickasaws who were conveyed from Memphis to Fort Coffee in the Steamboat *Fox*, under the contract of Mr. Buckner. The book notes the day of departure from Memphis 14th of Nov. 1837 and day of arrival at Fort Coffee on Tuesday 21st and contains a list of the names of the heads of families under the charge of McClish, exhibiting also the number of wagons, oxen and horses belonging to each head of family and stating the number of persons in each family. The book notes also the whole number of passengers that were conveyed in the boat at 260.

From the note book referred to there were 106 persons under the immediate care of McClish with 10 wagons, 28 oxen and 22 horses. The names of the heads of families as stated in the note book (and which also appear on a separate paper purporting to be an a/c by McClish) are John McClish, James Perry, Geo. Colbert, Mrs. Frazier, James N. McClish, R. J. Humphreys and Mimy Colbert.

Mr. Humphreys stated to me from recollection and with apparent reliance upon his memory that in addition to those persons, there were on board of the *Fox* other heads of families with wagons &c.; as McClure (two wagons), Bynum two, Kemp one, & Chegels one. He states that some of the wagons were ox wagons carrying but small loads – that he had not over one thousand pounds in his own wagon. He states that the whole of the baggage on board of the boat was conveyed by the 16 wagons (including the 10 noted by McClish) and a few packed horses – that perhaps half of the wagons were themselves conveyed by the boat (the others going by land from Memphis, as did the horses and oxen) and taking the whole of the baggage together he is willing to be qualified to the opinion that there was not exceeding twenty tons on board of the *Fox*.

I next fell in with Mr. Guy residing on Boggy, who was the Government Conductor of the party on board of the boat, and had a remarkable statement from him to this effect: that on arriving at Fort Coffee the captain of the boat, on behalf of Mr. Buckner desired him to certify to 125 tons of baggage; failing to obtain that, he said he *must* have a certificate for 100 tons – but the conductor finally gave him by *estimate* a certificate for 75 tons admitting to me that he believed it was more than there was on board of the boat, but that he had no means of weighing it. If the evidence in this matter is not sufficient for a Court of Justice, it would be quite sufficient to satisfy any man of common sense that Buckner was paid for the transportation of twice if not three times as much baggage as there was on board of the boat.

This view will fully bear out the very clear and judicious report of the Commr. of Indian Affairs adverse to the claim of Mr. Buckner for some $37,000, which was nevertheless unfortunately allowed him in 1840.

In connection with this subject I enclose herewith a statement made to me in writing by another conductor of Chickasaws, Mr. R. B. Crockett, who now resides at Webbers Falls near the mouth of Canadian river.

I have the honor to be Very Respectfully Yo. Obt. Servt. E. A. Hitchcock Maj. 9 Inf. Spl. Comm.

Camp Holmes, Little River, Creek Nation Feb. 11th 1842.

In January 1838 I was in charge of a party of Emigrating Chickasaw Indians of about one hundred and fifty and I made an arrangement with Capt. Boyd, Master of the Steamer *Itaska*, for the transportation of the Indians, their stock and baggage, to the Post of Arkansas and thence to Little Rock for as many of the Indians as might be disposed to go. The Steam Boat *Itaska* was one of the boats employed under the Buckner Contract for transporting Chickasaws. It was expressly agreed between the captain and myself that he was to be paid for the transportation of Indians from the Post of Arkansas to Little Rock, but only for so many as should actually be transported by him.

On our arrival at the Post of Arkansas, most of the Indians determined to take to the land, and there were only about fifteen transported to Little Rock in the Steam Boat. I am not sure of the number. When I arrived at Little Rock I met with Capt. Buckner, who became very polite and friendly in his manner towards me — taking me familiarly by the arm and asking me to drink, and then he suggested to me that my certificate of the number of the Indians that have been transported from the Post of Arkansas to Little Rock required some correction — that I ought to have given a certificate for as many as I had *wished* should travel by water, meaning the whole of the party except a few to drive stock. I told him I had given a correct certificate according to my agreement with Captain Boyd, and that I could not alter it. He stated that Capt. Boyd had told him that the agreement was that he was to bring ail of the Indians except a few to drive the Stock, and he appeared exceedingly anxious to get me to alter the Certificate until I told him plainly that I would not alter it.

At the time I left the Boat, as I did with most of the Indians at the Post of Arkansas, I had some controversy with Capt. Boyd about the baggage of the Indians. He was not satisfied with the Certificate of the quantity I was willing to give him, and he wished me to Certify to a much larger amount, saying that Mr. Roach, who had been with him with another party of Chickasaws, had certified to more than he had wished me to certify to, when Capt. Boyd said that he, Mr. Roach, had not half as much as I had with my party. I had no means of weighing the baggage and do not remember what amount I certified for; but I gave as liberal a certificate as I felt justified in doing – refusing to accede to the wishes of the Captain.

In the Contract with Capt. Buckner I did not understand that it was agreed to transport any stock at all, and therefore, when I arranged with Capt. Boyd for the transportation of the Stock of my party of Chickasaws, I refused to make any terms other than that it should be left with Col. Upshaw and Capt. Philips U. S. Agents, to make what settlement they pleased for it.

I certified to the number of horses &c but I never knew what settlement was made for it. R. B. Crockett.

New Orleans, La., March 20, 1842.
Hon. J. C. Spencer, Secy. of War. Sir:

Having heard on my arrival here yesterday of the invasion of Texas by the Mexicans, I make without further delay the following report of a state of things in the western part of the Cherokee Nation from which it will be seen that there is some reason to apprehend that several fragmentary tribes in that quarter may enter Texas with hostile purposes, if they have not already done so.

While I was in the Creek Nation and about to go to the Che-ne-hatche (or Little river about one hundred miles west of Fort Gibson) it was mysteriously intimated to me by an old Creek Indian without explanation that I "might hear something" in that direction. I travelled a circuit of several hundred miles, hearing nothing very definite, but concluding from a number of circumstances that certain Indians of the Cherokee, Shawnee & Delaware tribes had been in council on the subject of a war upon Texas.

A friendly Choctaw Indian gave a warning to an officer of Fort Towson a few days before my arrival at that post (mistaking the object of those Indians) intimating the existence of a design to go to war with the U. S.

I placed no reliance upon that story but made indirect inquiries on my route to Fort Smith and at one place had very unequivocal evidence that some evil purposes towards Texas had been agitated; on one occasion an inquiry was made of me as to whether the U. S. would interfere in such a case.

In the western part of the Creek and Choctaw Nations, there are several fragments of different tribes of Indians not properly belonging there – as Cherokees, Shawnees, Delawares, Kickapoos, Quapaws, and Piankashaws. Nearly all of them are on the Canadian extending some 60 miles above the mouth of Little River. The following facts will serve to explain the source of the hostility of some of these Indians towards Texas.

Many years ago, perhaps as far back as 1815 a Cherokee chief, Bowles, became dissatisfied in the Cherokee Nation and voluntarily emigrated to the West with a number of followers. He remained but a short time north of Red river. About 1818 he took possession of a tract of country in Texas north of Nacogdoches some 60 by 30 miles in extent. For this section of country Bowles procured a regular patent from the Mexican government – a fact not generally known; but I saw an intelligent white man who assured me he had seen the patent and that it was brought from Mexico by Col. Austin himself for Bowles. Subsequent emigrations from the Cherokee nation strengthened Bowles and besides Cherokees some Delawares & more Shawnees had wandered down into Texas and were living there when Texas declared independence. In the brief struggles that ensued with the Mexican forces Bowles took no part though it has been said he had a commission from the Mexican government. If he ever had such a commission he never used it and it must have been received as a stroke of policy by which to protect himself, a weaker party, from being destroyed.

After the battle of San Jacinto the Texans sought to remove the Indians by negotiation but failed, and a war broke out which resulted in the death of Bowles & the expulsion of all the Indians who crossed the Red river and for a time were scattered, between Red river and the Arkansas on the waters of Boggy, Blue and False Waschita rivers.

The Choctaws were not satisfied with their living within the limits of their country and ordered them out of it. When most of them excepting the immediate followers of Bowles (the Cherokees) moved to the Canadian above Little river where they have been permitted to settle by the Creeks. I could not learn the number of the Cherokees with certainty, but heard them estimated as high as 1500 men, women & children. They are living near the head-waters of the Blue, south of the Canadian and have resisted the pressing invitation of the Cherokee government proper to return to their friends in that nation, north of the Arkansas. They were represented as very much embittered against the Texans and it is quite probable that a number of Shawnees participate in that feeling.

The Shawnees, about 700 in number, are scattered along the Canadian on both sides of the river above the mouth of Little river. Some of these Indians have never lived in the country allotted to the Shawnee tribe, west of the State of Missouri, but wandered to the Southwest after the death of Tecumseh and the defeat of the coalition formed by him.

There are about 700 Delawares residing some 60 miles above the mouth of Little river, who with the Shawnees have carried on an extensive intercourse with the wild Indians still more west. Through these Indians the Comanches have received ammunition & other supplies in the way of trade, which have assisted them in prosecuting their predatory excursions among the white settlements in Texas.

About 15 miles up the Canadian from the mouth of Little river there are about 1500 Kickapoos living in a body with Shawnees above and below them. The Shawnees, Delawares & Kickapoos all cultivate to some extent – the Kickapoos more particularly – and all of them are permitted to live in the Creek Nation, by the Creek Chiefs, no doubt as a measure of policy to increase their own strength.

There are some 500 or 600 Piankashaws domesticated among the Creeks, living about 15 miles up Little river from its mouth. These were allowed last year by the Creek Chiefs $120 of their annuity and are regarded as a part of the Creek Nation – their chiefs attending the Creek general councils.

The Creeks are also very friendly with a village of some 250 Quapaws residing up the Canadian 8 miles from Little river. The Quapaws & Piankashaws both cultivate and will not be seduced into war.

Besides the Comanches in the Southwest who are at open war with the Texans, there are other wild tribes in that direction engaged in war; as the Wako, Witchita, Towaash & other tribes, some of whom are doubtless living within the limits of the U. S. – and of all the wild Indians it may be said they neither know nor care about a boundary in the establishment of which they have never been parties.

From the nature of the war carried on by those tribes, it was my intention to make a special report of a plan for quieting the whole country as a duty of humanity independent of any existing treaty obligations; and I would at the same time respectfully press the adoption of some steps for this purpose, not because the Texans are at war with the Mexicans for I do not undertake to judge of the international claims of either party, but because it is regarded as a general duty of all civilized states to prevent a savage war whenever it be possible to do so.

While I was on Blue river 70 miles south of the Canadian, I saw a respectable white man who related a shocking story showing the nature of the war made by the Comanches against the people of Texas. A party of those Indians killed the owner of a plantation and then scalped their victim before the face of his wife and dragged her by the hair of her head twice around the house, denuded her, & carried her and her three children into captivity in the great prairies where a Delaware Indian named Shaw, purchased her for goods to the amount of $150 and carried her to Blue river. An exposure of a fortnight to a burning August sun without clothing had scarified her body from head to foot in which condition she was received by the kind and humane man who related the circumstances to me, and who was instrumental in purchasing after hard efforts the surviving children, an infant having died — and the mother and her two children were restored to their friends, respectable planters on Red river.

Outrages of this character committed within Texas by Indians who may rove, if they do not reside within the U. S., have produced acts of retaliation and armed Texans have crossed Red river and committed acts of violence that have alarmed the quiet and peaceable Choctaws & Chickasaws, who availed themselves of the opportunity of my presence among them to express their hope that the government would interpose for their protection.

As a preparatory step, I would respectfully suggest that the Indian agents for the Creeks, Choctaws & Chickasaws be directed to warn the Indians within their respective agencies to abstain from acts of aggression in Texas; and I would direct through Gen. Taylor a movement of troops from Fort Towson as far as the False Waschitta with orders to the offr. commanding to give a similar warning at the head of his command under suitable conditional instructions. There are three companies of the 2d. Dragoons at Fort Towson and the grass in the country will furnish forage for their horses.

On my arrival in Washington I shall have the honor to make a further communication upon this subject.

Very Respectfully, Your obt. Servt., E. A. Hitchcock.

Washington City, April 29, 1842.

Hon. J. C. Spencer, Secy. of War. Sir:

I respectfully invite your especial attention to the condition of the Chickasaw Indians as exhibited to me in my late visit to that tribe.

By the treaty of 1834 this tribe agreed to emigrate west of the Mississippi and the government of the U. S. assumed the agency of selling their lands east of the Mississippi (excepting certain specified reservations) & becoming trustee of the proceeds after paying certain expenses. Large sums of money have been received by the government and heavy expenses on account of the tribe have been paid.

In the mean time the Indians have emigrated, and in their new country under the delusive expectation of wealth from their trust fund they have been exposed to a double evil. Their reliance upon their trust fund [133] for money has induced a general neglect of industry and has resulted in a dependence upon external resources. This has thrown the inconsiderate, far the greater portion of the tribe, into the hands of creditors who on their part having also looked to the prospective wealth of the tribe, have willingly brought them into debt.

No annuities having been paid, the creditors are gradually stripping the thoughtless of everything which constitutes an Indian's wealth; even, as was represented to me, to their very rifles in some instances. Their cattle and hogs are mostly used up – they have cultivated but little corn and while they are reputed to be the most wealthy of all the southwest Indians, they are absolutely in the very worst condition, almost grovelling in poverty and wretchedness.

They have purchased a residence in the Choctaw country for $530,000, the interest of which is regularly paid to the Choctaws, amounting to more than the Choctaws receive in the shape of annuity for the sale of all their lands east of the Mississippi. While this is paid from their funds year after year before their eyes, the Chickasaws find themselves destitute of every comfort they have formerly enjoyed; and by a misunderstanding on the part of most of the tribe they have become subordinate to the Choctaw government, a government utterly foreign to their habits and offensive to their national pride. They feel as if they had purchased themselves into degradation. They have not the general intelligence of the Choc-

[133] This trust fund held by the Government was considerable, as near four million dollars was realized from the sale of the Chickasaw lands.

taws – are more attached to their ancient customs (the life-blood of the wild Indian) and feel humiliated and broken-spirited under the operations of a government which they are told they *share* with the Choctaws.

There is no apparent remedy but time and increasing intelligence for removing their sense of subjection to the Choctaws, but I am induced to hope that by some appropriate action of Congress, a portion of the evils under which they are suffering may be alleviated by anticipating their prospective claims upon their trust fund; and that something in the shape of annuity may be paid to them the present year. Above all it is important that the payment to them should be uniform one year with another and punctually made.

E. A. H., Lt. Col. 3d. Infy. &c.

Washington City, April 30th, 1842.

Hon. J. C. Spencer, Secy. of War.   Sir:

It is my duty to report the opinions and wishes of the Indians in the Southwest on the subject of the funds set apart in various treaties for purposes of education and under the control of the government. On one point I found but one sentiment, and that was a most decided opposition to the establishment or continuance of Indian schools beyond the limits of the Indian country.

This opposition might be regarded as of less importance were it not for some of the reasons given for it, one of the most prominent of which is a general complaint of the habits with which most of the young Indian lads return from those schools to their homes.

They are said to return with almost every bad habit that can be named – gambling and drinking included and yet not the worst in their estimation.

I heard this complaint especially among the Creeks and among the Choctaws. A Creek chief, from the conduct of a son educated in Kentucky,[134] had imbibed the deepest prejudice against all education as the source of every enormity under the sun. A more intelligent Choctaw mourning over the destruction of a favorite son, was sure the fault was in the school or its location out of the nation and not in the fact that an attempt had been made to educate his son.

---

[134] Choctaw Academy in Scott County, Kentucky, was established by Richard M. Johnson, afterward Vice President of the United States. For an account of this Indian school see "The Choctaw Academy" by Carolyn Thomas Foreman, *Chronicles of Oklahoma,* (Oklahoma City) Vol. VI. 453.

It was also a general remark among the Indians that their children in Kentucky, besides the objection on account of their habits, came home with no knowledge that was of any use. This objection is of course of but little weight, as ignorant Indians are unable to measure the use of knowledge. This is a point indeed on which the judgment of many among ourselves is at fault, a vast amount of knowledge having a use which the uninitiated are not capable of appreciating and which may not be manifested to the world for ages after the seed has been sown. But with respect to the Indians the use should be very certain and of present application to justify the policy of forcing it upon them with an expenditure of their own money.

The proper place, therefore, for expending Indian money for education is in my opinion in the Indian nation, where the children are not removed from the observation of their parents. If the progress of the pupils shall seem more slow, it will be more sure and the benefits of instruction more diffused.

The Cherokees are prepared to take entire charge of their own funds for education and perhaps the Choctaws are not less so; but the Creeks & Chickasaws need the guardian protection of the government in the use of their education fund which should be expended in the payment of teachers employed in the nation under the supervision of Indian agents, unless, upon special recommendation from competent persons, it should be deemed advisable to place some portion of the fund at the disposal of the Agents of the societies in the U. S. who are intelligently connecting efforts for education with their missionary labors for the spread of Christianity.

These efforts for education have been attended with the most happy results in the Cherokee nation and I believe no less so in the Choctaw nation.

I had the pleasure to visit several teachers in the Cherokee nation and saw them engaged in their school rooms, and I witnessed remarkable results at one place in the Choctaw nation. In every instance the directors of those schools were zealously devoting their entire efforts to the cause to which they have assigned their lives. Many of them are not only mentally laboring for the spread of the gospel, but, they engaged with cheerfulness in any manual and even menial labor which they find necessary in discharging the duties of hospitality among a hospitable people, who, as they never turn a stranger hungry from their doors, so they expect food and lodging in their visits to the missionary establishments in their country. I have seen the head of one of those establishments lead the horse of a visitor to the stable and feed him, while his wife and daughters with their own hands prepared his evening meal. From these labors the family would gather around the evening fire and make their favorite topic the subject of conversation towit, the best means of spreading the light of the gospel and of civilization among the natives. I am satisfied that a zeal so devoted as that I witnessed, may safely be aided in that direction of labor recognized by the Treaties, as the object of the education fund – the government of course reserving its power to inspect and control its operations so far as that fund is concerned. I therefore do not hesitate to recommend this with the single remark that those who know me will not suspect me of any special sectarian views in the recommendation.

E. A. H.

Index

Index